L.A. Misérables, Too

More Adventures in Purgatory

Paul D'Angelo

L.A. Misérables, Too:
More Adventures in Purgatory
© 1997, 2019 - Paul D'Angelo

(originally registered with Writers Guild of America, West - February 25, 1997 #655830)

pdangelocomic@aol.com
www.pdangelo.com
ISBN: 978-0-9970340-3-5

(also available in eBook format)

Cover photo by Max Lane

For the best siblings a guy could ever have:
Jay, Chris and Shauna

Table of Contents

Foreword: — 1
Now, where were we?

Introduction: — 7
It's just like starting over...

Chapter One: — 14
I love that dirty water, oh, Boston you're my home...

Chapter Two: — 29
I'm back in the saddle again...

Chapter Three: — 40
Take another little piece of my heart...

Chapter Four: — 53
Send lawyers, guns and money

Chapter Five: — 63
I've become comfortably numb...

Chapter Six: — 73
Feats don't fail me now...

Chapter Seven: — 80
People are strange, when you're a stranger...

Chapter Eight: — 96
Wild horses couldn't drag me away...

Chapter Nine: — 105
Welcome to the Hotel California...

Chapter Ten: — 119
Ch-ch-ch-ch-ch-changes...

Chapter Eleven: 130
Mama, don't let your babies grow up to be comics…

Chapter Twelve: 148
Same as it ever was…

Chapter Thirteen: 166
I wanna be sedated…

Chapter Fourteen: 187
Livin' on a prayer…

Chapter Fifteen: 206
Living in my own private Idaho…

Chapter Sixteen: 223
The fool on the hill…

Chapter Seventeen: 233
I really don't mind if I sit this one out…

Chapter Eighteen: 243
Say goodbye to Hollywood…

Chapter Nineteen: 270
And the beat goes on…

Chapter Twenty: 283
I'm all shook up…

Chapter Twenty-one: 289
Hit me with your best shot…

Chapter Twenty-two: 299
Tomorrow never knows…

Epilogue: 301
Ba-ba-ba-baby, you ain't seen nothin' yet …

FOREWORD
Now, where were we?

I would think it's safe to assume that anyone reading the second installment of my *L.A. Misérables* series of chronological diaries would have already read the first book, *L.A. Misérables: The Amusing Misadventures of a Boston Comic in La La Land,* and I wouldn't have to provide the backstory... but I've always been taught "to assume makes an ass out of u and me," so let me very briefly explain to insure that I will remain the only jackass in this story.

My real name is Paul Murphy and I grew-up just north of Boston, in the town of Wakefield Massachusetts. I graduated with honors and a B.S. from the Boston College School of Management, then graduated from the Suffolk University School of Law with my Juris Doctor degree and passed the bar examination the first time I took it in 1982.

While I attended law school I worked in the Attorney General's office for the Department of Employment Security, researching and writing briefs to be used in direct appeals to the Supreme Judicial Court of Massachusetts.

I also worked for the Middlesex County Probate Court and was eventually promoted to a position as a judicial clerk, again researching and authoring written decisions for the justices of the land and divorce courts.

After I got sworn-in to the bar at a special ceremony right in Boston's historic Faneuil Hall, I went to work at the Essex County District Attorney's office as a state prosecutor. I went on to eventually supervise district attorney's offices in the Salem, Amesbury, Haverhill, Lynn district courts, as well as the jury sessions in both Salem and Peabody, the latter the highest volume jury session in the state for a year or maybe two while I was in charge.

After a couple years of valuable experience in the D.A.'s office, I was getting ready to look for a job with a private law firm in Boston when I performed at my first open-mike night at Stitches Comedy Club on Commonwealth Avenue. I was registered under the pseudonym of Paul D'Angelo to hide my true identity as an officer of the state court system. (Coincidently, it was on the very same night, and on the very same stage, that comedy superstar Louis C.K. first began his stand-up career. Louis and I stood in line together, signed in together, and lost our comedic cherries together.)

After only about a dozen or so open-mike appearances, I quit my brief foray into showbiz to take on a boring, tedious job in one of two medium-sized Boston law firms that had offered me a position... but I ultimately panicked and, instead, bluffed my way into a couple of auditions in front of Boston's two biggest comedy bookers.

I suddenly found myself performing all over New England, three to seven nights a week, every week, while I continued to hold down my very responsible and demanding job at the district attorney's office.

It was an extremely hectic pace and I seemed to always be on the brink of exhaustion, but they were arguably the best years of my life. I shared those years with several of my divorced friends who came to live with me when they got tossed out of their homes. Each desperate friend-in-need stayed with me until they got their shit together, at which time another poor soul who had lost everything to his ex would be standing in line to take his place... and we had a blast.

After working both full-time jobs for about eight of the eleven years that I spent as a prosecutor, while building-up an impressive resume as a comic, I left the DA's office near the end of 1993 with the intent of moving to Los Angeles and concentrating on my comedy career.

L.A. Misérables, Too

Through a series of serendipitous events, my move to the West Coast was unexpectedly postponed for several years when I got caught-up in a new career as a criminal defense trial attorney. I was very successful "doing good things for bad people," as I often described my new role, but I was not happy with having to constantly deal with other people's problems. As you might imagine, no client ever called me when they were having a great day.

Life's too short... Why was I torturing myself when I had the option of earning a living by making people happy?

Representing the unrepentant defendant in a disturbing motor vehicle homicide case was the final straw, and I eventually wound down my legal career and moved to an apartment building in Hollywood, California, a week and a half before my 40th birthday.

At the last minute, my girlfriend Kelly decided to make the move with me. Through neither fault of our own, we had been having some issues prior to relocating and, when it became apparent that my rise to stardom was going to be a long and difficult endeavor, if it ever happened at all, the challenging circumstances only added to the stress on our fragile relationship.

Most successful entertainers necessarily struggle at the beginning of their career, while they're developing their craft and gaining experience, before eventually making a name for themselves over time through a combination of sacrifice, dedication, and perseverance.

My situation was very different.

Because I had already built a notable reputation as an attorney when I first contemplated signing-up for amateur night, I realized that I didn't have the luxury of struggling for a lengthy period of time while I developed as a stand-up because my family, friends, and peers in the legal community would rightfully question whether I should get my head removed from my ass and then examined..

I didn't want to set myself up to be humiliated because that would discourage me from chasing my dream, so I worked very hard to write and compile a great deal of original, comedic material for a year or so before I ever considered stepping on stage. With regard to performing, I figured that the hundreds of bench and jury trials I had participated in would provide me with the stage presence and courage I needed to perform in a smoky comedy club filled with drunken strangers. It was basically the same thing, right? As a result of my advance preparation, I achieved headlining status after only a handful of open-mike performances and my career took off.

By the time I left for Los Angeles, I really had a great life. I had the support of many friends and an incredible family, I was financially comfortable, I was booked solid months in advance, I could walk into any club in town and be given stage time, and I was confidant, enthusiastic, optimistic and happy.

That all changed when I established a new residence on Hollywood Boulevard... not by mere coincidence known as "The Boulevard of Broken Dreams."

Now, to make things clear, I'm not claiming that I lived in abject squalor in the backseat of my car, or that I was literally becoming a starving artist, or that my life was now a living hell, like many unfortunate people suffer through on a daily basis. But things can be challenging when you choose to give up a comfortable lifestyle to essentially start over in a distant place, without the people around you who you could always depend on.

I couldn't get on stage; I couldn't get the attention of anyone significant who could advance my career; by my impatient standards, I was making excruciatingly slow progress; I wasn't getting paid gigs and money was becoming a serious issue; I was filled with angst, languishing in my apartment; I was convinced that I was disappointing my poor parents, the only people I ever really cared to impress; I was getting more frustrated by the day... and that crazy city I was living in didn't help the cause one bit.

But that's what makes it funny... the juxtaposition of comedy and tragedy.

Conflict... Tension... Frustration... Annoyance... Cynicism... Exasperation... Aggravation... Contradiction... Social Impotence... Discord... Humiliation... Awkward situations... Contempt... Stress... Pressure... Friction... Vulnerability... Apprehension...

That's where the best comedy comes from, and there was plenty of

L.A. Misérables, Too

it that was vented in the preceding book, the first of the *L.A. Misérables* series of six daily diaries that I kept when I "moved to L.A. and everything started to suck."

That diary covered a span of 130 days between my arrival in March of 1996 and July 16th of that same year. We pick-up right where I left off… and I won't provide a redundant overview of those first four-and-a-half months because I address it in the diary's introduction.

So here we go again…

Back to a time long, long ago…

In a land far, far away…

And one seriously fucked-up land, if I do say so myself.

Paul D'Angelo
June 2019

**Back in the good ol' days before I moved…
What the hell was I thinking?**

Paul D'Angelo

The law and the laughter
Assistant DA bound for Los Angeles comedy scene

By JOANNE MENESALE
News Staff

PEABODY — By day he is a clean-cut assistant district attorney, conservatively dressed for the courtroom in a navy blue suit and tie.

But by night, well, Paul J. Murphy is a wisecracking comedian, center stage, standing behind a microphone.

And his career as a comic just took a giant leap forward this week, as Murphy, who is known in the business as Paul D'Angelo, bested 108 other comedians to win the Johnny Walker Comedy Search held at Nick's Comedy Stop in Boston Wednesday night.

The $1,000 prize is the least of Murphy's joys. What's really important to the 32-year-old Wakefield resident is the trip to Los Angeles to perform April 12 at the Improv. There he'll compete against seven other regional winners from across the country.

PAUL J. MURPHY

Murphy, quickly editing his own speech. "Oh, don't write that. It sounds like something a little kid would say."

"Motion to strike!"

"It's just incredible exposure," he said, about being the Boston winner in the comedy search contest. One hundred and eight comedians auditioned throughout the day and the best were called back for finals that night.

Bud Freidman, who is big-time in the comedy world, with his own nationally syndicated television show and running the Improv in Los Angeles, Las Vegas and New York, liked Murphy so much he came up to him after the contest.

"He wants me to go out a week early (to L.A.) and do shows," said Murphy, who has spent vacations in Los Angeles and New York trying to get his name known in comedy circles.

"This is like all of a sudden you're in the door," he said.

Murphy began performing comedy about 3½ years ago, at first

MURPHY

Prosecutor by day is a comic by night

By ARIST FRANGULES
Times staff

It's a rainy Saturday night and a tall, slim man with neatly trimmed black hair, starting to gray, and a mustache takes the stage at Stevie D's Comedy Tonight nightclub in Middleton. Carrying an acoustic guitar and wearing a black jacket and gray pinstriped pants, Paul D'Angelo, that night's headliner, announces that he was driving so fast to get to the comedy club that his car was hydroplaning. "I know it's dangerous," he cracks, "but it saves on the tires."

SALEM — At age 30, Paul Murphy is one of a number of rising young prosecutors on the staff of Essex County District Attorney Kevin Burke.

Murphy, in less than five years after his graduation from Suffolk Law School, has moved through top posts in the Amesbury and Haverhill District Courts to his current job as prosecution supervisor in Salem District Court — which is second only to Lynn as the busiest district court in the county.

Burke calls Murphy an "excellent prosecutor" with "great legal sense."

In Murphy's district court office, which he shares with the clerical workers and prosecutors, there is a yellow piece of paper taped to the wall. It is a black magic marker sketch of a man with a guitar performing before a group of people. The man in the sketch, who appears to be a caricature of Murphy, is labled "Paul D'Angelo."

D'Angelo tells the responsive nightclub audience about one moment in his youth when he assisted his father at their basement workbench. "Hey, Paul, I lost a tack," D'Angelo quotes his father. "Take off your shoes and help me find it."

Murphy, page A10

Barbara Kennedy photo
Paul Murphy, alias comedian Paul D'Angelo, talks with his fellow assistant district attorney Robert Allison at the Salem courthouse.

INTRODUCTION
It's just like starting over...

When we last left our hero, Paul was slowly sinking deeper and deeper into deadly quicksand, desperately trying to reach for a vine that was just out of his reach, so he could pull himself out and get back on his feet again... while all of Hollywood stood around and watched and did absolutely nothing to help... like a bunch of assholes.

That's basically the situation I was in when the last book ended.

So let's make this like I'm pitching a script at a major motion picture studio in Hollywood.

"Imagine, if you will, *Punchline* meets *Justice for All* meets *Trading Places* meets *Death of a Salesman* meets *Down and Out in Beverly Hills* meets *Escape from LA*.

"Here's the scoop in a nutshell. After spending thirteen years as an assistant district attorney and successful criminal defense counsel in Boston, while at the same time managing a ten year career as a nationally booked, headlining comedian, the central character gives up everything and relocates to Hollywood to concentrate his attention on making it big in the entertainment profession... Then everything goes down the shitter from there. Ta Da!"

You see, like I tried to explain at the end of the last book, I really blew it when I didn't keep notes about my legal experiences as a prosecutor, so I made a commitment to chronicle my transition in Hollywood from the same sarcastic, observational perspective that I use to write material for my stand-up act.

The process of creating and writing each day was remedial in that it took my focus away from the actual day-to-day tests of my temperament, blows to my ego, karate kicks to my confidence, dope-slaps to my constitution, pile-drivers to my psyche, pipe-bombs to my career, drive-by shootings to my self-esteem, and small-scale, non-nuclear, conventional-weapon ground warfare to my future plans... and converted all of that negative energy into humor. Because I didn't have much stage time in LA to work out new material and vent my building frustration, I needed an outlet to exercise my funny bone and blow-off some steam, and the diary was it.

I recently got back a copy of the finished manuscript that I had sent to a literary agency for consideration. Basically, they said that they enjoyed the book, but it was more like a running stand-up comedy act than a novel. Ya, no shit... so what's your point?

OK, so here's the recap in classic movie screenplay format.

Introduce the main character and establish his environment:
I did that. My name is Paul Murphy. While I was working as a prosecutor in the Essex County District Attorney's Office, I snuck off most every night to work as a stand-up in New England's comedy clubs under the pseudonym of Paul D'Angelo. When I left the DA's office to move to LA in 1993, I came back to Boston temporarily and, through an unexpected string of circumstances, reluctantly began a successful career as a criminal defense attorney. My environment was secure. I was happy and carefree. I had steady income from two full-time professions. I was booked months in advance for comedy shows all over the country, and I was blessed with a very close family and many great friends. What kind of an idiot would give this wonderful life up?... Me.

Introduce the catalyst that will set the plot in motion:
Despite the security, something was missing. I needed a challenge. I'd gone as far as I could in the Boston comedy scene. Someone asked

me why I chose comedy over law and, when I thought about it, I realized it was because, unlike the legal field, my potential in entertainment was unlimited.

Event that throws the character into a new world:
I believe that would have been American Airlines, flight #11 from Boston to LAX.
(editor's note: Yes, the same AA Boston-to-LA flight #11 that was later flown into the World Trade Center in New York City on September 11th, 2001... which I took almost thirty times while I lived in Hollywood... Scary.)

Reveal central conflict (indicate what the protagonist will be up against):
The antagonist in this case would be Hollywood; both the city and the entertainment business it represents. How did I know that my apartment building would be inhabited with refugees from the *Village of the Damned?* How did I know that the section of Hollywood Boulevard that I chose to live in was a virtual 24-hour, 7-11 variety store of vice, where you could get crack, get a prostitute (with or without a penis), get shot at, get arrested, get a big vibrating rubber dildo, get a tattoo on your ass, get your nipples pierced, get cheesy souvenirs like matching Elvis salt & pepper shakers, or get robbed around the clock, in my neighborhood?

And between the drone of the LAPD helicopters searching for fugitives overhead, the constant blaring of car alarms, and the wailing of passing sirens, it's difficult to hear the subtle scraping sound of the massive, drifting continental plates, moving along the San Andreas Fault-line that runs underneath the city of Los Angeles, building-up enormous energy for "the big one."

As ring announcer Michael Buffer would bellow before a prize fight, *"Let's get ready to rum-m-m-m-m-m-mble!"*

Introduce lesser characters:
Let's see, I introduced Kelly, my girlfriend who relocated to Hollywood with me and now works as an assistant to a movie producer in Beverly Hills. There's Patty Ross, the Boston comedienne who's one of

my best friends. Patty's as tough as a truck driver and takes shit from no one... and that's her feminine side.

Then there's Max, the horror movie screenwriter who's looking to sell his first script. Our friend Timthy is a gay hairdresser from West Hollywood who is hilarious without even knowing it. Crazy Wayne, another Bostonian who waits up to ten hours in front of the Laugh Factory to sign up for three minutes of stage time; "Lola," the "ho" that lives across the hall from our apartment, and whose gender remains a topic of speculation. And, of course, the legions of people who went in and out of my life for four months; old friends, new friends, celebrities, nobodies, family, rivals and assorted strangers.

Introduce sub-plots:

There are all sorts of minor skirmishes that went on. Some examples: My ongoing battle against the army of cockroaches that has established a base-camp in my apartment; my struggle to protect the little money I have left from the never-ending deluge of homeless bums, constantly asking me for spare change that I can't afford to spare; my efforts to survive amongst the tattooed, body-pierced, struggling, alternative grunge-rock losers that inhabit my apartment and let their dogs shit in the hallways just outside my door; my uphill fight to break into the entertainment business in Hollywood; the daily challenge to endure the inconsiderate, hot-headed, demolition derby drivers on the roads of LA; sometimes, even the occasional conflicts between me and Kelly, the first female I ever lived with, other than my mother, creating all sorts of friction in our relationship; but, mostly, just me against the dim-witted people that torment me with their ignorance and cause me anguish, a broad category that includes myself in the role of "King Nitwit" on many occasions.

Introduce set-ups and payoffs throughout act:

Most of my set-ups didn't pay off yet. It took me almost three months just to get auditions at Los Angeles's prominent comedy clubs that afford the most industry exposure, The Laugh Factory and The Improvisation. After I was passed as a regular, the competition for spots, and the constant scheduling of showcases set-up by management and agencies, resulted in my shows at those clubs being very few and far between as I worked to establish myself.

I also got accepted into the Ice House in Pasadena and the Comedy and Magic Club in Hermosa Beach, which are premier venues for comedy, but those clubs are booked far in advance. I successfully made connections that booked me at several large theater venues, including the Ventura Theater, the Coach House in Capistrano, and 4th and B in San Diego. These gigs are all long drives for pocket change, but every little bit helps.

I even got offered a part in a proposed television show playing, of all things, a lawyer, but when it came time to finance the pilot, the producers went AWOL, disappearing from the face of the earth like witnesses to a Mafia slaying.

Introduce the "ticking clock":

The "ticking clock" would be my savings and checking accounts. Every withdrawal that I made to pay bills, without some type of income, sends some more sand through the wicked witch's giant hourglass. Meanwhile, I'm in Oz cooling my heels, waiting to get an audience with the television mogul-developer-producer Wizard himself, or even his manager, agent, lawyer, publicist or lackey administrative assistant... but I'd settle for anyone whatsoever who's at all loosely associated with the fringes of the entertainment industry and will give me the fucking time of day, so I can accomplish something that vaguely resembles progress in this heartless town.

And all this while those ugly flying monkeys, that represent the locust-like plague of assholes that seem to swarm around me everywhere I turn in Hollywood, are hovering over the city like big, hairy seagulls, shitting on me every chance they get in an effort to discourage me from my goals and dreams.

Whoaaaaaa, calm down killer, relax, take a deep breath, click your heels together and repeat three times, *"There's no place like home... There's no place like home... There's no place like home..."*

Paul D'Angelo

Moment of decision for main character-raises stakes, turns action in new direction:

At some point I realized that it is difficult to accomplish anything without management and/or agency representation to open doors for me at the comedy clubs, set up auditions for TV and movie parts, pitch the sitcoms that I created to development people, get a publisher for my books, get the talent departments of HBO, *The Tonight Show*, and other stand-up vehicles to take a look at me, include me in industry showcases, and book shows for me at significant venues.

I have been meeting with several agents and managers but, despite my seemingly desperate financial straits and growing discouragement about my career, I am being patient and waiting for the best opportunity to come along.

Emphasize the "ticking clock":

I know, I know… the money's running out. Do you think I like eating frozen dinners for lunch and driving two and a half hours into cow-country to do a show for a bar full of drunken rednecks, just so I can make a few bucks? Noooo! So every few months I've been going back to Boston to work the comedy clubs to help me pay the rent money in LA for a while longer.

Point of no return-character must confront central conflict:

There have been enough encouraging signs that inspire me to keep plugging. Despite the fact that I've been in "Tinsel Town" for over four months, I have just begun to make the connections that will hopefully lead to bigger and better things in entertainment. As I wait for that to happen, I'll continue to write down a chronology of what it's like to try and break into the biz and, in between, comment on the decadence of LA, the city's comedy scene, the life of a comedian, newsworthy events, my courtroom experiences, and general observations about the whacky world around me.

Tie up sub-plots / Climax and resolution:

Well, if we had accomplished that, we wouldn't need another book, now would we?

L.A. Misérables, Too

CHAPTER ONE
I love that dirty water, oh, Boston you're my home...

Genesis, Part 1: In the beginning... No. Not right.

It was the best of times, it was the worst of times... No, not that opening line either.

Call me Ismael... No, that's been done before too.

It was a dark and stormy night... Nah, doesn't apply here.

For years I have read the *Penthouse Forum,* but I never believed that something like could happen to me until... Ya, right. In my dreams.

OK, screw the dramatic beginning, Paul. Just continue to write down insignificant bullshit that no one really gives a damn about like the first book and let's get on with it...

DAY 131 - JULY 17TH, 1996

I'm back in Boston for a week and a half, trying to get some stage time and earn some rent money before I return to Hollywood. Tonight I had a show at the Comedy Connection at the Faneuil Hall Marketplace in downtown Boston.

Three gorgeous women sat stage-right. I started talking to them during my act and one of them was beautiful, with long dark hair and a killer tan, but she had to be one of the dumbest women in history. The only reason I kept going over and speaking to her in the middle of my stand-up routine was that I could look down her shirt from up on the stage and her nipple kept popping out like that plastic devise that tells you when your turkey is done cooking.

These comedy gigs don't always pay a lot, compared to what I could make as a hot-shot attorney, but I can never recall cross-examining a witness during a trial who would side-track me by flashing her titties.

"And where were *you* on the night of February 23rd, Miss Devine?"

"If you must know, Mr. Prosecutor, I was home, alone in my bedroom, playing *with THESE!!!*" (rips her blouse open)

It just doesn't happen.

DAY 133 - JULY 19TH, 1996

My friend Jim has two extra tickets to see the Who perform *Quadrophenia* at Madison Square Garden on Monday, July 22nd. I called my childhood friend, Kevin Foley, to wish him a happy 40th birthday, and told him that I had extra ticket. Kevin was supposed to baby-sit for his children, but he got someone to take care of them. When I told him I had seats next to the stage, I think he would have left those kids alone with a convicted child molester in a heartbeat.

I can remember being about fourteen years old in high school when Kevin's older brother Jackie would occasionally take the train to a Bruins game in Boston and leave his VW bug in the parking lot at the train station. Kevin had an extra set of keys made and he and I would go to the parking lot after Jackie left for the game and we'd drive around all night in the Volkswagen. Kevin's brother could never understand why his gas tank always seemed to be on empty. Jackie can't be too sharp anyway… he later became a lawyer.

Once we had the car, Kevin would drive by and pick up his girlfriend and they'd always get into a big fight. I'd be sitting in the back seat, listening to them go at each other, and Kevin would get so mad he'd threaten to hit a telephone pole until she'd apologize. He'd suddenly cut the wheel and veer straight toward the pole, waiting for her to offer an apology. Meanwhile, I'm in the back, pounding the back of the seat and screaming at her, "Tell him you're sorry! Tell him…

NOW!... Kevin, she's sorry... She's really, really sorry!... *PLEASE TELL HIM HOW SORRY YOU ARE!"*

Kevin is now married with small children, who he will eventually worry about when they get their driver's licenses, praying that they don't act anything like we did when we were their age.

DAY 134 - JULY 20TH, 1996

Mike Flanagan and Jim Roach came to my show tonight. Mike's a former agent who I met when he booked the Club Casino theater in Hampton Beach, New Hampshire. He now is a booking agent for all of the big country-western acts that come to the Northeast region. During a conversation relating to my career as a defense attorney, Mike reminded me that it was a Chinese restaurant such as this that he left before getting arrested for DWI many years ago. After having a few Mai-Tai's, Mike drove home with some leftover Chinese food and the smell was driving him crazy, so he started picking things out of the bag to munch on. Next thing you know, there were blue lights flashing behind him and a cop approached the car after he pulled over to the side of the road.

The officer leaned into the window and said, "Do you know that it's a crime to eat and operate a motor vehicle at the same time?"

Mike replied, *"Then why do they have drive-through windows at McDonalds?"*

"Get out of the car!"

It was the first night of the Summer Olympics, the opening ceremonies were going on, and I was doing a sold out show in a Chinese restaurant on the North Shore. A friend, Bucky, who is lawyer, was sitting in front table with his wife and family, and he was extremely shitfaced. He'd yell incoherent remarks up to the stage, I would give him a couple zingers to shut him up for a while, and then he'd start interrupting again. This went on throughout most of my set.

Lucky for him that he was a friend. An audience member once tried to heckle me... *and I ate his liver with some fava beans and a nice Chianti, fffffffff...*

Near the end of my act, I was right in the middle of a joke when there was a commotion at Bucky's table. Bucky was soooo drunk he had actually fallen over backwards in his chair. I mean feet up in the air, 3.2 degree of difficulty, don't try this at home because this man is a professional stunt person, 9.85 from the Korean judge, backwards flip to a prone position lying on the floor.

As the people around him were helping Bucky back up to his chair I announced, in my best echoing, public address system voice, "Well, ladies and gentlemen, the Olympics have officially begun. This is Paul D'Angelo reporting from the Olympic Chair Diving Competition where Bucky has taken an early lead with a spectacular effort... a double flip, triple lutz by a first-class klutz, with the help of eight double vodkas, dismount from the sitting position..."

In Hollywood they have a Chinese theater with impressions of people's hands and feet in the cement floor. This Chinese restaurant will have people coming to see the impression of the back of Bucky's head in the carpet.

"By the way people, Bucky here just happens to be a lawyer, so remember, if you're ever in jail, and you want to stay there... call Bucky at 1-800-YOR-FUKD."

DAY 135 - JULY 21ST, 1996

Sunday. I drove to my friend Dugie's house with my brother Chris. When I pulled up in front of the house and walked into the yard, I saw Dugie standing in his garden, slowly aiming a big rifle at a tomato plant and blasting it. Has he gone mad?

"Dugie! What the hell are you doing?"

He explained that there is a type of white butterfly that lays eggs which are harmful to his plants, so he blows them to kingdom-come with an air rifle.

"Dugie, do you know how bad this little scene appears from the street? You look like some deranged kook stalking tomato plants with a shotgun. Why don't you use a net or something?"

"The little bastards are too fast. I can't get 'em with a net. Quiet!

Paul D'Angelo

Stand still... There's another one... I'll teach you to wreck my garden, you son of a bitch!" He raised the gun to his shoulder and uttered an Al Pacino line from *Scarface* in a bad Cuban accent. *"Say hello to my little friend..."* BANG!

And another cute, little butterfly exploded into a million tiny pieces. I have a feeling, if there was a net anywhere around this neighborhood, Dugie should be in it.

I picked some string beans from Dugie's garden and brought them to my family in Magnolia. When I handed my mother the bag full of beans, my Uncle Dick asked if I grew them. I said, "Are you kidding? Anything that's growing in my apartment should be killed, exterminated, or wiped out with a harsh industrial cleaner."

At the home there were about twelve family and friends sitting on the front deck. My Uncle Dick was concerned because a well-to-do looking couple was looking at the piece of property immediately to our left, and he intended on purchasing it for himself to build a house. In an effort to discourage the potential buyers, Uncle Vito responded by telling everyone to "Man your battle stations!" and instructed his troops to make a lot of commotion, punctuated with a liberal use of profanity, while others dropped trou' and mooned the prospective purchasers from our kitchen window or threw empty beer cans off the balcony onto the front lawn. By the efficient manner in which the operation was carried out, it appears that they have gone through this drill before in an attempt to make would-be neighbors think twice before considering settling down next to a bunch of obnoxious, misbehaved, white-trash, lowlifes in the adjacent home.

It must have worked because the nice couple left in disgust, got in their car and drove off, as my family cheered in victory. The thought occurred to me that my family is a lot more like the Munsters than the Cleavers.

After dinner the family sat around the table and told stories. My other cousin PJ was there with his beautiful children. My mother looked at Uncle Dick and remarked, "The grandchildren got your good looks."

I couldn't pass up the opportunity to add, "Ya, but you were too generous, you should have kept some for yourself."

I'm an asshole, why should I be any different with my family?

My brother recollected about the retired fireman named Ray, who rented a store below my family's house years ago and turned it into an antique shop. Actually, it was more of a junk store along the lines of *Sanford and Son*, filled with useless, broken shit that no one would ever buy, and the crap kept piling up. It wasn't so much a business as it was a fire-hazard. My brothers and I used to call him "Mr. Haney," in reference to the backwards, country-hick character who owned the little general store on the *Green Acres* television show.

One day Ray went into the hospital after an apparent heart attack and my mother sent him flowers. My mom didn't know what Ray's last name was, but she had heard her sons refer to him as "Mr. Haney" on many occasions so, when she made out the card that accompanied the arrangement, she made it out to "Ray Haney."

After he recovered, my poor mother was totally caught by surprise when Ray snapped at her for the "tasteless practical joke" that she had pulled on him. I don't know what his problem was. My brothers and I thought it was hilarious.

I had a show tonight and some idiot parents thought it would be a great idea to take their eight-year-old kid to a late-night show and sit with him in the front row. What a buzzkill. Every comedian had to self-edit their presentation on the fly to avoid horrifying the one child in the full house who had no business being there in the first place.

The situation reminded me of a time when a show's producer pulled me aside, just before I took the stage, and said, "Paul, I need you to be squeaky clean and not swear tonight because there are a couple of young kids in the audience," and I did as I was told.

Ten minutes into my act, I saw a little brat in the front row pull on his mother's sleeve and whine, *"Ma, this fuckin' guy sucks!"*

DAY 136 - JULY 22ND, 1996

I woke up this morning and I was in pain all over. The last three days I golfed, went bowling, and played Whiffle-ball, and now I'm sore everywhere. I have a bad back, an aching arm, and I'm limping, and it's not like I was doing dangerous stunt work or anything like that. When I was younger, I could get drunk and fall out of the back seat of a convertible going 60 mph, brush myself off and walk away laughing. These days, if I'm watching TV on the couch and I stretch the wrong way when I yawn, I could end up in a full body-cast for a month.

Today I am driving to New York City with three guys to see The Who perform the rock-opera *Quadrophenia* at Madison Square Garden. Jim Murphy (no relation) had rented a big, gangster Cadillac Fleetwood for the 3 ½ hour drive. We met at Jim's house and only got 150 yards down the road when Jim realized that he forgot his wallet and had to turn back, leaving us baking in the car with the windows closed and the 90° sun beating down on the parked Cadillac for twenty minutes. If they leave puppies in a hot car, people know enough to crack the windows so they don't collapse from heat stroke, but Jim doesn't care about us because HE has the concert tickets in his pocket and knows we're not in a position to complain.

Kevin Foley has been my good friend since I played Little League baseball with him when I was about nine or ten years old. Kevin has held an eclectic variety of jobs over the years including construction worker, hairdresser, cancer researcher, substitute teacher, and collecting and selling bull semen to breeders. I would imagine the process is similar to milking a cow, except it would take a lot longer to fill up that metal bucket.

Kevin told us that a friend of his answered the door last week and there was a woman, standing there with an infant in her arms, who proceeded to accuse this guy of being the father. I told them he should have thought fast and said, "It can't be my child. The baby doesn't look anything like me. First of all, look at me and look at the baby... The kid doesn't have a moustache and I'm *much* taller."

Kevin lives on a farm in western Massachusetts. He swears that his baby-sitter's husband was raised by wolves. The guy wears one of those baby papooses and walks around with his little kid dangling in front of him all the time. Last week Kevin visited and found the guy in the backyard, cutting firewood with a big chainsaw, with the baby hanging off his chest. That's pretty responsible parenting. Maybe he can strap the infant to his body and take the kid bungee jumping, or do some rock climbing on a sheer cliff with the baby dangling on the end of a rope... preferably wrapped around his little neck, so he doesn't have to grow up and realize what an idiot his dad is.

According to Kevin, the mountain man's latest kick is working with metal and he has built a miniature cannon by boring out a big steel pipe. (Tell me you'd be surprised to turn on your TV one evening and see the FBI surrounding this guy's farmhouse in a standoff.) Kevin, who just had his horse castrated and is a little crazy himself, thought it would be funny to put the gonads in a shoe box, wrap it up with a pretty bow, and give it to his neighbor as a birthday present. When this nut received the present he retaliated by stuffing the horse's balls into his cannon and shooting them across the field at Kevin's home. "Incoming testicles!... Hit the dick! I mean deck!"

Ahhh, life on the farm.

As Jimmy drove us towards New York City, he asked me who the opening act was and it turned into a classic Abbott and Costello routine.

"Hey Paul, who's on first?"

"No Jimmy, Who's on second."

"I mean the band."

"The Band's not on the show tonight. They broke up."

"There's no band, Paul?"

"Yes."

"Yes is opening-up for them?"

"Oh brother..."

From the back seat Kevin asked, "Hey Paul, how's traffic?"

"Traffic's great, but they're not on the show either."

Jimmy: "Then who's on first?"

"OK, that's enough!"

I was sitting in the back seat with John, who is the booking agent at the Comedy Connection in Boston. John had a terrible hangover, because he spent the previous afternoon drinking beers at a Red Sox game and ended up closing a tittie bar in the wee hours of the morning. Now he was sitting in quiet agony for the entire ride when, suddenly, he bolted upright in his seat, tapped wildly on Jim's shoulder, and yelled, "Slow down! There's a cop car on the median!"

Jim decelerated quickly and we proceeded to drive past what turned out to be nothing more than a big blue sign. "You're hallucinating Johnny," I said as I cracked open a cold beer and handed it to him.

"Drink this Johnny, maybe it will restore your equilibrium."

After this episode it came as no surprise when John told us a story about how his friends dropped him off at his parent's house a couple years ago when he was passed out drunk. His friends didn't know what to do with John, so they propped up his limp body between the front door and the screen door of his parent's home, closed the door behind him and just left him there all night. When John's mother woke up the next morning and opened the front door, his lifeless body came crashing into the foyer and his mother started screaming because she thought he was dead.

John continued to drink before, during, and after the concert, then had a big meal at McDonald's before we started out for home. About half way home, I was beginning to doze off in the back seat when I smelled something that was so horrible it would make a medical examiner toss his cookies. John was laughing while I hung my head out the car window at 65 mph like a cocker spaniel. "Gross! You pig! Check your underwear, I think you had an accident! That's rancid! You disgust me!"

Once the coast was clear I sat back down with a sour expression on my face, like I just drank milk a month past the expiration date. It was about five minutes before I was hanging out the window again.

"You asshole! It smells like you're decomposing! I'm not putting up with this for the next two hours! I don't care if you book Vegas, I'll tie you to the hood of the car the rest of the way home like we bagged a moose!... And look what you're doing to the nice, new leather seats in this Cadillac. The leather smelled better when it was still part of the cow's ass!"

Ten minutes later he was at it again. It was like a bad episode of *Tales From the Crypt*. I tried to encourage Jim to run over a skunk for some relief, but he was too busy playing with his fucking radar detector that was constantly going off with an annoying whining sound every mile or so. Hey, the radar detector must have worked... we didn't get pulled over by any blue signs on the way home.

**Kevin, me, and John
on our way to the Who concert in NYC**

DAY 137 - JULY 23RD, 1996

We got in from New York City around 5:30 a.m. and I slept for a couple hours before I got a call from the management company in LA that's putting together the courtroom show that I got a part on. They told me I would be doing a run-through for the producers when I return to the West Coast. I better bring more suits with me when I return, because I only have one out there. I didn't think I'd need a suit in Los Angeles unless I got married, arraigned, or buried, two of which remain a distinct possibility in my scary neighborhood.

A short time later my friend, "The Prune," picked me up because I had a show at singer Carly Simon's nightclub on the island of Martha's Vineyard. Prune's gas tank was below "E," but he drove by about fifteen gas stations because he refused to pay their high prices. He was running on fumes to save one or two cents a gallon, and we were very close to being in a position where we would have to give some guy twenty five bucks to siphon some gas from his lawn mower so we could get to the nearest gas station.

We ended up getting gas and, while we drove to Cape Cod to catch the ferry to Martha's Vineyard, Prune and I reminisced about some funny moments we had together. When Prune was going through his divorce, I took him in at my "half-way house for estranged husbands" for a year and a half. Prune and his wife have one daughter who had just graduated from Vanderbilt University, where she majored in Russian and was now working in Washington D.C.

Prune was seeing a bunch of different women at the same time, all of whom thought that she was his one and only. One woman, who was not particularly bright, called the house one evening while Prune was on a date with someone else. She started complaining to me that she wanted to see more of the Prune, but he always seemed to be flying all over the world, canceling plans at the last moment, and she wouldn't hear from him for days at a time. Everything seemed to be a secret with Prune. Even when they would walk into a bar or restaurant, he would scan the place and check out the crowd before they could take a seat. I thought it was pretty obvious to anyone but the most naïve person that Prune was two-timing her, but she was obviously too dumb to put it together and insisted that I tell her where the Prune was that night, so I jokingly said, "Listen… you have to swear that you won't tell anyone that I gave you this information. Do you swear?"

"I swear. What is it, Paul?"

"I hope no one is listening in to our conversation now or we could both be killed. I don't know how to tell you this… but Prune is a secret agent working with the CIA and I can't tell you where he is now. It's top secret classified information."

I expected her to tell me to go fuck myself and slam the phone down, but instead she exclaimed, *"I knew it! I knew it! I knew it!* I was right all along! Ah hah! I'm not as stupid as you think I am! I had it figured out. It all falls into place! That's why he disappears without telling

L.A. Misérables, Too

me where he's going! That's why he always seems to be hiding things from me! That's why he can't take me to certain places! That's why he won't show up sometimes and he never has a good explanation! Ah hah! And he's always using my phone to call Washington D.C. and mentioning the Russians! I was right!"

I couldn't believe this woman could be so clueless to believe this story! I did everything I could to keep from laughing and just continued to lay it on thick. "Prune really likes you, but he can't get too close to anyone because he never knows when he'll be whisked off to another undercover mission in Russia"... and on and on.

The next night, Prune and I had a few drinks and I had Prune call from the apartment and tell her that he was on a nuclear submarine that had briefly surfaced in the North Sea from under a polar ice cap. While Prune spoke to the woman, I made beeping sounds like sonar in the background to make it authentic. Not only did she get off his back, she now feels that it's her patriotic duty not to ask questions and pry into his business. Prune always seems to fall into shit and come up smelling like roses. I would fall in a bed of roses and get up covered with fertilizer.

I had one of the best shows of my life at the club. I put a lot of energy into it, knowing that I would be flying back to Los Angeles and who knows when I would get on stage again.

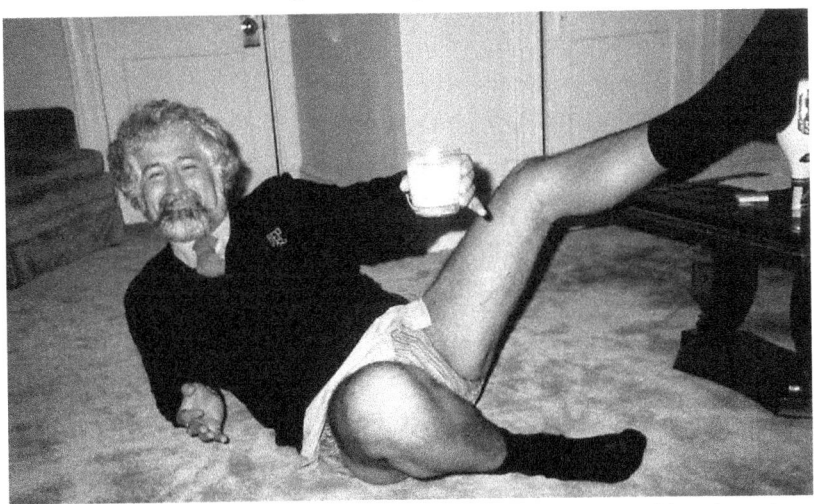

The Prune, living at my half-way home for divorced husbands

Paul D'Angelo

DAY 138 - JULY 24™, 1996

This is my last day in Boston before I have to fly back to California. My dad was nice enough to let me use his car for the two weeks that I was home and I have to return it to him today. I pushed the button to eject the cassette I had been playing in his car and it wouldn't pop out. I tried for a half hour to jimmy the cassette out with a screwdriver, or pull it out with pliers, but it wouldn't budge. Great. I'm forty years old and I'm afraid that my father is gonna yell at me for wrecking his car. I feel like a teenager all over again. How am I gonna handle this?

"Dad... thanks for letting me use the car... uh, I hope you like AC-DC."

I suspect I'll fly into town two or three months from now and my dad will pick me up singing in a falsetto screech, *"You... shook me alllll... night...long... yes you did... Yeah you... shook me alllll night long...."* and playing air guitar while he steers the car with his bad knee.

Believe me, I know what it's like to face my dad when I did something to his precious automobile. I tested the limits of my dad's patience the first week I got my driver's license. When I was seventeen years old, I had passed my driver's test and got my license in February of my junior year in high school.

The first week I after I got my driver's license, I begged my father to use his new company car, a shiny, bronze-colored Chevrolet Impala, so I could show off to my friends.

I picked up one of my closest buddies at the time, Chucky LeBlanc, and told him I had to stop by the high school to pick up something that I left in my gym locker. Because an arsonist had burned down half the school, we were on double sessions, with the juniors and seniors attending class in the morning and the freshman and sophomores going to school in the afternoon. Due to the staggered sessions, the school was full of students on the afternoon that I pulled into the snow-covered parking lot next to the high school gym. That's one of the reasons I went to the school at that time. I was hoping some of the underclass girls would see that I now had my license. "Mr. Big-Shot" had his dad's wheels. How could they resist?

I went into the building, came back out a short time later, and pulled forward to make one of those fancy three-point turns that they taught me in driver's ed. I pressed my foot on the brake so I could throw the car into reverse, but I had snow on the bottom of my shoe and my foot slipped off the brake and hit the gas pedal. Because of a lethal combination of my lack of driving experience, my typical teenage stupidity, and the sheer panic of the moment, I responded by immediately jamming my foot down on the brake. The only trouble was, my foot was not on the brake, it was still on the gas, and the car bolted forward, crashed through a snow-bank, flew across a lawn, and smashed head-on into the side of the brick school building at about twenty-five miles an hour.

After the impact, teachers and students ran to the windows of the classrooms as a cloud of steam shot out of the broken radiator that was behind the crushed and twisted collection of metal and plastic that, only moments ago, used to be the front end and grille of my father's new car.

I jammed the car into reverse and spun the tires as I fishtailed out of the parking lot, leaving a trail of auto parts and leaking engine fluids behind me. I looked over at my friend Chucky for support, but all he could do was stare straight ahead in a catatonic trance and mutter repeatedly, *"I can't believe you just hit the fucking school."*

"Chucky, what am I gonna do!?"

Still in a hypnotic state, *"I can't believe you just hit the fucking school."*

"Look at my dad's new car! It's totaled!"

"I can't believe you just hit the fucking school."

"My father's going to KILL me!"

"I can't believe you just hit the fucking school."

"I'm so embarrassed. I can never face those people at the high school again! I won't get a date until I move away to college!"

"I can't believe you just hit the fucking school."

I couldn't believe I just hit the fucking school.

I went home to face my mother and father and told them what happened. My parents took it well and all they seemed to be concerned about was that I was OK.

"We can replace the car, Paul, that's what insurance is for. As long as you're not hurt. That's the important thing. Were you injured?"

"No, I'm fine, Dad."

"Are you sure you're OK? You didn't hurt anything?"

"No Dad, I'm OK. I'm not hurt, really."

"You're positive you're all right?"

"Yes Dad, I'm positive."

"Good."

As soon as it was established that I had not been injured, I expected my father to beat me within an inch of my life, but he didn't. Instead he used that incident to tease me unmercifully for the next twenty-plus years… like on Thanksgiving, when my mother would ask me to bring the turkey to the dinner table.

My father would bellow, "Jesus Christ, don't let Paul carry the turkey, he'll drop the damn thing and we'll end-up eating cold-cuts for Thanksgiving dinner! Remember what he did to my new car?"

Of course, by saying that, it just made me all the more nervous and my hands would shake with anxiety as I cautiously carried the large plate to the table.

"See that? He's gonna drop it! Look at him. I told you, he's gonna drop the damn bird! Start making the sandwiches, Frances!"

Me and my dad, Jack "Tiger" Murphy

Chapter Two
I'm back in the saddle again...

DAY 139 - JULY 25TH, 1996

I got bumped up to first class for my flight to Los Angeles. Even though I fly a lot, I very rarely get to sit in first class. For a long time the concept of a first class section was very mysterious to me. The airline puts a curtain up to separate that area of the airplane from the people sitting in coach and then they pull the curtain closed right after takeoff, as if it's forbidden to know what's going on in there. Like they have something to hide from those less-fortunate losers stuck in coach class.

I often imagined that, if the curtain inadvertently got pulled aside during the flight, those of us sitting in the cramped, uncomfortable seats with no leg-room that don't recline more than about an inch-and-a-half, and eating our complimentary bag of peanuts that serves as lunch, would catch a quick glimpse of the first class passengers dancing through a limbo line to a live calypso band, with exotic rum drinks in their hands, served by topless Polynesian women, while a pig roasted on a spit... "Would you like some more complimentary cocaine, a full-body message, or a blow-job perhaps? Or maybe you'd like... Oh my God! The curtain is open! Quick, close the curtain! Don't let the losers in coach-class see what really goes on up here! Hurry, close the curtain!"... the pilot comes over the intercom in a booming Oz-like voice, *"PAY NO ATTENTION TO THOSE PEOPLE BEHIND THE CURTAIN!"*

The seat was so comfortable I actually fell asleep for a while, but I woke up when I had a bad dream. I have heard that it is a pretty common nightmare for people to dream that they are in school and have to take a test for which they're not prepared. I've had dreams like that myself, but I must be thinking about this courtroom television show because I had a dream that I prepared the case and had all of my important notes in my briefcase. The alarm didn't go off, so I had to get ready in a hurry, quickly snatched up my briefcase, ran off to the courtroom, and faced an angry judge who began the case immediately after I hurried to the defense table. The judge put me on the spot and asked me a legal question. In the dream I scrambled to find the answer in my briefcase, only to open it and discover that, in my hurry, I had grabbed my backgammon set by accident.

"Uh... uh, oh boy... you want to give my client two years in jail, your honor? Uh... I don't have a copy of the statute with me, but how about we roll the dice on the sentencing, double or nothing?"

Nightmare!

I took a cab ride back to my apartment and almost gagged from the unpleasant odor. I asked the driver, "Excuse me, sir, do you have a camel dung air-freshener in this car?"

He laughed and said, "No, I do not have an air freshener that smells of camel dung!" and, under my breath, I muttered to myself, *"Then it must be you, my friend."*

DAY 140 - JULY 26TH, 1996

Back in Los Angeles. Kelly has the day off and is blasting the Alanis Morissette CD on the stereo. I keep turning it down. She keeps turning it back up. Alanis has a really good voice... if you are someone who enjoys listening to bag-pipes.

I was driving through Beverly Hills when a cop on a motorcycle pulled out and got in traffic behind me. I knew he was there, so I was careful to do nothing wrong and even managed to slip on my seat belt as I drove. Next thing you know, the guy has his flashing blue lights on and pulled me over. For what?

The Eric Estrada wannabe (who the hell would strive to be Eric Estrada?) walked up to the side of the car and asked for my license and registration. They call the California Highway Patrol officers CHiPs as an acronym, but this cop could have earned the nickname from the cinderblock-sized chip on his shoulder.

"What's the problem officer?"

"You went straight ahead in a 'Right Turn Only' lane."

Oh shit. There's anarchy on the streets of Beverly Hills! You smoke a joint of that marijuana stuff and the next thing you know you're addicted to smoking crack cocaine and shooting heroin into your veins in a filthy flophouse... Go straight through an intersection in a "Right Turn Only" lane and it leads to failing to yield, making a left turn at 2:15 PM on a Wednesday that is prohibited from 9:00 AM to 6:00 PM Mondays through Fridays and, before you know it, you're smuggling a dozen illegal Mexican aliens over the border in a beat-up pickup truck and leading an armada of cops on a dangerous 100 mph chase through three counties.

Don't you have any real crime to fight in Beverly Hills? Can't you write-up some old Rolls Royce-driving millionaires for illegal distribution of Grey Poupon? How about issuing a citation for cruelty to animals when some high-society snobette forces her poodle to wear a little cashmere sweater? It must be a crime to carry an imitation Gucci bag in Beverly Hills and pass it off as an expensive accessory... Fashion fraud? No?

I told the officer that I was new to the area and anticipated taking a right, but realized that it was not the street I was looking for, so I merged back into traffic after realizing my mistake. He went back to his motorcycle and returned with a citation. Damn!

I told him that I had been an assistant district attorney for eleven years in Boston and he told me that I should have told him that before he wrote the ticket. I responded that, in my wildest dreams, I had no idea that he would possibly write me up for anything so trivial. I'll request a hearing and hope he doesn't show up out of consideration... that fucking fascist, Gestapo, storm-trooper, piece-of-shit-that's-making-my-life-miserable-so-he-can meet-his-ticket-quota-and-maybe-stir-up-a-little-overtime-at-my-expense asshole.

DAY 141 - JULY 27TH, 1996

It's Saturday and Kelly and I have plans to eat dinner with our gay friend Timthy tonight. Timthy picked us up and I sat in the front seat with him as we watched an older man in a big Mercedes in front of us throw a paper cup out the window of his car.

As we pulled up to a traffic light that had turned red, Timthy turned down the new Cher tape that was blaring over the car's sound system. (Thank God!) My relief was short-lived as Timthy proceeded to pull alongside the litterer, put down my window, lean across me, and yell out the passenger window, *"You're an asshole!* (pointing his finger) *You... are... an... ass... hole!"*

The man looked at us (Us? Leave me out of this, thank you.) and gave a puzzled expression, as if he didn't know what Timthy was so upset about.

Timthy countered by screaming at the top of his lungs, *"If you don't know what you did wrong, you've got other problems besides your receding hairline!"*

As I slid under the seat in embarrassment, pretending to be tying my shoe, I was thinking only one thing, "Please turn green! Please turn green! Please turn green!"

We went to dinner, then sat down at a little coffee house with an outdoor patio. You have to stand in line to order desserts, donuts or pastries, along with your choice of about twenty different types of coffee, expresso, cappuccino, latté, and other specialty coffees. I wanted to hide under the nearest table when Timthy got to the front of the line with me and yelled out to the guy behind the counter, *"Excuse me, is there a Starbuck's around here?"*

As I bent down in embarrassment, pretending to look at a slice of pie in the case under the counter, I was thinking only one thing, "Please don't let them think he's with me. Please don't let them think he's with me. Please don't let them think he's with me."

The guy didn't even bother to justify his question with a response of any type, but just stared at Timthy while I poked him in the ribs and whispered, "Why don't you ask him if it's OK if we call and have a pizza delivered to our table too?"

Timthy and Kelly

DAY 142 - JULY 28TH, 1996

My "cousin" Paul sent over a special comedy issue of *The Hollywood Reporter*, because it contained a number of articles that could be useful to me. One such article consisted of a discussion between six veteran comedy dealmakers and creatives representing the major studios, production groups, and talent management.

The reporter noted that the high failure rate for sitcoms could be attributed to the fact that many stand-ups are being plucked from the club circuit and thrust into comedy series before they were "ripe" by honing their craft for ten or fifteen years.

The panelists all agreed, but said that the studios were looking to make deals with comedians with any kind of experience and trying to develop them before they're ready. The executive vice president of Warner Brothers television noted that, "Tim Allen and Jerry Seinfeld spent years honing their acts and personas. I think the next person to be successful will be someone like that. That person may be out in the recesses somewhere undiscovered or just working the road for a long time."

That's *me* they're talking about!

The best part of the magazine was a full page advertisement for Comedy Central that had a picture of a Great White Shark with its jaws open, along with the caption, "There are over 747,000 lawyers in the United States... The world needs more comedians." Perfect! That's me they're talking about too! I brought it to the frame shop to be mounted.

I went to Kinko's Copies today and, according to her name tag, the black woman who waited on me was named "Valveeta."

I asked her, "What's your sister's name, 'Cheese Whiz?'"

She didn't laugh.

DAY 143 - JULY 29TH, 1996

I went to the Post Office near Highland Avenue, off of Sunset Boulevard, and the line was very long because there were only two windows open. The wait was annoying, but not nearly as aggravating as having to listen to some woman in front of me with an Eastern European accent complaining continuously about the poor service. She just wouldn't shut up for a second, going on and on about being inconvenienced by waiting in this slow line. I was on the verge of snapping and yelling at her, "What under-developed Communist country did you come from lady? Isn't the wait a little better than having your mail opened, read and censored, if it gets delivered at all, you ungrateful bitch?"

Then... after all her bitching... she got up to the window and spent about a half hour playing with herself up there. I couldn't believe it! I

L.A. Misérables, Too

could hear her, taking her sweet time, as well as our valuable time, "Do you have any stamps with flowers or animals on them? I want one Georgia O'Keefe commemorative stamp, two flower stamps... no, not Chrysanthemums, the roses, no... not the pink roses... Do you have red roses?... No? Then just make it one Lilac and one Sunflower, and three animal stamps, two from the endangered species collection... one spotted owl and, ooh... I don't like the colors in that one, they don't go with shade of the envelope... Make it one Amazon tree frog and one Red Breasted Tit Warbler, and make the last one a raccoon stamp... No, no, no... wait, are those American Indian tribute stamps? Who do you have? Geronimo?... Sitting Bull?.... Do you have any of the Northeastern tribes?... No? Well then, I'm going to go with the Pioneers of American Jazz collec..."

"Just buy the fucking stamps you Eastern Bloc pain in the ass! It's people like you that make waiting in these lines so miserable, Brumhilda! Did you do this when you were waiting for a handout in the cheese lines back home? No, of course you didn't, because your other cold, starving countrymen would have beat you by now and left you in a snow-bank! Please show your appreciation for this great country you now live in, buy the regular postage stamps with the simple, patriotic stars and stripes motif on them and get the hell out of line, because there are proud American citizens behind you patiently waiting to mail letter bombs to their congressman!"

DAY 144 - JULY 30TH, 1996

I had to make out the checks to pay the bills today. After I was done there was less than a thousand dollars left in my checking account. I'm screwed.

I'm gonna have to make money some way. I'm going to have to get creative or swallow my pride and take some shit job if something doesn't come up soon.

I was awoken by a phone call in the middle of the night. It was my friend Vinnie, the airline pilot, and he was shitfaced.

"What the hell are you doing, Vinnie? It's 3:00 AM!"

Vinnie slurred, "You'll never guess where I am, Paulie. Guess where I am. I bet you can't guess where I am?"

"I have no idea, Vinnie, where are you?"

"I'm standin' on a corner in Winslow, Arizona! Just like the song! Far out!"

"Ya Vinnie, but I'm nestled, all snug in my bed, with visions of sugar plums dancing through my head, just like the poem, so call back tomorrow, you fuckin' nut!"

(click)

Vinnie with my old Vette

DAY 145 - JULY 31ST, 1996

Last night Kelly and I watched a wildlife show on the Discovery channel. The documentary was filmed in Africa and the videographers followed a large pride of lions over the course of a year as they fought to survive by stalking various prey through the jungles and grasslands of the continent.

In one segment, it showed a majestic lion, hiding in thick brush, as he observed a group of gazelles drinking at a watering hole. He had his eye on one gazelle at the back of the pack that seemed to wander off from the others.

The lion waited patiently, then suddenly made his move, taking off in a gallop after the unsuspecting antelope… and the chase was on.

L.A. Misérables, Too

Kelly screamed, "HURRY PAUL! CHANGE THE CHANNEL!"

I said, "Huh?"

She was extremely upset and buried her face in a pillow, covering her eyes.

"HURRY UP, PAUL! CHANGE THE CHANNEL...NOW!!! ... BEFORE THE LION EATS THAT POOR GAZELLE! PLEASE HURRY!"

I laughed and said, "Why, Kelly? Do you think I'm going to save the gazelle's life if I switch the channel?"

"I DON'T CARE, JUST CHANGE IT!"

I attempted to explain. "That's the law of the jungle, Kelly. If the lion doesn't eat the gazelle, he'll die of starvation and its cubs will die too. It's a matter of survival. Eat or be eaten."

"I don't care. The gazelle is helpless. Put on *COPS,* where they just beat people senseless, I don't mind that at all..."

"What do you think, Kelly? Do you think that you'll save the gazelle's life if I change the channel? Do you think the lion will stop in his tracks, throw his paws up, turn around and say, 'Well, if nobody's watching, why bother?' No! Listen Kelly, the lion has a good reason to kill the other animals and eat them. He has to survive. It's not horrible. Animals are not like people. We're horrible. *PEOPLE* are horrible."

"Huh?"

"Think about it... The lion didn't kill the gazelle because he wants to steal his new Nike sneakers, did he?

"He didn't murder the gazelle so he can collect the life insurance money.

"The lion didn't randomly wipe out fourteen gazelles he doesn't know because he hates his job at the post office.

"The lion didn't blow himself up, along with a whole herd of antelopes, as he screamed *'Allahu ackbar!'* did he? He didn't kill the gazelle because his dog told him to, or because the gazelle happens to be a different color than he is.

"And the lion didn't kill the gazelle because his Uncle Mustafa touched him 'in a bad place' when he was a cub.

"Don't you get it? He's not horrible, he's just hungry!

Paul D'Angelo

"When a lion needs to eat, it's not like he can cut out the killing part of the meal by going to a drive-through at a McJungle's and order take-out... *'Ya... I'll have a medium zebra, two monkey meals for the kids, and some pond water to wash it down with, hold the crocodiles.'*

Of course, despite my logic, I ended-up changing the channel as my traumatized girlfriend had demanded.

After all, like the lion, I also have a strong will to survive.

Tonight I got a call to do an audition at Igby's Comedy Club on Pico Boulevard. It went well and I was told to call in my weekly availabilities each Tuesday afternoon. Good, that adds to the number of clubs that I can work-out at.

I was up at 1:00 AM trying to chip ice from the freezer with a hammer. I've never seen that much ice on a floor that didn't have two blue lines and a face-off circle in the middle.

I know one person that I'm not keeping awake with the noise. Business has been brisk for the gender-ambiguous 'ho' that lives directly across the hallway. Different men are coming and going out of her apartment at all hours of the day. (... and probably coming more often than going.) While I worry about where the money's gonna come from to pay next month's bills, she's raking in the cash. I guess that the only depression she has to worry about is the one she's been making in her mattress.

Hear the one about the assistant DA?

He chases bad guys by day, good jokes by night

DAY 146 - AUGUST 1ˢᵀ, 1996

I'm not much of an activist when it comes to getting involved in issues of any type, but I had to file a written complaint with my apartment building's management about the terrible condition of the equipment in the weight room. The exercise bike has been broken since I moved here. The Universal machine has two broken pulleys, a couple of damaged cables, ripped rubber grips on the bars, and it hasn't been greased in so long the weights stick to the machine. So I got a call from the office to inform me that the reason they have not maintained the equipment is because the complex is opening a nice new workout room with brand-new equipment next Monday.

What? You can't do this to me! Don't fix anything! Don't buy anything new! Don't efficiently respond to my complaints! If this place and the people in it don't suck, I'll have nothing to bitch about! I need to complain about the poorly maintained, smelly, filthy, insect-infested, asshole infested, shit-hole that I call my home. I can't write about the *nice* apartment building, and the *nice* facilities, and the *nice* management, and the *nice* people. Who wants to hear about that shit?

What are they doing to me? I knew something was up because I haven't seen a cockroach in my apartment for weeks. Next thing you know, there will be normal citizens moving in next to me, with normal jobs and normal sexual preferences, who don't let their dogs shit in the elevator, and don't cook things that make the hallway stink like a pig farm located next to a fertilizer factory.

What's going on here?... *What have you done to my wickedness? I'm melting... melting!*

They just painted the entire building. It looks a lot better. They even painted the doors on the elevator that looked so decrepit. Well, I don't think the new paint on the elevator doors was even dry before someone carved, "THIS PLACE SUCKS!" in huge letters.

Thank God. They can fix up the building, but the human vermin inhabiting it still remains. My well of misery has not run dry.

CHAPTER THREE
Take another little piece of my heart...

DAY 147 - AUGUST 2ND, 1996

You know, as if this town isn't filled with enough nuts already, one of the headlines in today's *Los Angeles Times* states, "RELEASE: KILLER LET GO BECAUSE OF CLERICAL ERROR."

What kind of bonehead filing error do you have to make to put a killer back out on the streets?

"Let's see," says the secretary as she looks through the Department of Corrections filing cabinet with the killer's file in her hand. "A - 'Assholes,' B - 'Bad Guys,' C - 'Convicted Murderers,' naw... ummm, D - 'Dead Men Walking?' hmmmmm.... no, no... G - 'Gangsters with Guns,' H - 'Hit Men,' I - 'Inmates,' no. K - 'Killers'... ooh, that's it, 'Killers'.

"But wait a second. Maybe it should be filed under 'M' for 'Murderers.' I can't decide.

"I know what... I'll put the folder in this file... right between the K and the M files. L - 'Let Loser Loose.' There we go! That's it, time for coffee!"

As if there isn't enough to be worried about in this city. It's scary. I know a friend who was concerned about getting broken into, so he bought a vicious pitbull to protect himself and keep criminals away from his home. It's been very effective... He hasn't been able to get near his place for two weeks.

Tonight I had a show at the Laugh Factory. I was scheduled to go on at midnight, but the show started late and Rodney Dangerfield came in to do a special guest spot, so I didn't get on until about quarter to one. Rodney fielded a couple questions from the audience at the end of his act and one guy yelled out, "Can you still get it up?"

Rodney answered, "What's the matter, don't you remember last weekend?" and then walked off the stage to riotous laughter. Fantastic.

My show went really well and a couple of the waitresses, as well as one of the managers, came up to me and asked why I hadn't appeared at the club for so long. I told them that I keep calling in my availabilities, but I can't get any spots. They told me that they were all going to submit recommendations to Jamie that he use me more often because I always do so well. That kind gesture really made me feel good.

Besides that, this week I have the scheduled presentation for the producers of the courtroom TV show that they are trying to procure financing for. I also have a meeting scheduled with the biggest personal appearance agent at ICM. After my show on Martha's Vineyard the booking agent for that show called up another major agency, APA in New York City, and recommended me to another personal appearance agent who has contacted APA's Los Angeles office on my behalf. I'm supposed to set up a meeting with their agent sometime this week. One of the assistants at ICM is setting up showcases with several prominent management companies and he needs a new videotape.

Elaine, who books the Ice House in Pasadena, is letting me do a set there Tuesday night so I can tape my performance. After my audition at Igby's this week, I was accepted as a regular and I'm supposed to call-in with my weekly availabilities every Tuesday. I also was informed that Mike Lacey from the Comedy and Magic Club in Hermosa Beach is trying to schedule me there for a week. Two literary departments from major agencies are doing coverages of my first diary for consideration from the publishing companies, and I'm supposed to play golf with a representative from a major television production agency next Saturday. I don't want to get my hopes up, but maybe things are finally starting to get rolling!

DAY 148 - AUGUST 3ᴿᴰ, 1996

It's beautiful out today but, then again, every day is beautiful in Southern California. I've lived in here for about five months now and I've seen like, maybe, two clouds.

It's so rare, when a cloud hides the sun and casts a shadow, people freak out like it's the movie *Independence Day*. Panic stricken surfer-dudes would look up, point to the sky with a look of horror on their faces, and exclaim, *"WHAT'S THAT? THAT PUFFY WHITE THING IN THE SKY?"* as well all the puzzled Californians start to run in terror.

"We'll ask the wizard....The wizard will know!"

Hey, snow sucks, but I'll take my chances with winter. If it's cold out, you can put on a heavy coat, mittens and a wool hat, and they'll keep you warm.

On the other hand, if there's an earthquake, a stocking cap won't protect you if your upstairs neighbor's entertainment center falls on top of your head while you're sleeping in your bed.

DAY 149 - AUGUST 4ᵀᴴ, 1996

Timthy needed help because he had to buy his roommate, Marshall, a birthday present, so he asked me and Kelly to go shopping with him. In the car we asked Timthy what he was thinking of buying for Marshall, and he said, "I'd like to buy him one of those laptop computers. How expensive are they?"

I said, "Gee, they start around $1500.00. Are you really going to spend that much on him?"

"I didn't know they were that expensive, Paulie. I was only planning on spending about seven or eight hundred dollars."

"Really? That's still a lot of money Timthy."

"That's OK," Timthy explained, "I've lived with Marshall for eleven years now and he's certainly worth it to me."

What a thoughtful guy.

Well, after shopping around and stopping for a couple drinks in-between stores, Timthy finally settled on a small, prewrapped box of Fanny Farmer chocolates as a birthday gift, which is a far cry from a laptop computer.

"Thanks for the chocolates. I think this one is caramel. And this one looks like nougat. Ahh... What's this one? Could it be? A 90 MHz Pentium processor with 8 MB RAM expandable to 40 MB, 810 million byte hard-disk with active-matrix color, 16 bit sound pro-compatible sound blaster, 4X CD-ROM and an enhanced port replicator, along with a video graphics accelerator, all contained in a milk-chocolate almond cluster?"

Nope, it ain't, Marshall.

So, is it *really* the thought that counts the most when you're giving a gift?

Answer: Yes... but it counts a little bit less when you're the one *receiving* the gift.

DAY 150 - AUGUST 5TH, 1996

Kelly gets up very early for work and I could hear the TV in the living room, so I decided to drag myself out of bed and keep her company. She was eating a bowl of cereal while she watched an exercise program on ESPN. I sat on the couch next to her and rubbed my sleepy eyes to get a better look at the three beautiful hard bodies that were bouncing around in skimpy, skin-tight outfits on a beach in Hawaii. I was mesmerized by these sweaty nymphets, but pretended to only be interested in the background scenery and the form and execution of the exercises.

Kelly remarked, "Wow, she's really in good shape."

I said, "Ya.... and she's hardly out of bed."

Oops. Freudian slip. Bagged. I'm screwed. "I-I-I... I mean out of *breath.*"

Kelly glared at me. "You said 'bed,' Paul. What were you thinking about when you said that?"

What I was actually thinking: "Truthfully, I was fantasizing about that tanned, taut and buffed little Energizer Fuck-Bunny performing some personal sex-aerobics with me in the sack, bouncing up and down like that on top of my naked body for a half-hour or so until the springs in the mattress gave out."

What I actually answered: "Truthfully, I'm still half asleep and I was just wishing I could go back to bed."

DAY 151 - AUGUST 6TH, 1996

So far, since I moved to Los Angeles to be "discovered," my comedy career has been a lot like a sale at a furniture store: "FIVE MONTHS – WITH ZERO INTEREST!"

As I walk around Los Angeles, I can't believe how many women have tattoos now.

When I was dating, it used to be widely assumed that the very few women who had tattoos back then were wild, uninhibited, promiscuous, loose and/or easy.

These days all of the women have tattoos and I don't like it… because now it's impossible for a guy to figure out which girls are the slutty ones.

DAY 152 - AUGUST 7TH, 1996

The newspaper reports that the state of Minnesota has signed a new state law ordering all counties to rename any lakes, rivers, or geographical features that contain the word "squaw" in them, because some high school students did some research and traced the word to "a French corruption of an Iroquois epithet for vagina."

I guess that means that "Muff Mountain" and "Cooze Canyon" are out too.

DAY 154 - AUGUST 9TH, 1996

You know that you're in Hollywood when you walk into a video store to rent an X-rated dirty movie and the guy behind the counter says, "Do you want a prerecorded video or do you want us to whip up a fresh film in the back room for you while you wait?"

It's a great idea. Made to order porno. It would be like ordering a sub in a sandwich shop.

(looking up at the menu on the wall) "Do you have any specials today?"

"As an appetizer we are offering a deluxe 'Creme d'Jeans' package consisting of a lovely young ass sautéed with scented body oils and, just in today, for the main course, we have a naïve, lovely eighteen year old, fresh off the bus from Kansas City. Very tender if I may say so."

"That sounds good, but I think I'll have the threesome... have them do it from behind... and can I have that with extra fellatio?"

"Sure thing... Would you like a lesbian scene with that?"

"No, thank you."

(Guy turns and yells into back room like it's a diner)

"TRIPLE PLAY, OVER EASY, MAKE IT A DOUBLE HEADER... AND HOLD THE CHICK-LICK!... Would you like to super-size that order and add a black actor?"

"No thank you, that should do it. Oh, and extra napkins, please."

"Of course."

DAY 155 - AUGUST 10TH, 1996

I placed a called to a woman manager who had been providing me with bookings at several theater venues outside of Los Angeles, including The Coach House in San Juan/Capistrano, The Ventura Theater, and Fourth and B, a 1500 seat auditorium in San Diego. I haven't heard from her for some time and, even though the money isn't great, it was a chance to work out on stage and put a couple bucks in my pocket.

When I got her on the phone, she said that the reason she hasn't called is that she went to see a fortune teller, who told her that she was in the wrong line of work and her true calling was to be a producer, so she is no longer involved with booking these gigs.

Whoaaaaa. Wait a second. Can you get a second opinion? I've been told that you should always have another doctor look at you before being operated on, why would you change your career based on this one fortune teller, leaving me without my shows?

Anything, a Ouija Board… that magic eight-ball that you ask questions to and turn upside down for the answers, "Should I really give up my management company and start a different career?" "ASK AGAIN LATER"

No good, I need money <u>now</u>. How bout we get some Chinese food and you consult your fortune cookie before you make any drastic decisions? We'll give a call to Dionne Warwick and her friends at the Psychic Network. We'll see what they have to say about this before you make any drastic decisions about your future. Have you looked at your horoscope today? Have you thrown a couple quarters in the "Voltar" arcade machine? You may be making a big mistake! Don't do this to me! I need the work!

I don't believe in any of that psychic, palm-reader, clairvoyant, astrologer bullshit anyway. Ya, I'm skeptical for sure but, then again, I'm told that's typical behavior for an Aries on the cusp of Pisces.

DAY 156 - AUGUST 11TH, 1996

There is an addition to the words, "THIS PLACE SUCKS!" that someone carved into the brand new paint on the elevator door. Some crime-fighting, social activist took a marker and added, "GROW UP ASSHOLES!" with an arrow pointing at the original graffiti.

That's very mature of you, also. In an effort to demonstrate how juvenile it is to carve graffiti into a newly painted door, this person found it appropriate to respond by <u>doubling</u> the amount of graffiti that everyone else has to read every time they ride the elevator.

I suppose that, later this week, we'll be seeing, "NO, <u>YOU</u> GROW UP, YOU STUPID SHITHEAD!" written in spray paint, then, "I KNOW YOU ARE, BUT WHAT AM I?" followed by "I AM RUBBER AND YOU ARE GLUE, WHATEVER YOU SAY BOUNCES OFF ME AND STICKS TO YOU"… and on and on until the entire door is covered and they have to paint it again.

I'm surprised that the people who live in this building can fill out a lease agreement without someone intellectually spotting them.

L.A. Misérables, Too

**St. James apartments on Hollywood Boulevard.
My second floor apartment is just behind the palm.**

DAY 157 - AUGUST 12TH, 1996

This is the day that I'm supposed to get the coverage back of my first diary from the literary department of one of the major agencies. You see, like a movie producer who is sent many scripts per week, a literary agent doesn't have time to read all the scripts or novels that are sent to him, so they get an intern to do a "coverage" of the work. The coverage gives a brief synopsis of the writing, along with that intern's comments, criticisms and recommendations, which the literary agent will review to determine if they want to take the time to read the entire piece of literature that has been submitted for consideration.

The obvious problem with this system is that the intern is the first line of defense that filters out many of the submissions before they ever get scrutinized by the agent. You are at the mercy of that particular person's personal assessment of your written material.

For example, in Kelly's job as an assistant to a movie producer, she occasionally is requested to write such coverages, along with her subjective remarks on the viability of the work. There was one script she had to read that was a futuristic science-fiction adventure, and she hated it with a passion because it wasn't interesting to her. Had she submitted a coverage for that screenplay, she would have panned it in the critique, recommended that the movie be passed on, and the producer never would have taken a second look at it. As it was, someone else read it, liked the premise and the dialog, and the movie is currently in production.

You take the chance that the snot-nosed intern who gets the assignment, fresh out of college and thinking that they know everything, is on your side when they read your work, or it will never get read by anyone else in the hierarchy of the literary department.

In my literary career crap-shoot, I rolled craps right off the bat.

My friend from the agency, Peter, told me that he had the coverage and suggested that we go to a cigar lounge and talk it over. I was all anxious when I picked him up, but started to get apprehensive when he talked about everything but the review on the way to smoke our cigars.

We got to the lounge, lit our cigars, and I looked over the review. My jaw dropped. I was reading the most scathing, derogatory critique I had ever seen in my life. Let's put it this way. If Adolph Hitler reviewed *Yentlel*, he would have more nice things to say about it. I guarantee, if the Fuëhrer was forced to watch *Fiddler on the Roof*, the next day he would be in the bunker and his generals would have heard him humming under his breath, *"If I ver a vich man... deedle deedle deedle..."* But not this miserable prick.

I was devastated. I took a yellow marker and highlighted everything on the comment page that was severely disparaging. When I was done, the only remark that was not highlighted read, "At least he never comes across as whiny or bitter." Oh ya?... You want bitter, you cocksucker? I can be bitter. After reading his belittling statements, eating my own shit can leave a very bitter taste in my mouth. I was so upset that I bought a six-pack of Bass ale on the way home and intended to drink it all before I went to bed.

If you look at this hatchet man's background, you'll probably find that he graded David Berkowitz's last book report, gave John Wayne Gacy his last job review, wrote Jeffrey Dahmer's last employment recommendation, and was Ted Bundy's guidance counselor. He set them off, and I'm going to be the next to snap and go postal.

But the longer I sat alone on my balcony and thought about what I had read, the less it bothered me for two reasons. First of all, it became obvious that Rex Reed's protégé, "Rex Careers," is a fucking idiot. I submitted a book and he reviewed it like a screenplay. "There is no storyline present... there is no plot... just a straight forward history. Characterizations are bland and poorly fleshed out... and never properly developed... It's not the sort of thing that will translate to the screen, big or small."

Well "Captain Conspicuous," that may be because there is not supposed to be a plot, a story, and a cast of reoccurring characters. The manuscript is a diary with comedic observations, but Vasco de Gama is oblivious to making that discovery. If someone put the *Los Angeles and Vicinity Yellow Pages* on this asshole's desk, he'd probably review it and mention that it has no plot and insufficient character development, because he had failed to recognize the most obvious fact that was staring him right in the face... which is that it is *NOT* a screenplay... *IT'S A FUCKING PHONE BOOK!*

The second issue was his criticism of my humor. Humor is very subjective and not all people react to the same stimuli. But, in my business, a comedian can either write material that arises from common experience and appeals to a wide segment of the audience, like a Jay Leno, or have a unique point of view that targets a particular market of loyal fans that can associate with that character or his particular type of humor, like an Andrew Dice Clay.

If my humor on stage was to be categorized, I would fit in the former style, because it's a form of observational sarcasm in which I make fun of myself, as well as others. To give you an idea, I took one routine almost verbatim from my memoirs and inserted it into my act when I performed in San Diego in front of an audience of over 1500 people of diverse backgrounds, nationalities, gender, ages and personalities, and got interrupted by four applause breaks during the course of the joke. The point is, I'm not someone who tried to write a humorous manuscript without any comedic background whatsoever. I've proven that I know how to make people laugh and have a talent for recognizing what's funny and what's not.

If this reviewer said that he only found certain parts of the book that were funny, or if he admitted that he didn't appreciate my sense of humor, I could understand it. But his criticism was so extreme, and his personal affronts were so excessive, that it's evident that there's a problem besides my lack of ability to find humor in everyday life.

"The material... has little entertainment value."

"Paul's comic observations are only mildly humorous, but rarely outright funny."

"As the manuscript unfolds, it quickly becomes apparent that this is a simple journal devoted to the banal."

"While jokes and witty aphorisms sometimes provide a chuckle, there are few real laughs."

"Paul's life is pretty ordinary (for L.A.) and his jokes are not funny enough to make one want to spend time with him."

"Comedian Paul D'Angelo lacks charisma and the manuscript is centered around his mundane life."

"There is a little humor here, but not nearly enough to overcome the material's fundamental flaws."

Holy shit, Batman! *Pow! Smack! Crash! Bang! Smash! Whack!*

Something's rotten in Denmark. Given the viability of the hypothetical example of random probabilities, which suggests that a group of chimpanzees, left alone long enough in a room equipped with typewriters, will eventually write the complete works of William Shakespeare, it seems reasonable to conclude that a person who makes a very successful living writing and performing comedy throughout the country would, during the course of a more than three-hundred page book, be likely to type at least *one* funny observation, even if it's totally by accident. There's more than meets the eye here. Something isn't kosher. I smell a rat. (Feel free to add your own appropriate cliché if you like)

Mundane?... Banal?... The whole point of observational humor is

L.A. Misérables, Too

taking ordinary, seemingly commonplace events, routines and items, and twisting them into exaggerated parodies of the obvious. My life is too boring to write about? If I spent every day in Hollywood in the back of a limousine doing lines of cocaine off the huge fake tits of some porno-starlet on my way to another movie premier I wouldn't have time to sit at my lap-top and write about the cockroaches in my Co-Co Krispies and the virtues of drive-through Mexican restaurants, you spoiled, apathetic prick.

I was hoping to get an objective assessment, but this isn't a critique, it's a personal vendetta. He couldn't have fit any more bad things on one page without switching to legal sized stationery and attaching Post-it Notes. Every sentence was devoted to personally slamming me and he used Satan's personal thesaurus to compliment his own venomous remarks.

It is apparent that this guy has a Crystal Gayle sized hair across his ass for some reason. It occurred to me that he seemed to dwell on the passages in which I mentioned my gay friend, Timthy, even though he only appeared in two brief segments of over three hundred pages of material.

"… a joke about Timthy styling his mother's hair is not exactly clever," he wrote. (A line attributed to me, but actually uttered by Timthy's companion which, along with several other misstatements of fact in the synopsis, indicates that dick-weed skimmed through the manuscript rather than reading it.)

Oooh. Do I detect a tinge of resentment there? It's less than coincidental that the only line he quotes out of the entire book is the one about my gay friend, and he totally ignores any interaction with my girlfriend, which presents many issues that anyone involved in a traditional male-female relationship can connect with. His little wisecrack and his blatant obsession with Timthy leads me to conclude, with good reason, that this gentleman is most likely inclined to be attracted to other gentlemen, which is just fine with me. I am very tolerant and accepting of any alternative lifestyles, which is evidenced by the fact that I have gay friends, but that doesn't mean that I am tolerant of being criticized for thinking like a heterosexual and being put down because a person thinks that his sexual preference is superior.

The point is this, pal. Live your life the way you please, you have my blessings, but don't try to inflict pain on me to reciprocate for the discomfort you feel every time your sphincter gets violated. Loosen up something besides your A-hole! You're taking life way too seriously! The reason I love Timthy as a friend is that we accept each other for what we are, which are opposites, but that's cool.

Actually, thank God this ruthless motherfucker came into my life. Things were starting to go pretty well for me. I lost my zeal for complaining. I had nothing substantial to vent about. This prick is the flatulence beneath my wings. He is the urine in the specimen jar that I have to hand in. He is the phlegm I need to clean my sunglasses. He is the open stall in a row of pay toilets when I have the runs, but no change. He is a wet-fart in the elevator of a meter maid who just gave me a parking ticket. Thank you for inspiring me to achieve new lows in literature that even you would be surprised at, you ruthless piece of shit!

Ahhhhh. I feel much better now.

CHAPTER FOUR
Send lawyers, guns and money...

DAY 158 - AUGUST 13TH, 1996

My financial situation is always on the back of my mind, and I wonder where the income will come from to pay the rent and the bills in the coming months. Why can't I win the lottery? I'm not asking for a lot of money, just fifty or sixty grand to get me through this dry period. Why God? Why can't you allow my luck to change and let me hit the numbers just once?

And God is looking down, shaking His head and muttering to Himself, "Paul, I'd like to help you out, but at least spend a buck and buy yourself a scratch ticket, you cheap bastard."

OK, Lord. You definitely have as point there. Entering the pool would certainly increase my chances of winning it.

So I went into a liquor store to buy myself a lottery ticket. I picked one in a shitty neighborhood, figuring that, if there is any justice in the world, a winning ticket would go to someone who is down on their luck and mired in a rat-infested public-housing tenement, spending the last dollar of their disability check for the dream of escaping from his private hell. Or maybe it's because I just happened to be driving through a shitty neighborhood when I got the idea to buy a ticket.

Anyway, I went in and asked the foreigner behind the counter if he had any five dollar scratch tickets for sale. He smiled and asked me where I was from, obviously because they do not sell five dollar scratch tickets in California.

"I'm from Massachusetts."

"Mahh... a... huh? Huh?"

"Massachusetts."

"Mass... hows... setitts... wha?"

"Mass-a-chu-setts! It's one of the fifty states, Punjab! Boston? Boston? Do you know Boston?"

He breaks out in a big smile, "Ohhh! Boston!... Boston Celtics! Larry Bird!"

Holy shit. Hey Hadji, I think it's great that you're doing well in our country... I'm fucking thrilled that you work in a liquor store and you're not robbing one but, if you're gonna live here and raise your family in the United States, at least *learn* the names of the states that are united. When someone mentions "Massachusetts," don't say, *"God bless you,"* like they'd sneezed.

Just like the other day, when I called a hotel and had to leave a message at the front desk for my friend, who was not in his room. By the time the foreigner wrote down the message, the guy was checking out.

"Tell him Paul called."

"Paul? How do you spell that? Is that P-A-L-L?"

Great, now this guy learned to spell from reading the brand names on packs of cigarettes. What's this country coming to?

I grabbed a burger on the way home. Is it me... or can the employees who usually work the drive-through window at fast-food joints act just a little too cheery for their own good... with their cute little smile and their cute little voice and their cute little head-sets, and their cute little uniform, in the cute little colors, and their cute little hat... They are reprogrammed by the giant corporation to act like robots... brainwashed to respond automatically, mechanically and unconditionally... without any mind of their own or a consideration for the particular circumstances.

"Welcome to McDonald's, can I take your order?"

L.A. Misérables, Too

"Yes, excuse me... My grandmother just died and I have to go to her wake... Can you tell me how to get to Mahoney's Funeral Home?"

(spunky and bubbly) "Sure! The mortuary is down the street. Take the second right and it's on your left-hand side... Thank you! Bye Bye now! Have fun! Enjoy the funeral!... Ooops, Hold on!... I almost forgot to ask, would you like french-fries with those directions?... No? OK, Bye Bye!... Have a great day!

"Welcome to McDonald's, can I take your order?"

The Boston Herald, Friday, March 13, 1987 **W17**

WEEKEND / MUSIC, COMEDY

Attorney has arresting sense of humor

By Dean Johnson

THE SCENE could have come right out of the NBC series "L.A. Law." The defense attorney proves the owner of a burglarized car went out after the accused carrying a nine-iron golf club for protection.

The prosecuting attorney posed a single question. "Could you tell me why you decided to use a nine-iron for that particular shot?" The courtroom dissolved into laughter and the prosecution won the case.

Pretty witty for a lawyer, huh? In this case, the lawyer was Paul Murphy, an assistant district attorney for the Salem District Court.

Murphy is accustomed to making people laugh, though. Several nights a week he appears in local comedy clubs as Paul D'Angelo.

Murphy, 30, is a Wakefield native who has been doing comedy since 1985. But he doesn't talk about or even mention his day job in his routines. He wants to become established as a genuine comedian, not just a novelty or someone with a gimmick. His stage name has kept his two careers totally separate ... until now.

"I went to the D.A.," Murphy explained, "and said, 'I don't want to embarrass you or cheapen my position,' and he said to go for it." So Murphy hopes the lawyer angle will get people to check out his comedy act for the first time. Once they see him, he's convinced they'll know he's for real and not just dabbling in comedy for his own amusement.

Being a comic is much more than just a sideline for him. Murphy worked long and hard on his material before he did his first open-mike night. "Before I went onstage for five minutes I made sure I had 20 good minutes of material," he said. After only half a dozen open mike nights he graduated to regular gigs.

Now, he works several nights a week and will be at Nick's Comedy Stop tonight and Sunday. A couple of weeks ago Murphy headlined at Stevie D's in Middleton, and he was on such a roll that some of the waitresses had stopped working to lean against a wall because they were weak from laughter.

"It's a lot of pressure," he admitted. "I get out of the court room shaking sometimes. But the most comfortable 45 minutes of my week is when I'm onstage. That's where I feel the best."

Though Murphy doesn't talk about his day job when he's performing, he can joke about it in conversation. He's thinking of billing himself, he said with a laugh, as "Paul D'Angelo, a comedian with convictions."

DAY 159 - AUGUST 14TH, 1996

I read something today that put the unfavorable coverage of my book in perspective for me. In 1982, to prove a point, someone took copies of the screenplay for what many critics consider to be the greatest motion pictures of all time, *Casablanca*, changed nothing but the title and the names of the characters, and sent the copies out to 217 production companies and agencies in Hollywood. Of the eighty-five agencies that responded, thirty-eight rejected the script outright.

In the book of Matthew, the Bible proclaims "... neither cast ye pearls before swine..." Apparently Matthew was unsuccessfully trying to shop a manuscript around Hollywood that also went unappreciated.

Paul D'Angelo

"Listen Matthew, I'm sorry babe, but I just don't think this *Bible* thing you got here is marketable... the book drags at times, maybe it needs some exclusive paparazzi pictures, you know... maybe a candid shot of Judas and Pontius Pilate together, or something scandalous... maybe we raise some eyebrows, go for the fringe audience...

"Have you considered changing the Adam and Eve characters in the opening scene to, say, Adam and Steve?... And seriously, no one's buying that Immaculate Conception routine. Do some digging and find out who the real father is... but, even then, we're talkin' mini-series at the most... I'm not saying it's a lost cause, but it needs something... Maybe spice it up with some blockbuster action scenes... part an ocean, burn a bush, raise someone from the dead, and we'll see what we can do.

"And this part with Madonna and the manger, that's hip babe, but let's see what kind of drawing power she has at the box office in *Evita* before we make a pitch to her agent... but, of course, that Christmas theme has been worked to death... enough already... we need something fresh...

"I know, I know I can be a prick, but hey, it's not like you're a fuckin' saint, right Matt babe?

"The crucifixion scene?... Oy vey! Every other director, producer, and important industry person in this town is a Jew, and you think you can sneak this image-burner by them without pissin' someone off? Get real, babe... Now, please excuse me, I have a power-lunch at the Ivy with Charlton Heston... I'll run your script by him and, hey, you never know... he's already reading for the part of Moses Malone in Shaq's new basketball movie, but I think playing Moses would be a real stretch for him, so maybe he'll be available to us... Stay in touch, you have my cell phone number. Ciao, babe!"

Max Reger was a German composer in the early 20th century who responded to the author of a negative critical commentary of one of his symphonies by writing, *"I am sitting in the smallest room in my house. I have your review in front of me. In a moment, it will be behind me."*

You know, like... uh... you know... I, uh wish like I could, you know like umm... express myself so fuckin' eloquently... You know?

DAY 160 - AUGUST 15TH, 1996

Yesterday, a grad student who was distraught about the poor evaluation he received on his master's thesis, shot and murdered three faculty members at San Diego State University who were on a committee that evaluated the work of graduate degree candidates.

The bastard who did the acerbic hatchet-job on my book's manuscript must be shitting in his pants about now. I could be armed and lurking around any corner.

Heh, heh, heh.

DAY 161 - AUGUST 16TH, 1996

I was trying to balance my checking account today and I was having the hardest time, like everyone does. Why did I waste so many years taking geometry, algebra and calculus that I will never, ever use because I am not employed as a chemist, computer whiz, banker, math teacher, architect or scientist?

The answer to the fourth math problem in exercise B of chapter three, $(X - Y^2) +$ (X plus the square root of Z) over the sum of the digits of X,Y and Z to the nth power minus π has never come up in my life since I was tested on it twenty-three years ago.

We needed to be taught more practical math that would be of use to people in everyday situations. Like, if I have less than $250 in my checking account, no means of income, and next month's rent is $865, how long will it be before my check bounces and we get our eviction notice?

If you have a Toyota pickup truck loaded up with twenty-six illegal Mexican aliens, how many more migrant farm workers can you fit in the back before the truck is full? If the truck is full, how much will you clear at 50% of their day's pay at $4.00 an hour for twelve hours minus any bail money you'll need to post if you have a 35% chance of being stopped at the border?

If you drive past twelve hookers in platform shoes and mini-skirts on Hollywood Boulevard, what is the percentage that the one you pick has a penis?

If the black guy standing on the corner near my apartment has 15 grams of rock cocaine in his pocket, and one of the buyers that approaches him is an undercover cop, how much state prison time will he do given ineffective counsel, a tough judge during an election year, and one-third of the sentence off for good-behavior?

If it's a white guy, how much money will it cost him to get one year's unsupervised probation for the same offense?

If I have $300.00 cash in my pocket and I walk to the cash machine in my seedy neighborhood to make a deposit, what are the chances that I will get back safely with the money if I leave after 10:00 PM?

If my car cost me $25,000, it's now worth $4000, but I still owe the finance company $9000, the vehicle needs $2500 of mechanical work, and my insurance costs me is $1000 a year, how much is a season's bus pass?

If it costs some nut $100 to go bungee jumping and risk plunging to an instant death, how much would it cost the same dummy to participate in an activity that could only possibly turn him into a paraplegic? What kind of deal to be merely maimed and disfigured?

If a guy spends an extra $4000 on a sports car to get the fuel-injected, twin turbo model with 425 cubic inches and 300 horsepower, that does 0 to 60 in 4.25 seconds, how much will the ticket cost that he gets the first hour after he drives the new car out of the showroom?

If someone cheats when they're keeping score during a golf game when he's playing with his friends for $10.00 a hole, how will shaving those strokes affect his handicap for the rest of the summer?

If it's 108° in the San Fernando Valley and 115° in Palm Springs on a typical summer day in Southern California, what SPF factor sunscreen would Satan have to wear if he left the fiery pits of hell and vacationed in the area?

If the expiration date on my strawberry yogurt is May 5, 1996, and I eat it without looking at the date on August 16th, 1996, how much will it cost to get my stomach pumped at the emergency room if I can't afford health insurance?

L.A. Misérables, Too

If a young boy is twelve years old, but he has the ass of an eight year old, how much will it cost Michael Jackson to keep his family quiet?

DAY 162 - AUGUST 17TH, 1996

I'm so broke I don't know what to do. Hey, what's this in the newspaper? Back in New Hampshire, of all places. Get this. A court in Providence, Rhode Island sentenced a guy to prison for pretending that he was dying of cancer for six years and raising $43,000 in donations from his family, employer and the church. This guy claimed he had kidney, lung and prostate cancer, and even his former wife and three stepsons believed him because he shaved his head to simulate the effects of chemotherapy, dropped red dye in the toilet to make it appear that there was blood in his urine, and would fake seizures, sometimes slamming his head into a wall to make the episodes look realistic.

Can you believe this? That lowdown, conniving piece of shit! Hey, I'm desperate for money and I'm worried if I'm gonna make next month's rent, but would I stoop so low as to fake cancer just to raise money from sympathetic people? Absolutely not, and you know why? Because I didn't think of it first! This guy may be sick (figuratively, not literally), but he's clever.

Just like the guy who started his own long distance service called, "I Don't Care." When operators asked people what long distance service they preferred, many answered, "I don't care," and they got connected to his service that charged double the going rate.

Why can't I come up with a money-making scheme like that? I could never fake dying of cancer. It's too serious. My family would be upset, it would bum the comedy crowds out and, besides, it's been done before. No, it would have to be something that invokes sympathy, but is not quite so depressing. I know, maybe I can attach a sandwich bag to my belt and tell people I needed a colostomy operation. Every morning I'll take whatever food is leftover in the apartment, throw it all in the blender, hit "puree," and fill up the bag. Then I'll approach people and say, "Give me some money or I'll toss the bag at

Paul D'Angelo

you like a toxic water balloon!"

I don't know about you, but I know that I'd dig into my wallet without hesitation. "Gross! Here's a couple bucks. Get the hell out of here! That's *disgusting!*"

Tonight I performed at a coffee house in the valley. I don't really want to do comedy at a coffee house, but I don't have much choice if I need the stage time to try out some new material that I've written for my comedy act.

I asked to be on first, because I had to be on stage at another location by nine o'clock. That was a lie, but I didn't want to have to stick around all night drinking espresso and listening to the insufferable open-mike performers.

There were maybe sixteen people in the audience and virtually every one of them was studying notes or writing things down in a notebook. This indicated to me that pretty much the entire crowd was made up of fledgling comedians who were waiting to get on stage that night. Since it was a rather informal atmosphere, the first thing I did, when I got up on stage, was to ask how many of those in the audience were comedians.

Everyone raised their hands except for one couple. I told them that I just wanted to know because I was there to throw out some brand-new ideas and other material that I had altered. Since my act was to consist of entirely untested routines, and I was looking for feedback so that I could see what worked and which jokes needed more work, I told them that, based on my experience with audiences consisting of comedians, I would have to use a different standard for evaluating the jokes.

Because this is such a competitive vocation, in an extremely competitive city, if the crowd of my peers laughed, I knew the joke sucked, because they would want me to *think* that it was funny and continue to use it, thereby increasing the chances that I would never amount to anything, and therefore improve their respective chances for success.

On the other hand, if a new joke was hysterical, I would expect to see the other comics somberly poking each other in the ribs and whispering under their breath, "Don't laugh, just stare at him. Don't let on that it's good. If he thinks it's lousy, he'll drop the joke and we can use it."

The comics in the audience laughed at my observation because they knew this to be more true than not.

DAY 163 - AUGUST 18TH, 1996

I just heated up a frozen dinner in the microwave and it really tasted horrible. I wonder if I did something wrong. I took the box out of the trash and reread the directions.

MICROWAVE HEATING INSTRUCTIONS:
- Puncture plastic film covering 3-4 times with fork to vent. (Yup, did that.)
- Heat on HIGH for 5 minutes. (OK, did that too.)
- Remove plastic film, rotate plate 1/2 turn and heat on HIGH for additional 5-6 minutes. (So far, so good.)
- Remove from microwave and enjoy!

That's it! No wonder the meal sucked. I missed an important step. I forgot to "Enjoy!"

This afternoon I went to the Beverly Center with Kelly, which is a huge mall on La Cienega Boulevard. She needed to get make-up at Macy's and asked if I'd like to go with her. Sure, I have nothing else to do. I went to the mall with her and sat in the make-up area of this big department store. There were women working there that had an entire line of cosmetics on their face, all at one time. One woman, who was made-up like a circus clown, came up behind me and scared the shit out of me.

"Can I help you?"

I turned to face her. "Aiieeeee! I'm sorry... You startled me... Shouldn't you say 'Trick-or-treat!' first?"

After all of this we were walking out of the mall when a cute little puppy in the pet store caught my eye. I went over to look at the puppy, believing that Kelly was right behind me but, when I looked around, she wasn't there. I immediately left to find her, which I did about fifteen seconds later, and she was absolutely bullshit at me for running off. She started screaming at me in front of all the people walking by, just like I was a little kid who got separated from his mother in the supermarket. I was humiliated.

Of course murder is out of the question as an option... every square foot of this city is either developed or covered with asphalt and there's just no place to bury the body.

DAY 164 - AUGUST 19TH, 1996

The day after I arrived in Boston to do shows for a week and a half in July, I got a call from the producers of a courtroom television show who begged for me to fly back to Los Angeles immediately so I could do a presentation to the distributors who would ultimately make the decision on whether or not the show's pilot would get financial backing. They weren't going to pay me for my services, or pay for my flight back, and there was no guarantee that the money would be allocated to the project. And besides, I had an obligation to perform every night in Boston, including a couple evenings opening up for country-western star Tanya Tucker in music theaters with a couple thousand seats. I told them "no way." If they wanted me bad enough they would have to wait, which they agreed to do, and they ended up rescheduling the presentation for the day after I arrived back to the West Coast.

That was over two weeks ago, and these people haven't been heard from since. The management company that set this whole thing up can't get a hold of the producers and they don't know where they are. The only reason I give a shit is that there was a slim chance that, if the pilot was made, I would get some money out of the deal that would hold me over for a while. Fat chance. They disappeared faster than a white guy thumbing a ride in South Central Los Angeles wearing a "Rodney King Deserved It!" t-shirt.

CHAPTER FIVE
I have become comfortably numb...

DAY 165 - AUGUST 20TH, 1996

I went down to the laundry room to do our laundry today. I was wearing a pair of shorts and a T-shirt and, after I put all the clothes in the washing machines, I left the laundry room and pushed the button for the elevator before I realized that I might as well throw the pair of underwear that I was wearing into the wash. I looked around the area near the elevator, then checked both sides of the adjacent parking garage, to make sure there was no one around. Then I ran back into the laundry room, took off my shoes, then my shorts, and finally my underwear, so that I was standing there, naked from the waist down. I threw my Calvin's into the washing machine, put my gym shorts back on, and then left to go back to my apartment.

When the wash was done, I put the wet clothes in the drier then, an hour or so later, I went down to check on the clothes to see if they were dry. They were still a little damp so I stood around trying to kill time for a few more minutes. There was a bulletin board with a notice of "HouseKeeper aBaiLaBle". There's someone you can trust won't be writing their doctoral thesis on your laptop when you're not at home. There was also a piece of paper tacked up advertising, "Full body massage and therapy for all types of injuries. Tarot card readings also available." (not to be confused with 'aBaiLaBle', of course) That's a good combo. She predicts when you're going to get hurt so you can schedule your therapy ahead of time.

I was getting bored, waiting for the stupid clothes to dry. That's when I looked up and saw the video camera. The one that monitors the laundry room. The one that sends a picture back into the main office where the women sit and do paperwork. The same camera that caught one of the perverted tenants running around in the laundry room with no pants on about an hour ago.

Ooops.

DAY 166 - AUGUST 21st, 1996

Tonight I had a show at the Laugh Factory and Barry Katz, a personal manager and one of my good friends, came into see me. When I got off stage, Barry told me that he had an extra ticket to see Hall & Oates perform at the House of Blues on Sunset. I asked how he got the passes and Barry told me that he was friendly with the band's manager.

Huh. That brings back a bittersweet memory. Back around 1990 or so, I opened up for Hall & Oates at the Club Casino in Hampton Beach, New Hampshire, which is a two-thousand seat concert venue on the seacoast. At the time, I was still employed as an Essex County assistant district attorney.

After the show, the managers and some other employees of the Casino came up to me and told me that Hall & Oates and their manager loved my show and they wanted to take me on the road with them as they began a national acoustic tour of small to medium sized theaters. Everyone was so enthusiastic, slapping me high fives and patting me on the back, that I began to realize what a great opportunity this would be. I was ready to leave the prosecutor's job soon and all I needed was a good excuse. Well, here it was. After Hall & Oates were done performing, the Casino people encouraged me to address their manager and see what was up.

I approached him near the stage as the roadies broke down the band's equipment.

"Excuse me, sir. I was told that you'd like to speak with me."

He held his hand up to me, like he was a cop stopping traffic, turned from me with a disgusted look on his face, and said, as he walked away, *"Ya. That's all we need... a fuckin' DA on the tour bus."*

My world came crashing down. In my mind I was thinking, *"No! You can't do this to me! I'll quit the prosecutor's office! I was going to leave anyway. Do what you want on the bus. I don't give a shit if you put crack on your corn flakes in the morning, watch a television stolen from the rectory at St. Joseph's Church, and sleep with your eight year old special-needs sister every night. Do you think I'm gonna turn you in?"* but I just stood there speechless and watched him walk away... along with my dreams.

On stage at the Club Casino, Hampton Beach, NH in 1989, opening up for Huey Lewis and the News

DAY 167 - AUGUST 22ND, 1996

It took what seemed like five minutes of struggling, grunting and swearing to get the top off of the new bottle of Listerine I bought. Is a child-proof safety top really necessary on a bottle of mouthwash?

What kid is going to climb into the medicine cabinet and overdose by drinking a bottle of Cool Mint Listerine?

I envision a paramedic, giving a child mouth-to-mouth resuscitation as his frantic mother tearfully pleads, *"Oh God! Is my little Johnny going to make it?"*

The emergency worker looks up at her and answers, "I don't know lady, but I gotta tell you… his breath is *fantastic!"*

Tonight I had a show at the Ice House in Pasadena, where I was set-up to have a ten to fifteen minute videotape shot. I wanted this to come out OK because I have at least fifteen management companies, literary agents, booking agents and TV producers waiting for a tape. The show went perfect and I slept with the tape under my pillow.

DAY 168 - AUGUST 23RD, 1996

The first thing I did when I woke up was to watch the video recorded last night so I could time it for dubbing. I turned on the TV, popped in the tape, and pressed "play." All I could see was a blank screen. I started to get nervous and hit the "search: forward" button. Still nothing. Oh no. My stomach was starting to hurt. I hit "fast forward," and got nothing but snow on the TV. Fuck!! This show was perfect and it will be weeks before I get another night to tape there. I got on the phone to call the club to reschedule.

"Hello, the Ice House, can I hel…" (click)

I hung up when I realized that I forgot to rewind the tape before I watched it. I better make a strong pot of coffee before I do something else that's stupid this morning.

DAY 169 - AUGUST 24TH, 1996

I'm getting ripped-off left and right in this town.

If I don't get my copy of the *LA Times* by 9:30 in the morning, someone always takes my newspaper, even on the weekends. I was so pissed-off, I planned to wait one morning with my eye to the peephole, for hours if I had to, to catch the culprit.

Upon reflection, I realized that this was a stupid idea. No, I have a better plan. I'm going to tie a string to the newspaper, run it underneath the door, and tie the other end to the handles of some pots and pans in the kitchen. Then I'll grab the nearest weapon, spring out into the hallway and nab the bastard. I'm sure the dirtball will be trembling when I suddenly pounce after the Sunday paper in my boxer shorts, with a bad case of "pillow-head" and a plastic spatula raised over my head in a threatening manner.

DAY 170 - AUGUST 25TH, 1996

This morning I drove down to the Ralph's supermarket on Sunset Boulevard, at the end of my street, to get some milk. When Kelly and I pulled into the parking lot there was a confrontation going on between two men who were yelling threats at each other as a security guard tried to break it up. One guy, who was wearing no shirt and looked wasted already, seemed to be the aggressor and wouldn't back down. The guy who was retreating looked like a gangsta, wearing his pants slung low on his hips with his underwear showing, and the crack of his ass peeking through like a plumber working under the kitchen sink. He was screaming that he was going to kick the other guy's ass, to which the shirtless man repeatedly replied, "You'll have to shoot me, motherfucker!"

It seemed that the second man was willing to comply as he reached for his waistband in the back of his pants. How clever… he's using the crack of his ass for a holster.

As we watched the drama unfold from the car, my stomach was growling because I couldn't eat my Co Co Puffs without milk. I said,

"Kelly, cover me, I'm going in," and, before she could stop me, I ran for the store entrance in the crouched over position that I see people on the evening news using when they are running for cover between buildings during a rebel uprising.

"Will that be all, sir? Just the half-gallon of milk and the medium saucepan you're wearing on your head?"

"It's not a pan, pal, it's a helmet."

DAY 171 - AUGUST 26TH, 1996

I had to get the oil changed in my car today. I drove around until I found a Jiffy-Lube quick oil-change shop. I said, "Can you change my oil and filter?"

The guy says, "We're pretty backed up. It'll be about a two, two and a half hours until we can get to ya."

I said, "Two and a half hours?!... Boy that's real fuckin' 'jiffy.' Maybe 'Lazy Lube' would be a better name for this place."

He told me that he'd do his best to get to my car sooner, which is garage talk for, "For all I care, you can shove a can of 10W-40 up your ass, mister."

DAY 172 - AUGUST 27TH, 1996

My friend Max and I had dinner in a new bar/restaurant on Sunset Boulevard called Red Rock. We sat out on the deck facing the street to watch the world go by. After our food was served, our waiter disappeared and Max needed a spoon, so he called the maître'd over and asked him for a table spoon.

The young man looked perplexed and replied, in broken English, "Spoon? I do not understand, spoon."

You know, if they're gonna have a foreigner work in a busy restaurant, it should be a minimum requirement that they learn at least some of the basic words that are necessary to provide effective service to the customers. Nothing fancy, just some fundamental English words that would be important to understand in a food service situation. I'm not asking a lot, but essential words and phrases like....

"Quick! Where's the fire exit?"
"Help!... I'm choking!"
"Heimlich maneuver."
"All employees must wash hands before touching food."
"Board of Health."
"This is a stick-up, don't move or I'll kill everyone in here!"
... and *"SPOON,"* for starters.

DAY 173 - AUGUST 281H, 1996

We drove down Hollywood Boulevard tonight and it was filled with hookers. I swear half of them are men, but you really have to look close, if you can be certain at all, because a lot of the men dressed as women look damn good. Some guy who has a few drinks in him would never know the difference.

Here are some things that you don't want a beautiful "woman" to say as "she" looks up at you while performing fellatio:

- "How 'bout those Packers?"
- "Hey Joe! It's me, Lester, from the Elks Club!"
- "Ow! You just hit my Adams Apple!"
- "After this, you should check out the new table-saw I got at Sears."
- "Let's go... I gotta piss like a race horse!"
- "Don't you hate it when your balls hang below your hemline?"

DAY 174 - AUGUST 29TH, 1996

There is a huge wildfire raging out of control about forty miles north of Los Angeles. It should come as no surprise if people are searching for a cause. The temperature has been in the upper hundreds the last couple days. I saw a woman sitting by the pool with no sun-block on who spontaneously combusted. All that was left was some smoking ashes, a bottle of Evian, and an issue of 'Cosmopolitan' on top of a beach towel.

Paul D'Angelo

DAY 175 - AUGUST 30TH, 1996

There are many double standards in Hollywood.

Here's an observation regarding one of those double standards that I made while stuck in traffic on Sunset Boulevard today:

If you see someone driving alone in their car, and it appears that they are talking to themselves... and the car they are driving is an expensive model, like a Mercedes, Lexus or Jaguar, you would automatically assume that this person is talking over his speakerphone... maybe making a big business deal.

If, however, you see someone talking to themselves in a shit-box... you will immediately conclude that they are a friggin' nut having a delusional conversation with an imaginary friend.

The truth is, there are probably just as many fruitcakes in the nice cars as there are in the crappy ones.

DAY 176 - AUGUST 31ST, 1996

I can't believe this retro-fashion craze. Every store window display... every magazine advertisement... every young person I see on the streets or in the clubs, is wearing clothes right out of the '60s and '70s. Bell bottom pants... platform shoes... lime greens and orange together... wide lapels and brightly colored polyester jackets... leisure suits with white stitching are back... gaudy leopard skin everything... knee-high, white patent leather go-go boots... velour pullovers.... tacky disco jewelry around the neck... flood-water-length plaid pants... fake-silk polyester shirts with butterfly collars... cat's eye sunglasses.

You don't see anyone my age getting caught up in this trend. Why? Because we already went through that phase and eventually realized that we looked like tasteless assholes. One day we all woke up, looked at ourselves in the mirror and collectively asked, "What the fuck were we thinking?"

Don't worry... their time will come.

DAY 178 - SEPTEMBER 2ND, 1996

I see in the newspaper today that lawmakers have introduced a bill to sanction the chemical castration of repeat sexual offenders. Apparently, scientists have developed a drug that has Federal Food & Drug approval, which will suppress your sex drive and make you impotent. Convicted sex fiends could be forced to take the drug once a week for the term of their parole.

Hey, I think it's probably a good idea to render child molesters incapable of being able to have sex, or even desire to have sex. It just worries me that such a drug exists. These are tough times for a guy.

In its aftermath, the Lorena Bobbitt incident created an appreciable degree of paranoia and vulnerability in any man who went to bed after having an argument with his wife or girlfriend. There were countless hours of lost sleep as American males lay with their eyes open until dawn, attempted to sleep in the uncomfortable, but protective, face-down position, or went to bed wearing their old hockey cup. Now, with this impotency drug available, after a big fight we'll need to have a food taster, like a South American dictator.

(whispering to someone under the table) "She's in the kitchen... quick... Here, try this meatloaf... Did you eat it? Good... Now go into the bathroom. There's a *Penthouse* in the book rack... Look at the centerfold and see if you get aroused. I'll stall her until you give me the results."

The article mentions that the drug's possible side effects include depression and breast enlargement. How true. Any guy would be gloomy if he suddenly grew a pair of beautiful, firm breasts that he could fondle with his left hand, but at the same time, his equipment wouldn't get aroused enough to manipulate with his right hand.

And therein lies the tragedy.

DAY 179 - SEPTEMBER 3RD, 1996

On the way to the ICM office on Wilshire Boulevard, I was stuck in traffic and noticed a huge bronze statue of John Wayne riding a horse in front of the Western Bank building. I'm not saying that this city doesn't have a real sense of history but, for example, in Boston's North End there is a bronze statue of American patriot Paul Revere sitting on the horse he heroically rode to warn the colonists that the British were coming, before he went on to become a legendary statesman, craftsman, and brewer.

In Los Angeles, they would erect a statue in tribute to the guy who *played* Paul Revere in some movie.

DAY 181 - SEPTEMBER 5TH, 1996

I was in traffic on Sunset behind a car called a Daihatsu *Charade*. What kind of a lame name for a car is *Charade*? It's a pussy, fruitcake name. What happened to tough names like Thunderbird or Barracuda or Mustang or Firebird?

I looked around me. To my right was a Volkswagen Golf. Huh? It's called a "Golf?" If you bring the car into to have it aligned because it pulls to the right, does the mechanic say, "Actually, your front end is fine… the reason it's pulling to the right is your car has developed a wicked slice."

The way I play, I'd end-up driving the car deep into the woods and wouldn't be able to find it.

Chapter Six
Feats don't fail me now...

DAY 182 - SEPTEMBER 6TH, 1996

It's been around twenty-six weeks since I moved to Los Angeles. For twenty-six weeks I have been calling the Improvisation every Friday and telling Ross, who books the room, which days I will be available to perform the following week. (Which is basically every day) Then every Monday afternoon for twenty-six weeks in a row, I would call Ross and he would tell me that I was not on the week's schedule.

After about, say, twenty two weeks of this shit... I figured that I had nothing to lose by calling Ross and speaking to him about my absence of bookings, despite the fact that the club's owner, Budd Friedman, told me that they would use me after I auditioned for him. After all, what's less than doing zero shows in twenty-two weeks? Still nothing, so what's the worst that can happen?

I told Ross that I had been patiently calling every week for over five months but got the impression that he no intention of using me at the club, and it occurred to me that Ross had never seen my act, so I suggested that we set up a showcase in which I would perform at Ross' convenience. He told me that he didn't have time to see me and I should just keep calling. I got the impression that each week I was wasting my dime and my time.

Paul D'Angelo

The good news was that I just heard that Ross is out and one of the Improv's managers, Richard, would now be booking the club. Tonight I dropped by the Improv and someone introduced me to Richard. He was a very nice man and told me that he's heard a lot of good things about me and plans to give me some dates when they become available. Great. That's encouraging.

I headlined other Improvs, but was lucky to get a whiff of the stage in Hollywood

DAY 183 - SEPTEMBER 7ᵀᴴ, 1996

I got a phone call from my friend Barry Katz today. Barry asked me if I'd like to tape a seven to ten minute set on NBC for *Friday Night Videos*.

Yes!

DAY 184 - SEPTEMBER 8ᵀᴴ, 1996

I can't believe how many people in Los Angeles are driving around in those Hummer vehicles. These things were developed specifically for the armed forces as an all-purpose, all-terrain vehicle to replace the Jeep. It is very impractical and very expensive and very stupid to have in the middle of a major city.

Hey!... Stupid rich people, listen up. When people say, "It's a jungle out there," you're not supposed to take them literally. They don't mean *that* type of jungle.

You don't need the heavy-duty, steel-reinforced cage over the front bumper to deflect a charging rhino... You don't need the four-wheel-drive to make it home to Beverly Hills in a raging drizzle... You certainly don't need three feet of ground clearance to make it over the speed-bump behind The Coffee Bean...

Understand, you dummies?

DAY 185 - SEPTEMBER 9ᵀᴴ, 1996

I'm disgusted. It's my brother Jay's birthday and I couldn't even afford to buy him a present. Sometimes I wonder how I ever got involved in such a crazy business. It's funny how people change their priorities.

For instance, when I was a young, immature, stupid and naïve kid, I thought the best job in the world would be to work on the back of a big garbage truck, slinging trash barrels into the back of the compactor, pulling the handle to crush the stinking refuse, and then standing on that little step in the back, taking in the fresh air and holding on with my gloved hand as the truck took off on its daily route. What a great way to make a living, I thought. You get to work outside, ride around on a cool truck and pick through people's trash.

God, was I stupid or what? What a loser! It's amazing how far I've come... How much I've matured... How much more motivated I've become... How I've learned to set my goals higher and not settle for less. Yes, I've grown quite a bit.

What I really wish for now... What I really want out of life... What I really want to do now....is to *drive* that big truck and be able to blow the horn really, really loud.

What can I say? My goals are lofty and I'll settle for nothing less.

DAY 186 - SEPTEMBER 10TH, 1996

Tonight is the night that I shoot a stand-up spot for *Friday Night Videos*. The show is shot on the same set where they film *The Tonight Show* at NBC studios in beautiful downtown Burbank, as Johnny used to say.

Kelly accompanied me to the shooting and we were let in at the gate and told where the sound stage was located. We walked past a beautiful 1950's Buick that was in showroom condition. It was a big beast and its chrome glistened in the moonlight. As we suspected, the car was in the parking space assigned to Jay Leno.

I was tenth on the list to perform and Kelly and I watched my predecessors from the bleachers in the studio. For this taping they basically constructed a separate backdrop to the right of the *Tonight Show* stage and sat an audience in that half of the studio only. As you looked at the area where the stand-ups were performing, behind and to the left of the temporary background were the desk and chairs where Jay interviews his guests. As exciting as it was to tape this nationally broadcast show for a major network, my mind looked ahead to the day when I might appear on this same stage on *The Tonight Show*.

Unless I'm appearing at an audition and need to be precise in my presentation, it is my usual custom to step on a stage with a general set-list in my head from which I can loosely follow a series of routines

L.A. Misérables, Too

and deviate if I happen to go off on a tangent. I approached this set much differently, first because I was under a time restriction, and particularly because I was doing one rather involved routine in which I narrate a five minute monologue and/or dialogue with myself that is comprised primarily of acronyms.

I wrote the routine almost ten years before I ever thought about performing stand-up comedy, while sitting in the lunchroom at Boston College during my senior year, in 1977-78. When I became a comic, it became a staple of my very early act in 1986.... the concept has often been copied since, but my version was written and performed long before anyone else did so...

It starts out:

"I recently moved to Hollywood, but let me tell you about one of the first trips to California... I flew from Boston to LA but I couldn't get a direct flight to LAX so we had to go through JFK on TWA... the FAA delayed our ETA and, when we got to baggage claim, my f'n luggage was MIA ... anyway, when I got to LA, I got invited to one of those TGIF parties....you know, BYOB, RSVP...

(slurring my words) "Well, I had enough V.O. and J&B to send me to A.A. with the DT's...

I staggered into the parking lot and there was this AH...The guy was a CPA with IBM and he got his PHd from MIT, but now he's a big CEO with MGM (jerk-off motion)... He was getting into his brand-new BMW with the ABS brakes, and an AM-FM radio with a CD, a GPS navigational system and he had the A/C on... but I wasn't impressed... I looked at him and said, (slurred with an attitude) *'well B.F.D.!'*

"Anyway, this AH started giving me some B.S.... I got P.O.'d at the S.O.B. with the BMW who wouldn't mind his P's & Q's and thinks he belongs on the cover of *GQ*... and I was ready to KO him and send him to the E.R. where the EMT's can give him some CPR so he doesn't D.O.A. in the. I.C.U. because he has a shitty HMO like me.

"That's when my friend DJ came out of the party... DJ got his M.B.A. from U.C.L.A., but he's been working with the D.P.W. 'cuz he did a lot of L.S.D and now he's got the I.Q. of an M&M!... Nice guy, but a bad case of B.O.... P.U.!

"DJ said, 'Calm down! Don't fight! You need some T.L.C., A.S.A.P.'

I said, "Thanks, I.O.U."

"He was right, so I remembered this girl Dee Dee... Dee Dee is an R.N. from D.C. who moved out here to Riverside, EIEIO... and now she lives in LA near the YMCA, next to the IHOP, by the KFC., close to the T.G.... T.C.Y... T.B... whatever the hell that stupid yogurt place is.

"I have no idea... anyway, I heard that she's E.Z... so I got in my 300ZX and put KLOS on the FM... but the G-D Dee-Jay was making me O.D. on the Bee Gee's... so I said 'F-this' and put in a CD... it was REM and it sounded great on my JBL speakers...

"I pulled a U-ey, hit the ATM, and started to head over to Dee Dee's place. That's when I started thinking, 'Gee, If Dee Dee's that E.Z... she could have STD's... or she could be into B&D... or S&M... she could be AC-DC... or have an I.U.D. as big as the Q.E.II... I'll end up with V.D. on my pee-pee... and my pee-pee could fall off in my BVD.'s... and that thought gives me the Hee-Bee Gee-Bee's!'

"That's when I decided to go home and watch some HBO on the TV... or E.T. on the VCR (I have it on VHS *and* DVD!)... R.E.M. on MTV... E.R. on NBC... the N.B.A. on ESPN... or a Mr. T interview on E!...

"... and make myself a B.L.T. and Spaghetti-O's, and wash it down with some Hi-C (slap side of head) I could have had a V-8!...

"... then I put on my *Star Wars* PJ's with R2D2 and C3PO... and slept till 9am when I was woken up by a tele-marketer... "I don't know! AT&T or MCI? AT&T or MCI?"... then watched *Mayberry RFD* with Aunt Bea and Opie (O.P.)...

"... but instead I got CNN with the LAPD chasing O.J. and A.C. trying to go AWOL because he left behind his DNA when he killed his 'ex.'

"Now I live in LA... the land of T&A and B.S. ... where I'm going to have to give somebody a BJ. just to get on the TV."

L.A. Misérables, Too

Even though I've been doing this routine in my act off and on since I wrote it early in 1986, and I can repeat it in my sleep, I had added some LA references, made some edits for television, and rewrote some of the subtext, so for the last three or four days I had been repeating the routine over and over and over to myself, perhaps a hundred times or more, to make sure that I knew it inside and out and the presentation would flow naturally.

I even used a lint brush as a prop microphone to simulate my body language during the narrative. By the time I stepped on the stage in front of the cameras I was like a machine and it went off without a hitch. In that respect, stand-up is like a court hearing, because there is no substitute for preparation if you want to look like you know what you're doing.

On the NBC studio to tape my appearance on Friday Night Videos

CHAPTER SEVEN
People are strange, when you're a stranger...

DAY 187 - SEPTEMBER 11TH, 1996

The "ho" who lives across the hall has become a mysterious enigma. Even though, from all outward appearances, "she" seems to be a woman, now we're not so sure. The ho's roommate is a petite, dusky-skinned woman with breasts, but has a large head like a Rottweiler and a piercing stare that will give you the creeps. The consensus is that it's actually a transsexual. As for the ho... we don't know for sure. The jury is still out. Max swears that he saw her walking toward him on the street and she had a little package between her legs that was, how would you say... uh, inconsistent with a vagina.

Tonight the ho and her roommate were having a fight in the hallway and the roommate's clothes were packed into boxes and thrown out of their apartment. Like the nosy asshole that I am, I went to our door and watched the drama unfold through the tiny peephole.

What have I turned into, Gladys Kravitz the snooping neighbor on *Bewitched*? They were yelling loudly, but I couldn't make out what they were saying because of their unidentifiable accents and exaggerated lisps. I saw this trick on a movie once where some guy was spying on his neighbors and put a glass against the wall, then put his ear to the glass, and it worked to amplify the conversation. I tried it and all I heard was... well, nothing. Just like a seashell, I swear that the only noise I could hear was the sound of milk being poured into the glass. In any event, the bottom line is that we still can't pick "the ho's" sexual status out of a gender line-up.

"That's the one, officer! I'm sure of it... I'm absolutely, positively sure it's a woma... um, then again, maybe not... oh, I don't know. Can I go home now?"

C'mon...sing with me! *Lola...L - O - L - A...Lola...La-la-la-la-Lola....*

DAY 188 - SEPTEMBER 12TH, 1996

I was watching A&E channel's *Biography* tonight and the subject was Hugh Hefner who built the Playboy empire.

Hugh is getting along in age and, from time to time, the thought must go through his mind that there is no way that the Kingdom of Heaven can be any better than Hugh Hefner's life on earth.

There's no way that he will enter the pearly gates and some saint will direct him to a mansion where hundreds of the most beautiful, and sexual liberated, large-breasted women in the entire world walk around half-naked in nighties and string bikinis, and are at his disposal twenty-four hours a day... and he doesn't even have to wear a necktie to work. He can just lounge around in his silk pajamas, throw parties, fondle women and sip cocktails.

Heaven has *got* to be a letdown for Hugh Hefner.

If there is any equity in the afterlife, what kind of horrific past lives does one have to endure to get Hef's gig on this earth? What kind of horrific suffering would he have to experience to be blessed with every man's fantasy life?

I can imagine God going over an unborn child's past-life chart with St. Peter...

"Let's see now... Check this out, Pete... this guy made his debut as early man and got eaten by a Tyrannosaurus Rex."

"Terrible... terrible."

"Yes, but that's just the beginning. In his next life, he worked as a slave on the Pyramids in Egypt and did hard labor, eighteen hours a day in the 110° heat, for thirty-seven years until his death by whipping."

"Tragic, Lord."

"Just wait, it gets worse. Upon reincarnation as a Roman, he lost his home and family in the volcano at Pompeii, then he was a galley slave rowing a ship until he was eaten by a lion in the Coliseum. In his subsequent lives, he got the Bubonic Plague, was beheaded during the French Revolution, burned as a witch in Salem, took a musket ball to the groin during the Civil War, spent one of his lives as The Elephant Man, went down on the Titanic, was imprisoned at Aushwitz... and, whoa, look at this! The poor guy... This man was the fifth Beatle!"

"He was Pete Best? Oooooooh... now *that* was a rough one.."

"Whew!! Talk about getting the shaft! How did this poor bastard slip through the cracks? He really got a bum deal. What do you think Peter? Let's give him that pajamas and big titty naked girl thing we've been saving? I'd say he deserves it!"

"I couldn't agree more."

"But wait, Peter... one last touch to help make-up for all of his suffering. As an added bonus, right around the time he's getting too old to 'do it,' we'll have them invent Viagra!"

"Brilliant!"

The show informed us that Hef personally chooses the centerfold each month. I guess that's not a job you retire from so you can play more golf.

I remember a traumatic experience from my childhood when my parents came home early from a party and my father caught me going through his *Playboy* books. I'll never forget the extremely embarrassing father-and-son talk that we had afterwards.

My father, who was obviously every bit as uncomfortable as I was, spoke clumsily and said, "Son... I know that you, um... well, you see... your body is going through a lot of... uh, changes and you have to take things slow... I know it's kind of awkward, but... well... these books for instance... once you get used to seeing naked women, it's really no big deal... and, basically, if you've seen one breast, you've

L.A. Misérables, Too

seen 'em all."

And I vividly remember my hormone-charged, adolescent self, blurting out, with a stupid grin on my face...

"Dad, if it's all the same to you, I'd rather see them all!"

Then... WHACK!

DAY 190 - SEPTEMBER 14TH, 1996

I went to the Foundation Room at the House of Blues with Kelly tonight. It is a "members-and-guests-only" private club, but Kelly is friendly with some people who put our names on the guest list. While we were up there I saw Mickey Dolenz of the Monkees. I approached Mickey and introduced myself, because I had been the opening act for the Monkees at the Club Casino in Hampton Beach, New Hampshire, in 1989 or '90.

I realized that I was never actually introduced to the band members (Mickey, Davey and Peter... Mike Nesmith didn't join in the reunion) and, after a couple cocktails, I recalled the circumstances. Actually, I forgot about it until last year, when I ran into some former employees of the Casino. Unbeknownst to me, they had been cleaning up after that Monkees show and overheard a conversation I had with the group's manager. They gleefully related the story and everything came back to me.

Before the performance was to begin, I was backstage in the dressing room area when the theater's stage manager told me that the Monkees' road manager wished to speak to me regarding my set. I approached him and was told that, even though the crowd of 2200 or so was primarily made up of adults, there were some young children in the audience. The manager asked that I avoid the use of profanity in my act because they just had trouble with a comedian at another venue who was filthy and it generated a lot of complaints from the children's parents. I told him that it would be no problem whatsoever, then asked him if he would be so kind as to introduce me to the members of the band, who were standing only a couple arm's lengths away from us. The manager dismissed me, said that he was much too busy at that time, and told me to wait until after the show was over.

OK… that's fine. No problem. I can do that.

I did my set and everything went great.

Then I stayed and watched the Monkees perform.

After the show, I stuck around because I wanted to meet the band that I was so obsessed with when I was a kid. I was going through puberty, but I was much too insecure to actually talk to girls. Instead I wore out my Monkees record albums as I played air guitar with my Little League bat and fantasized that the girls were swooning over me like they did with Davey Jones.

I patiently hung out as the crowd filtered from the club. I waited for more than an hour and a half as the road crew broke down the stage and loaded the equipment into several 18-wheelers by the back entrance. Late in the evening, the band finally came out from their dressing rooms.

Once again they were only a few feet away from me, but I wished to be formally introduced, so I approached their manager, as he had earlier suggested, and said, "Excuse me, sir… but you promised me that you'd introduce me to the guys if I waited till the end of the evening. So I've waited like you said and here I am."

The manager threw up his hands in disgust and shook his head from side-to-side as he moaned, "Awww man… I'm way too busy. I don't have time for this shit. I have things to do!"

More stunned than disappointed, the stagehands recalled that I picked up my guitar, looked at the manager and, in my most obnoxiously sarcastic voice, said, *"Don't get carried away, pal… Hey, hey it's the Monkees, not the fucking Who,"* then turned around and walked away as his jaw dropped.

As I left in disgust, I apparently didn't notice the Casino employees cracking up behind us. When they refreshed my memory, the incident all came back to me. That's why I didn't meet Mickey, but I thought it best not to relate that story to him.

What is it with me and band managers? Bad voodoo.

DAY 191 - SEPTEMBER 15^(TH), 1996

After discussing my situation with several knowledgeable people, I have come to the conclusion that getting ahead in this town can be a hopeless situation without the assistance of a manager and/or agent to represent your interests.

I spoke with two club owners about my lack of stage time and both explained that many of the evening's schedules were preempted by industry showcases. In the comedic world of LA, managers can arrange for you to "showcase" or audition for industry (i.e. network representatives, casting companies, television or film development people, or production people who are looking to actors to fill specific roles, or for characters around which they can create a program) as well as personal appearance and film agents, commercial agents, club or college booking agents, representatives from comedy festivals, etc. etc. etc. These showcases can take several forms.

A film company, television network, independent production company, or casting director may need to locate talent that fills a particular need. For example, if they are looking to find a cast for a new TV pilot. In addition to their regular casting calls, those people might set up a show in one of the three major comedy clubs. (The Laugh Factory, The Improvisation or The Comedy Store) Word of the pending showcase would be circulated, managers and agents informed of the audition, and the roster would be filled with performers whose manager or agent, or sometimes the club owner or booker where the show is taking place, managed to get them on the list.

Another version of a showcase occurs when a manager or agent contacts the networks, film companies, casting personnel, directors, producers, development people, and so on, directly, and informs them that he has a hot talent who he wants them to come and see, hoping that they may want to build something around that person's character or may have something in mind that he or she could get plugged into.

Sometimes a management company or agency will set up such a showcase to display a number of their clients to those in a position to make one, or some, of those performers… and consequentially their manager or agent... wealthy.

There are other scenarios that are variations of the above, and the list is not exhaustive, but the point I'm trying to make is that you really need valid representation to set this stuff up for you if you want to get anywhere.

I have a directory that lists the management companies and talent agencies and, from that guide, I have narrowed down the field to a couple dozen that I would consider to handle me. I have met with several representatives of different firms and I haven't been overly impressed or comfortable with any of them. There are some people who have advised me just to sign up with anyone who's reputable, so at least I can get some television auditions, showcases, TV spots, and club bookings, instead of wasting my time. I don't know. It is tempting to settle, especially when the money becomes tight and the frustration builds, but I think it's best to be patient and wait for the best opportunity.

DAY 192 - SEPTEMBER 16TH, 1996

Today I found out that yet *another* one of my friends is having trouble with his marriage and is getting a divorce.

They should get a bit more realistic with the wedding vows.

The traditional "I do" response doesn't reflect reality anymore.

How about this...

"Do you promise to love, honor, cherish and obey..."

"I'll try... Love and cherish I can't argue with, but don't give her any unrealistic expectations with this *obey* shit. You're just lookin' for trouble down the road."

"... through sickness and in health..."

"What can I say? I'll do my best... How sick and unhealthy are you talking? You gotta draw the line at, say... Leprosy, Elephant Man's Disease or turning into a hardcore liberal, dont'cha think?"

"... through richer and poorer..."

"I promise to give it my best shot, but it sort of depends on which one of us becomes richer or poorer... and maybe you should throw in

L.A. Misérables, Too

an escape clause if she grows one of those big, fat, dimpled, cellulite-filled, saddle-bag, trailer-trash asses because, and I'm gonna be honest with ya, I'd be out'a there in a heartbeat... *See ya!*"

"... till death do you part?"

"Ooh... That one could be tricky. Are we talkin' natural causes here?"

Lifestyle

From court lawyer to court jester

Lynn court's assistant D.A. relishes role as comedian

By MARY MacISAAC
For The Item

DAY 193 - SEPTEMBER 17TH, 1996

I watched several episodes of those real-life police television shows, *COPS* and *LAPD: Life on the Beat,* for about an hour and a half tonight. It's disturbing to think that they film the show *COPS* throughout the entire United States, but they have enough crime in Los Angeles to justify their own show. What's even more disturbing, as I watch the LAPD investigate a double stabbing in a crack house, is that the location of this sordid incident is less than a five minute drive from my Hollywood apartment.

Usually, there is nothing that can desensitize your reaction to bad news like great distances.

Paul D'Angelo

"Ahhh. Here's the morning newspaper. Let's see… '600 FEARED DEAD AS MONSOON HITS INDIA'… sad… ho-hum (sigh)… 'MASS GRAVES FOUND IN BOSNIA, THOUSANDS FEARED MASSACRED'… humph, borrrrrring… 'FERRY CAPSIZES IN THAILAND - HUNDREDS MISSING'…(yawn). '100's KILLED BY AFRICAN REBELS'… too bad… 'HOTEL FIRE IN BEJING - 64 PERISH IN FLAMES'… shame, mmmmm… Wait, what's this? Holy shit! Please God, say it isn't so! The Patriots lost to the Jets? The fucking *Jets?* You gotta be shitting me! The heartbreak! Life can be so damn cruel… Woe is me… Oh, the humanity!"

Well, on the show I'm now watching, these knife wielding crackheads are not in India… or China… or even in another part of the country. No. They're my *neighbors*. That frightening thought will shrink your scrotum quicker than skinny-dipping at a beach in Maine. Hell, in this vicinity our Welcome Wagon is used for drive-bys.

In the next segment of *LAPD*, the police were called to break up a domestic dispute. When the cops entered the filthy apartment, they encountered a hysterical woman in the kitchen who was difficult to understand because she was a) brain dead b) highly intoxicated c) missing a front tooth d) there was a lit cigarette butt stuck in the gap between her remaining rotting, yellow teeth e) all of the above.

This *Hee-Haw* spokesmodel was about 22… looked 72… has 4 kids by five different fathers, and she's pregnant again.

A fashion show commentator would likely describe her rather smashing entrance by saying, "Modeling the newest look from this fashion season's hot, new 'White Trash' collection, Gertie's cheap, cotton moo-moo is the perfect outfit for watching soaps, beating your husband, or getting arrested on national TV. Its bright flower print is more than just a 70's 'retro' look recreation… it's the real thing, worn daily and washed infrequently for over twenty years.

"The eye-catching oranges, greens and yellows of the smock blend smartly with the rich earth-tones present in the many food and sweat stains running throughout the fabric. This stylish house-dress nicely complements her 260 pound frame. If you have the body tone of a water balloon, this tent is for you ladies. Gertrude's running mascara

L.A. Misérables, Too

creates that oh so trendy 'Alice Cooper' look, which makes an obvious statement ("Please shoot me!") and goes nicely with the shiner under her eye and various black and blues scattered about the model.

"If you've been in line at the welfare office, you know that greasy, stringy hair is *in* this year, and the cold-sore on her lip is the perfect touch for adding a little color. She has accessorized nicely by supplementing her outfit with a number of tasteful tattoos, indicating her love of Satan and Harley-Davidsons. For footwear, Gertie's rubber flip-flops complete the ensemble with the 'refugee' look that is so popular in many third world countries."

Ironically, their wedding picture is in the background and, if you look closely, she's a 105 pound prom queen with a beautiful smile. And the cops wonder why the husband's drinking? One look at the social quicksand that this guy is sinking into, sucking him further and further into a hopeless future and a dead-end life, and you'll realize that the only reason that he's getting wasted on Old Milwaukee and cheap bourbon is that he can't afford to hire Dr. Kevorkian to assist him in a mercy killing.

"Why are you intoxicated, sir?"

"Why am I intoxicated officer? Are you serious? Look at what I'm married to! She used to be a cheerleader! Look at her!"

The cops take a good look at his wife, "Jesus! You're right! Give me a swig o' that shit!"

I love it. Every time the cops pull a suspicious car over on the highway they ask the driver, "Do you mind if we search your vehicle?" The fact that I am also a criminal attorney (no, that's not a redundant term) makes me want to yell at the television screen, "Don't do it! He has no probable cause to search the car unless you give him your permission!"

But what does this poor bastard know about the law? He does know that there are twenty pounds of uncut cocaine underneath the spare tire in the trunk. Even with absolutely no knowledge of the legal principles of search and seizure, even the dumbest person's gut reaction would tell him that the responses, "What are you, fucking nuts?" or "You must be kidding… right?" are not appropriate because they're a dead give-away.

So they always choose option "B," which is to say, "Sure... I've got nothing to hide officer." Like this nonchalance might throw the cops off track and they'd say...

"Well, if you say so, sir... why should we waste our valuable time searching for something that isn't there... Thanks for saving us the trouble. Sorry for any inconvenience we may have caused you and your best friend, on your way home from Mexico to visit your sick uncle in East LA... although the passenger separately told us that he's never seen you before, and you picked him up hitchhiking because he's heading to a class reunion in Colorado. It's just a minor discrepancy. You're free to go. Take care now, and drive safely."

No. Once you give your "voluntary" consent you're screwed.

The police might as well be honest and ask, "Do you have a problem allowing me to discover the illegal contraband in your trunk that will give you a one way ticket to eight to ten years of forced anal rape in the prison shower room?"

"Sure officer."

Another thing. I'm noticing that a lot of the criminals they arrest are wearing those camouflage pants and shirts... and yet, they still get caught. You think they'd catch on. Pal, you're in the middle of a city, not the jungles of 'Nam. If you want to blend in with the concrete and asphalt, you have to wear a gray sweat-suit and stay close to the buildings.

It seems to me that the police on these programs are like the creatures in the old monster movies I used to watch. In every scary film, some helpless and terrified woman would take off in a sprint, with a frightful ghoul in pursuit. Even though the monster had just risen from the grave, after being buried for a couple hundred years (presumably without access to a treadmill or cross-trainer) and is dragging a lame leg behind him as he trudges along... he inexplicably happens to gain ground on the poor victim.

On *COPS* they'll show some chubby, out of shape policeman hopping out of his car to chase after a young, athletic kid, who has abandoned the stolen motor vehicle he was driving and is now flying through a series of backyards, taking fences like an Olympic hurdler. With the cameraman right behind him, the policeman plods through the yards, with his big, donut-belly jiggling, huffing and puffing from his two pack a day cigarette habit, and struggles over a fence, ripping his pants in the process... but, somehow, it always ends with the officer catching-up to the fugitive. It's another example of life imitating art... or vice versa.

When they film the show *COPS* there's a camera following the action that records everyone doing their job. I expect that the people they film change their conduct somewhat when they're under the microscope like that. Don't tell me for a second that some of these cops wouldn't give a guy who's struggling with them and going out of control an extra little whack with the baton if it wasn't all on film. The LA police would have picked Rodney King off the street, brushed the gravel off his jeans and offered him a cigarette if they realized they were being videotaped.

For example, on the TV show, whenever they bring a wounded guy into the emergency room, they treat him right away and the hospital gives him immediate medical attention because the camera is right there, recording every move they make.

Anyone who has ever been to an emergency room knows that they make you wait forever and the staff won't touch you until admissions asks you an endless amount of questions first.

Under normal circumstances, without the camera, if you were a shooting victim, the admissions procedure would be more like:

"Height?"
"Prone."
"Weight?"
"With or without the heavy blood loss?"
"Any identifying marks or scars?"
"You mean *besides* the bullet hole in my ass?"
"Social security number?"
"I believe that would be .38 - .357 - .22 tonight."
"Mother's maiden name?"
"Her maiden name is Frances What's-this-have-to-do-with-the-

fact-that-I-have-a-bullet-lodged-in-my-ass… It's Greek."

"Occupation?"

"Target."

"Marital status?"

"Single, but I'm going to be married to a life support machine if you don't attend to my ass soon."

"Date of birth?"

"That's not nearly as relevant as the fact that my date of death will sneak up on me very soon if you don't take this fucking bullet out of my ass!"

"Any allergies?"

"Yes… I always have a bad reaction whenever I get shot in the ass. I experience several unpleasant side effects such as bleeding, intense pain, and diminishing vital signs."

"Insurance?"

"Yes… but it's not a good policy because I have been in the emergency room for forty-five minutes and, apparently, I have a one bullet deductible."

"Who should we contact in case of an emergency?"

"A fucking *doctor* would be nice."

"Reason for admission?"

"The reason is that I will have a tough time riding my exercise bicycle with a slug buried in my buttocks… not to mention the embarrassment when I try to get through the metal detector at the airport. This is not a Bruce Willis movie! This slug is real and it hurts!… *NOW PLEASE TAKE THE FUCKING BULLET OUT OF MY ASS!"*

DAY 194 - SEPTEMBER 18TH, 1996

I got a spot at the Laugh Factory tonight. They put me on first. Even though the club filled up later and was packed with people, when I went on there had to be only about twenty people in the club.

Given the choice of performing my act for an important audition in front of twenty people, who together make up a tiny, but enthusiastic crowd, and the alternative of having a room packed with moron

L.A. Misérables, Too

schmucks who sit through the act like they are holding-in a big shit. I would always pick the small, but appreciative, audience.

However, if a small crowd is made up of schmucks, you have the unique experience of completing your set while you watch your career getting towed out to sea in a garbage scow to be scuttled off the coast while your material is being sold for scrap to anyone who's interested.

No problem. This crowd was nice.

The Laugh Factory on Sunset Boulevard

DAY 195 - SEPTEMBER 19TH, 1996

Tonight was interesting. My friend Max and I joined my gay friend Timthy for dinner. After dinner, Timthy insisted that we go to an outdoor café in West Hollywood for a cup of coffee. We walked in and it was immediately apparent that Max and I were the only "breeders" in the overcrowded establishment. Now, I'm very cool about stuff like this but, in this case, I have to admit that I felt a little uneasy because Timthy, had an endless supply of embarrassing comments to casually blurt out, and has absolutely no idea how loudly he talks.

"Amsterdam? I was in Amsterdam once and sodomized a fourteen year old prostitute, because it was legal for young boys to peddle their backside there. It was heaven," Timthy screamed out in the quiet courtyard with the closely arranged tables.

"Hey Paulie, look at the nice asses on those two butch guys!" As I suddenly bent to tie my shoe and hide, out of the corner of my eye I could see Max covering his face with a menu.

When Timthy went up to get coffee, I tapped Max on the arm. "Is it just me, or do you feel a little uncomfortable Max?"

"Definitely", replied Max as he cracked his knuckles and scrunched up his neck, "Some guys have been checking me out."

All of a sudden I was applying logic to our predicament that I learned from watching an old, late-night vampire movie.

"Max", whatever you do, just don't look in their eyes. I'm telling you Max... for God sakes, avoid making eye contact or they'll turn you! Do *not* look into their eyes!"

As if Max would say, "Oh, shut up, Paul! That's ridiculous! As if I would catch someone's eye and..." as he met the gaze of one another man... "I... I... I... Oh, my goodness (giggle)... Paul, I don't know what's come over me, but I suddenly have the silly urge to style someone's hair while I listen to the soundtrack from *Oklahoma*."

After coffee, Timthy suggested that we rent a dirty movie and go to his house. OK, I think it's time to run to our car, lock the doors, make a crucifix out of the antenna, load the window washer reservoir with holy water, and order delivery of a garlic pizza, heavy on the garlic, with some more garlic on the side, as we wait for the morning's sunrise to drive Drag-ula away.

If my memory serves me correctly, almost every victim statement that I have ever read, or heard in testimony, in which a teacher or cub scout leader molested some little boys, followed a particular pattern which invariably began with, "He told me to sit next to him on the bed, then he made me a drink, and put in some dirty movies on the TV... and the next thing you know he had his hand on my leg and... a-a-and...and... then he used my ass like a butter churn."

DAY 196 - SEPTEMBER 20TH, 1996

I brought my car to the car wash today. For $16.95 you can have "The Works." After they vacuum out the entire car, it goes through the car wash, and then a guy wipes it down, cleans the wheels, and goes through the interior.

And what a great job that little Mexican guy did. He cleaned my wheels, he cleaned my floor mats, he cleaned my dashboard, he cleaned my windows… and he also cleaned-out all of the loose change that was in my ashtray. How thorough.

CHAPTER EIGHT
Wild horses couldn't drag me away...

DAY 197 - SEPTEMBER 21ST, 1996

When women talk about their sexual fantasies they are always very romantic... you know, pretty flowers... a sensual mood... candles... an intimate dinner... body lotion... quiet walks on the beach.

Men, on the other hand, are pigs.

Kinky, perverse, insensitive degenerates... all of them.

Not me, however... I'm different. I'm very sensitive and caring and sensuous. I'm traditional, even corny perhaps, by today's standards.

My fantasy would be to get snowed in at a ski chalet on a scenic mountain in the middle of nowhere, on a cold, winter's night during a big blizzard... there's a warm fire blazing, a nice bottle of wine, a bear-skin rug in front of the fireplace... and a pair of bisexual Siamese-twin hookers with shaved heads and a bag full of sex-toys...

Call me old-fashioned.

DAY 198 - SEPTEMBER 22ND, 1996

Sometimes I wish that life was like a Hollywood movie... and I was the star of the movie, this really blew my mind, the fact that me, a noble... wait, that sounds like an old Eric Burdon song... No, again...

L.A. Misérables, Too

Sometimes I wish that life was like a Hollywood movie, so I could second-guess my decisions, correct my screw-ups and, hopefully, avoid unnecessary arguments. For instance:

"Hi, Kelly. I'm home…"

"Where the hell were you, Paul?… I cooked dinner and it was getting cold and I had no idea where you were because you didn't bother to call and let me know what you were doing tonight… You don't care, do you? Where were you? Out with *your friends?*… Huh?"

"Relax, honey. I was just shooting a couple of games of pool down at the billiard hall, had a few beers and lost track of the tim…"

"I KNEW IT! YOU DON'T GIVE A SHIT, DO YOU? DO YOU EXPECT ME TO…"

And the director yells out, *"CUT!!!…* Let's try that again, Paul. We'll take it from the top… OK, take two, everybody… Ready? Let's go 3… 2 and… Action!"

"Hi, Kelly. I'm home…"

"Where the hell were you, Paul?… I cooked dinner and it was getting cold and I had no idea where you were because you didn't bother to call and let me know what you were doing tonight… You don't care, do you? Where were you? Out with *your friends?*… Huh?"

"I'm sorry, honey, but I was out shopping for a nice Columbus Day present for you down at the Beverly Center Mall in Beverly Hills and…"

"Really, Paul?… That's sooo sweet of you! How was your day?… Why didn't you go play pool with your friends? You haven't seen them much lately… I hope you're hungry! I'm reheating the meal I made for you, Honey."

"OK, THAT'S A WRAP!"

DAY 199 - SEPTEMBER 23rd, 1996

I'm ready to sign with a personal manager. OK…. maybe he's not my first choice. Not that he's incompetent or not well connected or is incompatible with me. It's just that I'm not convinced that he truly believes in me. You really need a manager that has a passion for your talent and abilities. Someone who will make you a priority, will fight for you, will aggressively market you, and won't take "no" for an answer. They can't be wishy-washy about you or your relationship will be like being stuck in a bad marriage.

Anyway, even though I'm on the fence about this decision, I reluctantly set-up a meeting with this manager because I'm going nuts and I need to make some progress. The first question I want to ask him is if he's truly committed to me, because I have a lingering doubt about his motives.

So we finally sat down alone and the first words out of his mouth were, "So you want me to manage you?"

I answered, "We're getting off on the wrong foot, because I was hoping that you'd tell me that *you* want to manage *me*."

"I never said that I wanted to manage you. Whatever gave you that idea?"

"You gave me that idea when you told me that you were interested in being my manager."

"I never said that."

I said, "I didn't imagine that you made that statement. I'm not stupid, and I didn't make it up because, if I didn't get that impression, I never would have set up this meeting."

"Well you must have misinterpreted me."

I said, "Listen, that's really all I need to know, because I was worried that you weren't the right person for me, and it looks like my suspicions have been confirmed."

He responded, "Well… I'm not saying that I wouldn't be interested in, like, three months or six months from now… things can change quickly around here."

Ayyy… there's the rub. The more he kept talking, the more I realized that he was hedging his bet. He wanted to wait until I had someone interested in giving me a television show or the equivalent and *then* he wants to jump on the bandwagon. He doesn't want to be the one that does the work, and takes the risk, to get me a show.

I'm so glad I learned this before I was contractually committed to him. It was a good lesson. I have a lot to offer. Just stay patient.

DAY 200 - SEPTEMBER 24TH, 1996

Today's the day I had a hearing scheduled in Beverly Hills Municipal Court for my traffic violation of going straight in a lane marked "Right Turn Only." What a fucking menace to society I am... going straight when I should have taken a right. Please.

From my years of experience in the courthouses of the Commonwealth of Massachusetts, I learned that traffic hearings are such a kangaroo court, I'm surprised the judge doesn't hop up to the fucking bench. Why should this court be any different? My only hope is that the cop doesn't show-up and the case will be dismissed. As I waited to be called, I put together a defense just in case he appeared.

But he did show-up, damn it. Just to illustrate what a prick he was, the hearing before me involved a driver who was pulled over and issued a citation for not wearing his seat belt. The man tried to explain to the officer that he was exempt from the statute because he was making frequent stops to deliver the *LA Times* to homes, offices and apartments, but the cop wouldn't listen. The judge told the cop that that man did, in fact, fall under the exception and let him go.

As is often the case, there is usually something behind the stop. This cop slipped up during the hearing and mentioned that he thought the defendant's son, of the same name, had outstanding warrants out on him. That means that the cop was just looking for any reason to pull the car over... a defective tail-light... failing to use a turn signal... a loud muffler... no seat belt. In my case, I think the officer saw my Massachusetts plate and wanted to check out my papers because my infraction was awfully trivial, if you ask me.

A bit of advice from my experience: If you're ever going to contest a traffic ticket and your defense is directly contrary to the officer's testimony, you are going to lose. If the defendant's story contradicts the cop's version, or alleges that the cop was wrong, the judge would have to give your story more credibility than the policeman's account, therefore implicitly indicating that the policeman's judgment was flawed, his observations were inaccurate, or he was exaggerating the facts, or even lying about them.

You, as a defendant, are going to come and go. On the other hand, that clerk magistrate or judge will have to deal with that particular officer on a continuing basis and does not want to piss him off or undermine his credibility. So ninety-nine percent of the time... you lose.

Knowing this, when they called my case, I tried to tell the judge that I was not questioning the facts as related by the officer, but rather I wanted to offer some mitigating circumstances that would justify my going straight ahead; namely that I had directions to take a right after Santa Monica Boulevard, I was unfamiliar with the area, and I got in the right hand lane only to find out that the next street was Burton Way and not the right that I was looking for, so I proceeded cautiously across the intersection and merged left as soon as it was safe to do so.

The judge didn't give a shit about what I had to say. I tried to tell him that I knew there was a uniformed officer on a marked police motorcycle one car length behind me... why would I blatantly commit a moving violation? It would be legal suicide to do that in front of the cop without a good reason. Forget it... Guilty.

As a criminal defense attorney I had the good fortune to win every single trial and motion hearing that I participated in. I represent myself once and... POW! And I was my favorite client. Besides paying about $140 in fines, now I have to go to traffic school for eight hours to keep this scar off my record.

As it is, since he stopped me, every time I drive through Beverly Hills, I'm so paranoid I drive as if I have a dead body in the trunk of my car.

This whole incident upset me so much I called my friend Prune in Boston to get a little sympathy. All he could do was convulse in laughter.

"Some big trial attorney you are! Ha, ha, ha! You can't even beat your own ticket! Ha, ha, ha! You'll never represent me! No way! Ha, ha, ha!"

Thanks, pal.

DAY 201 - SEPTEMBER 25 TH, 1996

Kelly had a ten dollar gift certificate for a restaurant in Burbank and told me that she wanted to take me out to dinner... and I could pay the balance of the check. After getting lost and looking for the place for almost an hour, we were disappointed to find out that it was a Denny's-quality restaurant but, by the time we arrived, we were so hungry that we decided to eat there. Besides, we had the gift certificate.

When we walked in, we were overcome with the overwhelming aroma of strawberry scented disinfectant. If this was the atmosphere I craved for dinner, I'd buy a sub sandwich to go and eat it in a gas station restroom. Not only that, the air conditioning was blasting and the place was absolutely frigid. After I looked around and saw that most all of the other diners were elderly, I figured they keep the place cold to help preserve the clientele's decomposing bodies.

When the check came it was over thirty-seven dollars with the tip. Kelly handed me the ten dollar gift certificate and laughed.

"Thanks for taking me out to dinner, Kelly."

On tonight's news, a major freeway in LA was closed down for eight hours while the police negotiated with a crazed woman who hijacked a cab and was holding the cab driver hostage with a gun. The police SWAT team eventually shot tear gas into the cab and rescued the hostage, only to find out that the "gun" was actually a curling iron.

Did she threaten the cabbie with a bad hair day?

"Don't try anything stupid or the driver gets a cowlick right in the back of the head!"

No wonder the guy was frightened. If he's a typical cab driver, he has no idea what any instrument associated with hygiene or grooming looks like. This being true, she could have got the same results by terrorizing Abdul with a bar of Irish Spring.

"Ayyyiiii!... Please,.nooo!... Not a bath! The winter is not yet over!"

DAY 202 - SEPTEMBER 26TH, 1996

One of the big stories in today's news is about the uproar caused when a little 6-year-old schoolboy from North Carolina was suspended from school for sexual harassment simply because he kissed a female classmate on the cheek.

Most people think the school board is being outrageous but, the truth is, it was an irresponsible thing for that child to do.

Doctors report that the little girl has just tested positive for cooties.

Sexual harassment... really? You've got to be shitting me. And believe me, I know sexual harassment from personal experience, and that was certainly *not* sexual harassment.

Sexual harassment is an adolescent boy eating lunch in the junior high school cafeteria, when the girl you have a crush on walks by with her lunch tray, contemplates sitting next to you as your heart races, then notices the big, ripe zit on the end of your nose, drawing her attention like the flashing red light on the top of a fire engine, and she walks away, giggling and thinking to herself, "Eating for two, Paul?"

That is sexual harassment that's gonna have an impact on a kid.

Sexual harassment is having a few beers to get up your nerve, approaching a cute college cheerleader that you like during a sold out BC-Texas football game, and asking her out, only to have her laugh and say no, then ask "Why not?" and have her lead thirty thousand fans in the stands with "Gimme an L!!"

"L!"
"Gimme an O!"
"O!"
"Gimme an S!"
"S!"
"Gimme an E!"
"E!"
"Gimme an R!"
"R!"
"What's that spell?"
"LOSER!"

"What's his problem?"

"LOSER!"

Sexual harassment is being in a disco and feeling too shy to approach the babe who you've been staring at for two hours, while she's been bumping, grinding, twisting, turning, shimmying, shaking, and hopping around with every guy in the club, then overcoming your insecurities with your friends' encouragement, and finally asking her to dance, only to be told, "No thanks…I don't feel like dancing tonight," then walking back to face your friends as she grabs the next guy who walks by her and pulls him onto the dance floor so she can grind her crotch against his leg while your buddies bust your balls.

That is sexual harassment.

I didn't tell my parents. I didn't call the newspapers. I didn't sue. What a bunch of pathetic, whining, wimps the world is turning out these days. I'm ashamed of these people. And believe me, I know ashamed… from personal experience.

DAY 203 - SEPTEMBER 27TH, 1996

I booked a trip back to Boston from October 9th to October 21st and I have scheduled shows on the weekends and a couple weekday evenings. I really didn't give the booking agents in Boston enough notice, but I had to book the flight in a hurry when I realized that the free flight certificate from my frequent flier miles was due to expire on October 17th. As it was, they had to jockey around some of the previously scheduled acts in Boston so I could get the shows that I did.

This will be my third trip home since I moved to LA about six months ago. I went back the first time because I had one trial leftover from my legal career. At the time I didn't want to go back because I was just getting settled and I was excited about the possibilities that were presenting themselves in Hollywood. It was good to go home, but I was anxious to get back.

My second trip, in July, was a different story. I was getting discouraged by the slow progress of my comedic career and the numerous letdowns I was encountering, not to mention the fact that my lack of in-

Paul D'Angelo

come was becoming a constant source of concern. I had a great time in Boston and didn't particularly look forward to returning to the bullshit, lack of self-esteem, and low standard of living that I was experiencing on the West Coast.

On this occasion I really need to go back and recharge my comedy batteries that have been drained by my absence of stage time in the LA clubs.

It wouldn't hurt to eat some of my mom's lasagna either.

As discouraged as I am, I will not give up because to do so would mean that I just wasted all my time and money for nothing. I need to try a new approach.

DAY 204 - SEPTEMBER 28TH, 1996

OK… I need management and I can't just wait for these people to come to me. I have decided to go after them. I called NBC and got a copy of my eight minute set on *Friday Night Videos*, then I brought the tape to a service to have twenty dubs made. I spent the next two days taking my list of management companies and agencies, as well as *The Tonight Show* and HBO productions, and putting together press kits, addressing envelopes, and writing cover letters indicating that I was seeking representation and inviting each of them to watch the enclosed video and set a up a showcase at the Improv or Laugh Factory if they're interested. I hate to do a general mailing like this because, unsolicited or unaccompanied by a personal recommendation or referral, it isn't likely that the package will get much attention. But what harm will it do? None.

As the French say, *"Fuck eet"*.

CHAPTER NINE
Welcome to the Hotel California...

DAY 205 - SEPTEMBER 29TH, 1996

Kelly was going through the Sunday *LA Times* and read a headline aloud to me, "TOILET PAPER THEFT BRINGS 40 YEAR TERM."

I asked, "Third strike?"

She said, "No, third swipe."

I should just have her write the book.

It's a sunny Sunday afternoon and Kelly has to go to the Beverly Center Mall. I've been watching college and pro football on TV for two days, so I told her I'd accompany her just to get my fat ass off the couch.

First we went to the Thrifty pharmacy at the corner of Fairfax and Sunset. As Kelly parked the car in the parking lot, she looked in the rear-view mirror and gasped, "That man has his dick out!" I turned around and saw a bum peeing all over the side of a new Lexus. He saw us and tried to walk away as he continued his business, soaking his pant-leg in the process.

When Kelly's mother visited her a couple weeks ago, they were pulling into a Thrifty's parking lot at LaBrea and Santa Monica during the mid-afternoon and surprised a vagrant with his pants around his ankles, doing the same.

Paul D'Angelo

What is it about a busy Thrifty's parking lot that attracts bums like Mecca, inspiring the homeless to make a pilgrimage to a location where it's perfectly OK for them to relieve themselves in public?

What are the diuretic qualities inherent in the combination of parked vehicles, fluorescent lighting and pedestrian traffic? You can be a homeless bum and still retain a semblance of decorum and a small sense of self-respect, can't you?... Or maybe not.

Maybe I'm wrong. So what, 'cause here's another thing... Why do these bums appear so imposed-upon when people discover them relieving themselves in public and stare?... They act just as if they've been totally caught by surprise. They're shocked, as if some intruder just opened the door to their private stall, in the private locker room, of the private clubhouse, on the private golf course, at the private country club, past the private security guards, on a private drive, in a private neighborhood, in a private community. What's with that?

Excuse me, but why do you think they call that part of your body "your privates" and *not* "your publics" anyway? There's no reason for your "pubic areas" to be exposed in our "public areas." Even though the two territories are only differentiated by one lower-case letter, they are not to be confused with each other or associated under normal circumstances. Keep 'em to yourself, if you don't mind.

The preceding has been a pubic... uh, *public* service announcement.

After our Thrifty experience, we drove to the mall and parked the car in the outdoor parking lot across the street from the Beverly Center, carefully casing the lot to make sure we weren't interrupting anyone doing their business. After shopping, we came out of the mall and walked to the car. As Kelly backed out of the space, some spoiled-brat, arrogant Hollywood-type, with his GAP model haircut and designer sun-glasses, sitting in his convertible sports car, let out a big sigh and banged his steering wheel because he had to wait for us for three seconds. As we left the lot, another car tried to pull-out out in front of us and the "center-of-his-own-universe" hit the wheel again and impatiently muttered "Let's go!" like it was our fault and he was too important to have to wait for anyone. Who the fuck does he think he is?

Kelly and I looked at each other as we approached the two men at

L.A. Misérables, Too

the booth where we had to present our parking ticket. We did not have to exchange words. When we pulled-up we began to ask directions in broken English, confusing the parking lot attendants, who themselves spoke broken English. Before you knew it, the two of them were leaning into the driver's side window and pointing in opposite directions as they fought for the longest time over the location of the fictitious street that we had asked about. All the while, Kelly and I kept looking back at the fuming asshole in the convertible and laughing. Quoting Al Pacino in *Scarface*, "Don jou fugk wi' me man!"

Tonight I picked up my friend Seamus at LAX. (pronounced like Shamus... which is how I thought it was spelled until he told me tonight) Seamus is the cousin of Paul Barclay, the owner of the Comedy Connection in Boston. Seamus used to be the one who booked the club and we became friends through my association with the Comedy Connection. Anyway, he's moving to LA and is staying with us for a couple of days until he gets settled.

Seamus would like to get a job in one of the comedy clubs, so I brought him to the Improv for a beer. While we were at the bar, I saw Richard, the gentleman who now books the Improv, and introduced Seamus to him. I spoke to Richard for a while and he was very nice to me, assuring me that he would get me some spots at the club. I told him that I would really appreciate it, because I have been calling in for six and a half months without success.

A few minutes later, Richard had me by the arm and brought me into the showroom. He introduced me to Brett, the stage manager, and told him to put me up if he had the chance. The next thing I knew, I was being asked for my introduction by the host and told that I would follow Dom Irrera's set.

Things were happening so fast, and this was so unexpected, that my head was spinning. It was around 11:30 and I was introduced to a small crowd that had sat through at least twenty comedians on a Sunday night, but I proceeded to rip the room, probably because I didn't have any time to think about what I was doing.

When I got off the stage, I was so grateful for the opportunity and wanted to thank Richard. He acknowledged that I had a great set and told me that I "was in" now, and that I could expect plenty of spots. He had plans to use me a lot in the Melrose Ave. club, as well as in the Improv's satellite clubs around the country, and asked if I would be available.

Well let's see. I just completed an entire 86-game season and four rounds of playoffs on the way to the Stanley Cup on my Sega-Genesis Hockey '96 video game... I suppose I can fit a few comedy shows into my hectic schedule.

And just like that.... after six and a half months of frustration... six and a half months of being told that they had no stage time for me... six and a half months of disappointment... I was "in."

DAY 206 - SEPTEMBER 30TH, 1996

My elation was short lived. Last night I couldn't get into my regular parking space, so I took an open space. When I got into the car this morning, there was a note on my window that said, "This is NOT your space! Please do not park your car here! Signed: The person who parks in this space." It was written in a woman's handwriting and I told Seamus that it was a good thing that it wasn't a guy's space or he may have taken it out on my car. As I was backing up and making that statement, I cut the wheel to the right and smashed the front fender into a large, yellow cement pole. I knew my happiness wouldn't last long on this roller-coaster ride that I'm on, but, geez... how about a *couple* hours without pain?

Good news. I finally got a spot at the Improv on Wednesday night.

My friend, Larry Myles, arrived in Los Angeles this afternoon. Larry and I actually stood in line on the very same day for our first open mike night in 1985, along with our friend Louis CK, who was also making his comedic debut along with us. We also shared a great experience when we got booked together to do shows on St. Thomas and St. John in the Caribbean for eight days. Larry's in town to do a showcase at the Laugh Factory on Tuesday with several other Boston comedians and he's going to be staying with us for a couple of days as well.

Tonight Kelly was in her room reading a script, while Seamus, Larry and I watched television together. Out of the corner of my vision, I imagined that I saw Larry hitting himself repeatedly with a metal hammer. I looked again and verified it.

"What the fuck are you doing, Larry?"

Seamus said, "I'm glad you asked Paul, I was wondering the same thing."

"I'm breaking-up the heat in my body and rechanneling the bad energy, or Chi, from my kidneys through this special magnetic hammer."

"Larry, when did you start treating your internal organs with shop tools? Who's your primary care physician, Larry, Bob Vila?... I didn't know that the 'H' in your HMO stood for 'Home Depot.'"

Weird. Just weird.

I know the drill. I'm screwed and I need to get hammered... That's awl.

DAY 207 - OCTOBER 1ST, 1996

I woke up this morning and thought I was experiencing my first earthquake, but the tremors kept coming and going. "Maybe it's the aftershock," I told Kelly. Then we realized that it was just Seamus snoring in the other room. Oh my God, he was so loud we could hear him through the wall, through the closed door, and could actually feel the vibrations from the other room.

Poor Larry is sleeping on the floor next to him. How can he sleep through that horrible noise? Seamus sounds like earth moving equipment.

I looked in on them and Larry is out like a light. He must be dreaming that he's putting in a foundation. Good thing he has his hammer with him.

DAY 208 - OCTOBER 2ND, 1996

Seamus and I had to run some errands and we had lunch on Sunset. Since the weather is nice all year round, most of the restaurants put a few tables and chairs out on the sidewalk for anyone who wishes to eat outside. And why not? It provides so much more atmosphere when you're sitting on the sidewalk of a busy, four lane, main street during rush hour.

You can take in the sweet smells of the many buses and diesel powered trucks that are stuck in traffic, just a few feet away from your food. Why put pepper on your pasta when you can have some fresh soot? Besides the respiratory diseases that are available with your meal, you can also catch some cancer from the hot sun, hepatitis from the pigeons under your table, and maybe get crushed by a runaway tractor-trailer for no extra charge. And the bums… there's always the ever-present, drunken winos to add to your dining experience.

"Can you guys spare any money for a guy who's down on his luck?"

"No, I'm sorry, but we spent our money on food. You should try it sometime."

Tonight I got my first scheduled set at the Improvisation since I moved here. Just after I arrived at the club with Kelly and Seamus, Larry walked in with a dazed look on his face.

"What's up Larry, you're late?"

"My wallet is missing. I can't find it anywhere."

I tried to help. "Did you have it when you went out today?"

"Ya."

"Retrace your steps, Larry. Where'd you go?"

"I walked out of your building and started talking to this strung-out hooker slash junkie, who introduced me to a street hustler that was hanging out in the lobby and I gave him a ride uptown."

"You gave a ride to a street hustler? What kind of hustler did you give a ride to, Larry?"

"You know… the guy was a swindler. He explained to me that he makes a living by scamming people out of their money."

"And you gave him a *ride*?"

"Ya… he was cool, Paul."

"And you can't figure out where your wallet is? I'm not Colombo, but I've narrowed down the suspects to an exclusive list of one."

Where do I find these people?

L.A. Misérables, Too

When I confirmed my booking tonight I was told that my spot was scheduled for either 8:30 or 8:40, and I should get to the club a little early. We arrived about 8:00 to find that I wasn't going to go up until 10:10. By the time I went up on stage my bar tab was three times more than what they were paying me.

DAY 209 - OCTOBER 3RD, 1996

This afternoon, I was driving my car into the parking garage when I drove past a sexy chick in a tight halter-top, shrink-wrapped hot-pants, and a tight ass that had an exaggerated wiggle in it. I turned my head as I drove by and, to my surprise, she caught me checking her out, turned to me with a big smile, winked her heavily made-up eye, waved, and gave me a big, bright, "Hiiii!"

As I smiled and raised my hand to wave back, my immediate reaction was, "Wow! She really digs me!"

My secondary reaction was, "Fuck! It's the He-She from across the hall!"

I'm screwed. I can't take that little display back. I can't see her/him in the elevator and say, "Um... Hi. Uh, remember when I waved to you the other day? Well, um, you see, I really didn't mean that... I... I... I thought you were someone else... with tits... like, like... like, a real woman, for starters."

Nothing was going on at the clubs. Seamus and I decided to rent the new James Bond movie and watch it at Max's apartment. Max buzzed us in and we got in the elevator together. I sniffed the air, looked at Seamus, and wrinkled my nose.

"Man, it smells like shit himself in here!"

Seamus took a couple big whiffs.

"No, it smells like a steak and cheese sub."

"Really, Seamus? Where do you eat lunch? Remind me to skip that place."

Watching the movie at Max's place was just like watching a movie at the cinema. We could sit back, eat popcorn in the dark... and throw our trash on the floor.

Paul D'Angelo

The James Bond movies always have spectacular chase scenes and stunts. A Hollywood stunt man just died on the job a couple months ago, and he was at least the second stuntman to lose his life this year, which is not too unusual considering the risks they take. I mean, if you're a movie stunt man, and get killed doing something crazy, no one should really be surprised.

I can't imagine a family member getting the news and weeping, "No, not Johnny! I can't believe it! He's done that 400', two-and-a-half somersault with a 3/4 twist, free-fall from a suspension bridge into the back of a burning, unmanned, out-of-control speedboat a hundred times without a problem! What happened out there? The family wants some answers!"

You want an answer? He was a fucking nut.

If you're married to a Hollywood stunt man, you should have been surprised on the days he came home *without* getting himself killed.

"Honey, I'm home from work!"

(to herself) *"Damn."*

DAY 210 - OCTOBER 4TH, 1996

I got a call from radio disc-jockey and comedy show host Frasier Smith today. Frasier is a great guy and I worked with him several times at both the Laugh Factory and the Ice House in Pasadena. Frasier asked me to perform at the Alex Theater in Glendale before a special screening of the movie *Metropolis*. He told me that an assistant director from *Seinfeld* and a producer of the *Larry Sanders Show* are supposed to be there.

I hope so.

Kelly, Seamus and I arrived at the theater and the place was just beautiful. I believe that this is the theater where the local symphony performs. The venue held about 1,400 people and it had been recently renovated. The show went great except for one faux pas by yours truly. The event was a special screening of the silent film classic *Metropolis* and we were kidding on the way over in the car, pronouncing the name of the movie like a country hick... Metró-polis. Well, in the middle of

L.A. Misérables, Too

a routine about a guy in the audience being dragged out by his girlfriend to see *Metropolis* when he really wanted to see the new Steven Segal movie, I inadvertently slipped and pronounced the name of the movie like we goofed around about. I think I could hear Kelly and Seamus giggling in the back of the theater. Damn! I may hold the distinction of being the most highly educated illiterate in the performing arts.

After the show we went to a place to watch some bands. What a difference in venues. The club was so grungy I papered the handle on the men's urinal.

DAY 211 - OCTOBER 5TH, 1996

I was on the throne in the bathroom, reading a magazine that was making a big deal about Ellen DeGeneres, star of the hit sitcom *Ellen*, coming out of the closet. Who cares? Who would be surprised? Lesbian female stand-up comedians are like Jewish accountants and gay hairdressers. If you can't find any, you ain't lookin' very hard.

DAY 212 - OCTOBER 6TH, 1996

We met a woman who has been a vegetarian all of her life. Her parents were vegetarians and they raised her that way, so she has never had meat, chicken or fish in her entire life. I'd hate to get invited to that home at Thanksgiving. I can see it now… a freshly killed, wild zucchini in the center of the table… with tofu stuffing and bean curd gravy. Yummm Yummm.

"Paul, will you do the honors and carve the pumpkin?"

"Sure."

"No, stupid! Look at what he's doing! Paul!… *not* like a jack-o-lantern… that's the wrong holiday! Cut it into serving portions."

"You realize that you vegetarians have lost your fucking minds… They say, 'You are what you eat' and it's true, because you people are acting like real vegetables… I'm tellin' ya, keep it up and you'll develop roots, then you'll never be able to leave the house. You'll feel the need to spend half the day in a tanning bed and all your hair will fall out right after the summer and stay off until the next spring... every year. My advice to you? Eat a big, juicy prime rib and get some color in your *Addams Family* faces besides the big chunk of green spinach that's caught between your two front teeth."

The thing that amazed Kelly was, "I know she didn't eat any meat, but... um, how do I say it?"

"What, Kelly?"

She hesitated... "Even though she just eats plants, she's still a... a big girl... You know, Paul, you've met her... She's... she's chubby. I mean, is that possible to get that big from just eating plants, Paul?"

I said, "Sure it is... Look how big a brontosaurus got... and all they ate were leaves."

"Paul, you're mean! My friend's not *that* big! Be nice."

"I'm sorry, Kelly. You're right. I take it back... I meant to say 'stegosaurus.'"

"*Paul!*"

I'm leaving for Boston early Wednesday morning and Seamus hasn't found an apartment yet. I don't want him to join the ranks of the homeless, so we went over to Patty Ross's place to see if she knows of any comedians that are looking for a roommate. Joey Carroll was staying with Patty. He is another Boston comic who had performed on the same showcase as Larry. Joey mentioned that Wayne Previty was looking for a roommate. Wayne? Last month Wayne flew home to pick up his girlfriend and drive three thousand miles back to California with her. He' alone now so, apparently, that cross-country trip lasted longer than their relationship.

Joey stayed at Wayne's new place and I asked him where Wayne's apartment was located. Joey told me it was "a big building" and all he remembers is that "you have to take an elevator to get there."

Patty lit a cigarette and, in her own charming manner remarked, "Heh, heh, heh. Paul, if you were the prosecutor how'd you like Joey to be your only eyewitness in a murder trial? Heh, heh, heh. You'd be so fucked, heh, heh, heh."

DAY 213 - OCTOBER 7TH, 1996

I can't believe it. I got another spot at the Improv tonight! This is two weeks in a row. What a good man that Richard is. Seamus, Max and I met Larry Myles at the club. Larry's a real pussy hound. He was all over every girl at the bar. Seamus and I confronted him about the woman in my apartment building that he met the other day. I found out that he spent the afternoon with her and I wanted to make sure he didn't do anything foolish because, if it's the girl I'm thinking of, she's pretty skanky.

Larry says, "No, no, no. Don't worry about me." He looked around the dining and bar area where we were seated. "See that wholesome, pretty, well-dressed blonde girl over there. She looked *just* like her... exactly like her... except for, like...well, imagine that girl, but she's been on heroin for three years or so... and... and she just walked in after doing tricks all night long... and... she had ripped nylons and a butt hanging out of the corner of her mouth... and, uh...um, like dark... *really* dark roots... and heavy, kind of like, you know, caked on makeup and bags under her eyes... and chipped nail polish and she's kind of out-of-it a little... like a little unsteady when she stood up... you know, like she couldn't stand on her own."

"Ya Larry... kinda like... sort of like... <u>absolutely nothing like</u> that girl over there. A totally different woman."

"Well, ya... OK...you win... But I was careful man, I swear, Paul."

You gotta love Larry.

My friends came into the showroom to see my set. The crowd was pretty good I was all anxious to perform. I started for the stage when the host addressed the crowd.

I knew the host from the 1989 Johnny Walker Comedy Search, when we both were national finalists. We ran into each other in the bar area of the Improv before the show.

"Paul? How are you doing? What brings you out here?"

"I live here now. I've been here for a few months already."

(biting his lower lip) "Really, that's fantastic. Good luck to you."

Bullshit... He didn't mean it. And he proved me to be a good judge of bad character when he brought me up to the stage.

"Before I bring on your next performer, how many people were here to see Damon Wayans, who was advertised to perform tonight?"

The crowd clapped and whistled enthusiastically.

"Well I have some bad news for you people… Damon just canceled (collective groan of great disappointment from the entire crowd) and I'm sorry to let you all down, because he really is a funny guy. (At least a third of the crowd got up from their seats to leave) I guess you'll just have to go see his new movie… but hey, all I can say is we're very sorry. What a bummer, but these things happen sometime. It's very disappointing. Sooooooo, let's bring on our next comic! What a'ya say?… Ladies and gentlemen, Paul D'Angelo!… Come on, let's hear it!" (feeble reaction from the devastated crowd that couldn't care less at this point if I whipped out my noodle and did a whirly-bird with it)

Doesn't that suck? He's trying to bury me! Thanks for whipping the crowd into a frenzy for me, my good friend.

Needless to say, it took a couple minutes to win them over after they had the wind taken out of their sails by that asshole. After the crowd failed to respond to my first two jokes I said, "Fuck it" and addressed a couple in the crowd who revealed that they were acrobatic gymnasts from the Cirque du Soleil. I climbed on the piano and simulated their lovemaking which ended with the dialog:

"How was I?"

(smoking a cigarette) "Only a 7.2. I took off points for the early dismount."

The crowd went nuts and the rest of my set took off.

The stage manager had a big smile on his face and came over to shake my hand.

Then the host approached me and said, "Great job, Paul! You handled that well."

I gave him a dirty look and said, "That was a lousy way to bring me on stage."

Comedians can be so territorial at times. I'm surprised he didn't lift his leg and pee on the four corners of the stage before he sniffed my ass and introduced me.

L.A. Misérables, Too

We sat around and had a beer after the show. It was the first time that Larry had been introduced to my friend Max, the horror film screenwriter.

"Larry, this is my buddy Max, he's a movie writer."

Larry says, "No kidding. I wonder if I've ever seen any of your work. Did you ever write a porno movie?" (C'mon, what else would you expect Larry to say?)

I cut in. "Ya Larry. Max is famous in the skin-flick trade. You know the line, 'Oooh yeah baby... Fuck me harder... Don't stop... Give it to me, OOOOH, GOD!'? That's Max's line. He wrote that!

"He also wrote such blue-movie classics lines as, 'Hi, my name is Candy. Let's fuck!' and 'Pull it out and come all over my tits... yes... yes...*YES!*

And don't forget, 'Faster baby, *faster!* I bet you didn't know, that's his dialogue too, Larry... That verse is in a league with *'I'll be back!' 'Play it again, Sam'* and *"Go ahead, punk. Make my day'* to the X-rated community... He gets a residual check every time they use that line... I'm telling you, Max is a legend in the XXX business."

Oh boy.

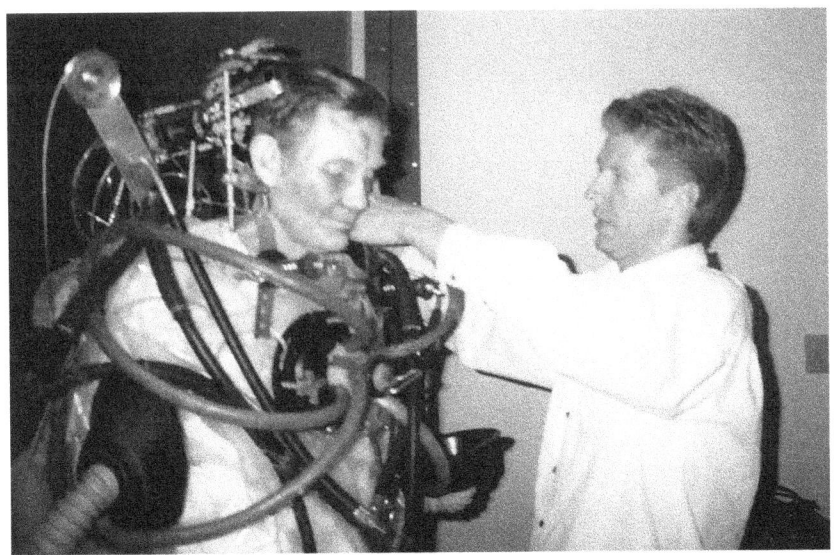

Max preparing to film a horror movie

Paul D'Angelo

DAY 214 - OCTOBER 8\ :sup:`TH`, 1996

I sent out copies of the videotape from NBC's *Friday Night Videos,* along with press kits, to over twenty pre-selected management companies and talent agencies, and explained that I was seeking representation and was looking to set up showcases with anyone who's interested. I've met with many agents and managers since I moved to Los Angeles, but I never got the feeling that any of them were right for me or my career. Some people in the business encouraged me to just sign with anyone who can open some doors, set up some auditions and industry showcases, get me some TV and club work, and be my mouthpiece.

The thought has been tempting, especially as my savings have dwindled down to almost nothing, but I have been patient with my career so far and I don't want to make any decisions that I'll regret once I've made a commitment. It's like a single woman who has a lot to offer, but feels like her biological clock is ticking, panics and marries some guy that she knows is not right for her, just so she can have a kid. She has the baby. She's very happy that she's got a child, but then reality sets in and she realizes that she's stuck with this schmoe for the rest of her life. I think I'll wait.

CHAPTER TEN
Ch-ch-ch-ch-ch-changes...

DAY 215 - OCTOBER 9th, 1996

The shuttle bus was supposed to pick me up at 7:00 AM for my flight to Boston, but the driver was late.

"I'm sorry I'm late," he tried to explain, "It's because of the fog we're having this morning."

Only in Los Angeles can a bus driver lose his way because it's foggy out. You're not flying a jet. All you have to do is read the street signs on every corner. How the hell did this moron manage to park at my building? Did he make an instrument landing or did the apartment manager talk him in from the tower?

No first class this time. My window seat is in the very last row of the plane, row number thirty-three. I sat down and looked out the window to my right. I was staring at the inside of a jet engine about eight inches from my face. I have a vivid recollection of reading a tragic story, just a couple months ago, about two people who were decapitated on a commercial jetliner when a piece of the engine broke off and the spinning turbine shot the shrapnel through the fuselage and into the passenger compartment, right where the unsuspecting victims were sitting. Great. Now, besides the in-flight movie, I have the added entertainment of anxiously waiting for a jagged fragment of metal from the nearby jet engine to sever my head at the neck.

If it does happen, I hope it puts me out of my misery before they serve that horrid airline food.

Even if I survive the breakaway engine, at the very least I suffer the indignity of having to stare at the side of an engine for the entire trip cross-country.

"Ladies and gentlemen, good afternoon, this is your captain speaking. If you look out your windows you will see a spectacular panoramic view of the Grand Canyon in all its magnificent majesty, except of course, for the gentleman in seat 33F who will have a fabulous view of gray sheet metal, twenty-two Phillips screw-heads, and the stenciled words 'NOSE COWL ATTACH BOLTS ACCESS,' whatever the fuck that means.

"As we continue eastward across the Midwest, we expect clear weather with visibility over a hundred miles... except the schmuck in the back whose visibility will remain at eight inches throughout his miserable little trip. Enjoy your flight."

I'm reading the newspaper. Earlier in the week, a thirteen-year-old high school girl was suspended from school because she was possession of Midol, a non-prescription, over-the-counter pill that women take when they're on their period. Now, in an unrelated incident, another young schoolgirl was suspended by a school board for having Advil on her person during school.

You know, .this country's priorities are really getting convoluted. It's not the casual user that we have to target... it's the drug manufacturers and pushers that demand our attention. We've got to step up efforts to stem the flow of Midol at the Mexican border, where it is being smuggled in right under the noses of drug enforcement agencies.

We need the cooperation of third-world nations in wiping out the Midol fields where local farmers are growing and harvesting the Cramp Plant without government intervention. We must bring the kingpins of the Midol Cartel to justice before more of our children fall under its spell.

Sure, the kids start with Midol, but pretty soon they won't get the same kick out of it, even when they exceed the recommended dosage.

L.A. Misérables, Too

Before long they've graduated to popping medicated, cherry-flavored cough drops like they're candy. Next thing you know, they're abusing vitamins and taking two-a-day instead of one-a-day. Before they know what hit them, our children are caught in a downward spiral and they're hooked on Pepto Bismal, drinking it right from the bottle in a dumpster at the end of a filthy alley.

Midol use leads to violence.

(taste, taste) "Hey man! This shit ain't pure Midol! This shit has been stepped on! You're trying to rip me off, Amigo! This is cut with Bufferin! I'm still exhibiting menstrual symptoms… cramps, nausea and fatigue. This is a drug war!"

Expect retaliation in the form of a drive-by cookie-tossing.

DAY 216 - OCTOBER 10TH, 1996

I called Los Angeles to see if I got any responses to my mailing of videotapes to the management companies and agencies. Kelly told me that there was an envelope from one of the prominent management companies with my promotional tape inside and a rejection letter. The postmark on the firm's envelope was the same day, Monday, October 7th, that I mailed it out. She says that it looks as if they never even viewed the tape.

No, I disagree. Not if the postmark is the same day I sent it out. I didn't even mail it until the mid-afternoon of the seventh. From the evidence, it appears that the company's in-house psychic had a premonition that my tape was in the mail and had an intern track the mailman down on his route and intercept the package before it could ever reach the office. Now that's an efficient rejection process if I ever saw one.

Tonight I had a show at the Comedy Connection in Boston. It was good to see all of my old friends from the club. They asked if Seamus was still at the apartment after almost two weeks. I told them yes, and asked them if they had seen the movie, *What About Bob?* with Bill Murray.

"Ya, we both saw it."

"Seamus is my 'Bob.'"

Welcome to the Hotel California, where you can check out, but you will never leave.

It felt great to be back on stage. During the show, I saw my black friend Chris, the doorman, standing by the entrance watching my act. I love Chris and have rarely done a show at the Connection without directing the crowd's attention to him and making some kind of wise remark to embarrass him. He will always come up to me after the show, laughing, and ask me why I always bust his balls but, if I didn't, I know that he would be disappointed because he enjoys it when I include him in the show.

Tonight I acknowledged him in front of the audience, "That's my friend Chris working the door. I think that you should know that Chris is the man personally responsible for ruining the Million Man March in Washington D.C. because he promised that he would go, then ended up sleeping late and missing the bus so, all because of him, they had to change the name of it to 'The 999,999 Man March.'"

I actually got a standing ovation from the front part of the audience. I don't understand it. While I was up there I worked the crowd a lot and, in my own mind, I was all over the place because it seemed like it had been a long time since I got the chance to stretch out at a comedy club. Maybe it was my obvious enthusiasm for doing live stand-up. Not so much that I had lost my zeal for performing, but more like a renewed appreciation for the opportunity to get on stage after being deprived for six months in Los Angeles.

DAY 217 - OCTOBER 11TH, 1996

My family makes it soooo easy for me to write this book. I don't even have to use my wit or imagination. I just listen.

I visited my parents today. After fifteen minutes of several unsuccessful and frustrating attempts at communication with my father, I asked, "Dad, why aren't you wearing your hearing aid?"

"What?"

I yelled louder. "I said 'WHY AREN'T YOU WEARING THE

L.A. Misérables, Too

NEW HEARING AID THEY GAVE YOU?'"

"What are you talking about, dummy? I don't need a damn maid, I got your mother!"

Then my mother walked into the kitchen. "Jack, where did you put that check for the Alzheimer's Foundation?"

He says, "I don't remember where the hell I put it... What check?", then he proceeded to scroll through every one of his children's names until he correctly called me Paul.

"Uh, Jay... uh, Chris, I mean... ah Sha... What the hell's your name?... Paul, come with me to the living room, I want to show you this new hearing aid they gave me."

"That's great, dad."

"What?"

"I SAID 'IT'S GREAT THAT YOU HAVE THE NEW HEARING AID.'"

"It's the best money can buy, you know. This is top-of-the-line. The best."

"Good for you, Dad."

"Paul, I need you to help me fix the kitchen faucet that's been dripping, get me the wrenches in the garage."

I said, "Sure, dad. Regular or metric?"

He answered, *"Who's from Medford? Do I know him?"*

"Ha ha ha..."

"What was that?"

"I said, 'Your new hearing aid is really working great.'"

"Ya, you can say that again."

"I know I can... I'll need to."

Two of my old roommates, Paul and Richard, and another friend, Danny, came with me to my show at Giggles tonight. It's my version of *The First Wives Club,* but this is the first husbands club... they're all divorced. I was working with Kenny Rogerson, who is a long-time veteran of the Boston comedy scene and extremely funny, and comedian Jackie Flynn, who brought the producer and director of the Jim Carey movie *Dumb and Dumber* to see Kenny's act. Jackie told me that his friends wanted to leave after Kenny's set, but he convinced them to stick around for ten minutes so they could catch part of my act, and they did. It sure can't hurt.

DAY 218 - OCTOBER 12TH, 1996

I can't believe it. My privacy has been invaded! I just yelled at both my brother Jay and my other brother Chris, and accused them of stealing some dirty videotapes that I copied and kept in the back shelf of my closet. Now they're missing and heads will roll. I told them that they could borrow anything of mine they wanted, but I was very upset that they had gone through my closets while I was living in Los Angeles.

My brothers told me that, if in fact they knew about my hidden stash of X-rated films, they certainly would have pilfered them, but they had no idea that I kept any dirty movies in my closet. That was an honest answer.

Then who could the culprit be? No one else has had access to my apartment since my trip to Boston. My brothers must be lying. They had…. Hey, wait a second… My mother and father told me they had a key to my abode and they let themselves in to vacuum the floors, change the sheets, and clean-up before I arrived home to visit. The last time I came home in July they cleaned my place and, the next week, I saw a bunch of my old *Playboy* magazines in my dad's bookcase at my parent's house. Now *Love Potion #69, Analmania 9, A League of Their Moans, The Load Warrior, Sex Trek: The Next Penetration,* and *Against All Bods* are missing, and all the evidence points to one man as the looter… my father. How do you like that? My dad is stealing my porn!

That's so cute.

After all these years, our father-son relationship has finally come full-circle.

L.A. Misérables, Too

My siblings: Chris, Shauna and Jay

DAY 219 - OCTOBER 13TH, 1996

I have one of the worst Boston accents you will ever hear. Since I moved to California I have working haaaaaard on pronouncing my "R's." I am very conscious of my R's and try to emphasize them when I speak to break myself of the habit of eliminating the letter R from my words.

As a result of my efforts, I have not improved at all, *but* I am now including R's in words that don't have an R in them.

Some examples: "I am going to the supa-maaaahket to buy bananers."

"This Mexican salser is hot! Hand me the root beahhh soder!"

"Yes... I'd like to orda a peppa-roni and peppa pizzer. Do you take Masta Chaaaahge or Vis-er?"

People have trouble understanding me back in Los Angeles and I can't seem to understand them either. A few weeks ago I was having dinner with a married couple and the husband got up to use the men's room.

I asked his wife where he was going and she answered, "He's going to the potty," meaning the bathroom... but I thought she said he was going to a *party,* so I got all excited and exclaimed, "Ooh, I want to go too!"

She gave me a puzzled look and inquired curiously, "Why do *you* want to go?"

I smiled and said, *"If it's a big one, I don't want to miss it!"*

She didn't talk to me for the rest of the night and I had no idea why.

DAY 220 - OCTOBER 14TH, 1996

You won't believe this, but I heard that Jay Leno was signing his new book at Copley Square in Boston today. I had planned to drive in, buy a book, ask him to sign it, and just happen to mention that I was now living in Hollywood and would like to be on his show.

Only problem was, it was a beautiful 70° mid-autumn day in New England and I blew off Jay to ride my motorcycle with my buddy George. We rode over one-hundred and seventy miles up the seacoast of Massachusetts, through New Hampshire, into southern Maine and back. Jay would understand.

The air was so clean compared to the Super-Chunk-Style Jiffy Peanut Butter air that I breathe on Hollywood Boulevard. We were on the shore road near Hampton Beach, New Hampshire, heading toward Portsmouth to get something to eat, when we got behind some leave peepers that were driving at an excruciating crawl. The fall attracts hordes of people during peak foliage and the couple in front of us were so old they reminded me of my golf game: in the high nineties to low hundreds. The old man driving was continuously checking his rear-view mirror for a large glacier that may be slowly gaining on them.

Women and old people are the most ardent foliage fans. It's not that the old men are crazy about taking a field trip to view leaves, it's just that, by that age, they are simply too weak to put up a fight.

L.A. Misérables, Too

So George was on his racing Ducati 900 motorcycle, revving the engine and impatiently looking for a chance to pass the car on the winding road. He finally couldn't stand the smell of burning brake-pads, from the parking brake that has been engaged ever since the couple left their driveway, and he gunned the bike, passing the slow moving car on the inside of a tight turn. I was in the process of twisting my throttle and following suit when I heard the siren of the unmarked police car following directly behind us. Bagged.

Damn, this could put a damper on a nice day. One thing's for sure, I'm not making the same mistake I did with the Beverly Hills cop. I walked over to the cruiser before the officer wrote the ticket and asked if I could speak to him. I informed him that I was a former assistant district attorney in Essex County and George was a close friend from law school. I also told him the I had met most of the cops in the area from the shows that I opened at the Club Casino theater in Hampton Beach and asked if he could take it into consideration. He said he would and I never dreamed that he'd let this one slide, but he did. I talked to him for a while and thanked him for being so understanding and, as I walked away, I added, "Now I think I'll have George buy my lunch."

As we mounted the bikes, the trooper pulled the cruiser alongside us, put down his passenger-side window and said, "You have it all wrong. I think the *two* of you should buy *me* lunch!" and pulled away.

Good guy. Good point. Good day.

I have got George out of so many driving violations I can no longer count them. It only rubs salt in my wound to think that the only client I couldn't get out of a jam was me.

DAY 221 - OCTOBER 15TH, 1996

Seamus finally bought an airplane ticket back to Boston and left our apartment today. I had invited him to stay for a couple of days and he was there for two and a half weeks. Either his math is lousy or he's from Alaska, where the nights last much, much longer than they do Southern California.

Paul D'Angelo

After two and a half weeks he was no closer to getting a job or apartment than he was the day he stepped off the airplane at LAX. It's difficult to find employment when you sit like a lump on the couch all day long, playing video games instead of making calls, taking interviews, and filling out applications... unless, of course, you plan on going professional with that Sega-Genesis video-sports-thingy.

DAY 222 - OCTOBER 16TH, 1996

Last night, my two brothers and my friend Gary Gulman hung out with me at my apartment and we had quite a few beers while we watched a playoff baseball game. Around midnight, I got a call from a man who introduced himself as the assistant to Jim Brogan, the booking agent for *The Tonight Show with Jay Leno,* to whom I had sent a videotape and press package last week.

He told me that Jim had received my tape and was interested in having me appear on *The Tonight Show,* but they needed to hear some more of my material before they could make a final decision. He then asked me if I could perform a couple routines over the phone to assist them in determining if I would be appropriate for the show.

I said "Come on. Who is this? Is this a joke or something?" I was skeptical because this was not common practice, but he told me that he got my Boston phone number from Kelly, and no one else knew that I had mailed the tape out, so this could possibly be a legitimate call and I didn't want to piss him off and blow my chance.

"I'll tell you what. Let me call you back at the NBC studios, so I can verify your identity."

The caller got angry and told me that this was no joke, and if I wouldn't cooperate there were several other stand-ups under consideration for the appearance. Shit! What am I gonna do? I began to wish I hadn't been drinking, because my mind was in turmoil and my stomach was feeling a little nauseous to boot. So I started to go into one of my jokes, then... bang!... I stopped.

"I'm sorry, but I can't accommodate you. This just doesn't feel right to me," and hung up wondering if I had just told the assistant to the booking agent for *The Tonight Show with Jay Leno* to go fuck himself.

L.A. Misérables, Too

I nervously paced my living room floor as I related the phone call to Gary and my brothers, who unanimously agreed, in their intoxicated opinion, that I had just made a huge mistake. I had a very difficult time falling asleep that night.

The first thing I did when I woke up this morning was to call Kelly to ask her if anyone from *The Tonight Show* had called the house looking for me. She said that she attended the taping of our friend Anthony Clarke's NBC show, *Boston Common,* last night and met Jimmy Brogan, told him about me, and convinced him to have his assistant contact me about doing the show.

"You did? What was the assistant's name?"

"I think it was Bob something."

That's what the guy's name was! Oh no, I'm fucked! I'll never get a chance to do *The Tonight Show* now! I wanted to throw up when Kelly told me that she couldn't torture me any longer. While Kelly was attending the taping at NBC, a couple of Boston comics who were sitting with her convinced Kelly to participate with the crowd's warm-up comic in placing a crank phone call to me. The call was carried over the studio's sound system in front of a couple hundred audience members, but I wouldn't fall for it.

You bastards!

And, for your further entertainment at my expense, a father-son conversation we just had:

"Dad... I was just wonderin'... Uh, I'm not accusing you or anything... I just, uh, well, you see... How can I put this?... Umm, oh, it can't be.... Never mind. It's not important anyway... and, besides, I must be wrong about the... uh... just forget it."

"What, Paul? Spit it out," my dad said.

"Um... you see, the other day I was upset and yelled at Jay and Chris because I thought that they went snooping in my closets and took some things of mine that..."

"Are you talkin' about the dirty movies, Paul? Ya, I took 'em. You can have 'em back, yours suck. I have some real good ones I'll let you borrow."

Well, I'm glad we got that matter straightened out.

CHAPTER ELEVEN
Mama, don't let your babies grow up to be comics...

DAY 223 - OCTOBER 17TH, 1996

Early this morning my brother Jay woke me up when called me from the salon where he gets his hair cut.

(taken from my original stenographer's notes)

"Paul, talk to Jeannie. She wants to know where you're playing this weekend."

"Sure... Hi Jeannie. I'll be at the Comedy Connection in Boston and then I hop over to Andover for a 9:30 show on Friday and Saturday. Hope you can make it. Hey, by the way, what's your secret? My brother Jay goes to you. You cut my brother Chris' hair. And you're my dad's stylist and a bunch of his friends too. You must be really good."

"Oh, they don't like the way I cut their hair, Paul. It's because I have huge tits!"

Ha ha ha. That's sure a fine way to start the morning.

Yesterday my mother bought me Jay Leno's book, *Leading With My Chin*. She read the first few pages and remarked, "See how sweet he is? Did you read all the nice things he said about his family in his book?"

Yes I did, Mom, but I somehow sense that our family is a wee bit crazier.

L.A. Misérables, Too

It's another gorgeous fall day. I went golfing with my friends Randy and "The Cat Man." I realized that golf and women play similar roles in my life. With both, I really have no idea what the hell I'm doing, even though everyone wants to give me advice.

In addition, I keep going back because I want to have a good time, but I usually end up angry, frustrated and upset, so I just want to say 'Screw it!' And just when I'm thinking of giving up, something good happens that misleads me into believing that maybe I'm finally getting the hang of this thing, which I'm not. But what it comes down to is, after it's over, I feel that I'm lucky just to come you out of the experience with the balls I started with.

Tonight I had a show in New Hampshire for a booking agent that I typically don't deal with. I picked up the Prune and, on the way up there, he reminded me of one of the shows I did in Manchester, New Hampshire, when he was with me.

The opening act of the show had to be the world's worst magician.

He was very amateurish, had a horrible delivery, and screwed up every trick he did. Hidden objects would fall out of his sleeve in the middle of an illusion. He'd bump into the table that was set-up on stage and knock his magic props onto the floor. And for his grand finale, he made some item appear in a puff of smoke and set fire to the background curtain. The crowd was in hysterics at his incompetence but, through it all, the kid maintained a cocky, arrogant attitude toward the audience.

I watched the fiasco in disbelief at the back of the room with Prune and the club owner. As the brat was frantically trying to snuff out the drapes, I said to the owner, "Where the hell did you get this kid? He sucks!!! I can't believe it! What an obnoxious little prick!"

The owner answered, "That's my son!"

"Ohhh, you don't say so… Uhhh… Um, uh… He has a lot of potential."

Just say the magic words, idiot… *"Hocus Pocus!"* and… Voilá! And right before my very eyes, all of the future shows that I have booked at that club have suddenly disappeared!... POOF!

"Thank you, ladies and gentlemen! And for my next trick… "

Paul D'Angelo

What a disappointment when we arrived at the gig. I get very discouraged when there are less people in the audience than the total number of hours I drove to get to the club.

Now let me say that I've done shows in biker bars... I've performed at a bachelor party where the guest of honor was puking into a green trash barrel three feet in front of the microphone stand during my act... I've done a show at a college frat house where a huge melee broke out in the middle of one of my routines... I've done a show for a construction company where they interrupted my act, mid-performance, to bring in some strippers, then wanted me to continue when they were done... I've done shows at a Chinese restaurant where I've had to talk across a sunken bar with three blenders going at once... I did a show on the SS Norway in front of 800 passengers who only spoke Spanish and didn't understand a word I said... I opened a show for Joan Jett and the Blackhearts, where hundreds of spur-wearing, leather clad, dykes yelled out, "Fuck you! We want Joan!"... I performed on the deck at a pool party where a dozen elderly Italian ladies wore black wool dresses in the ninety degree heat because they were widowed during the fifties... I had to do a mid-afternoon show in a courtroom as a favor to a judge... I did a show at a Mexican restaurant where the cook was drunk and holding hostages with a meat cleaver because his wife and girlfriend both showed up on the same night, and I had to be the one to talk him into giving up because he liked my act... I did a show in the store-front window of Sal's House of Calzone because Sal was the uncle of one of the big comedy club owners in Boston... I did a show on a cruise ship during a hurricane where everyone was seasick and audience members would intermittently run from their seats to throw up... I did a comedy show on a floating barge in St. Thomas harbor that had a sound system that sounded like the speaker at a drive-through fast food place... I had to do a show into a PA system from the front of a moving bus... I did a show in an outdoor tent during a driving thunderstorm that drove a family of skunks into the music theater during my act... I did a show where most of the audience was comprised of two busloads of special-needs adults... I was on stage when a drunk sitting up front took off his prosthetic leg and threw it at me because he thought it was funny... I was late for a show because I was stuck in traffic on the highway and was asked to do part of my act over my cellular phone, with the club's telephone held next to the microphone on stage, while the club's manager held up one of my headshots for the crowd.

The point I'm trying to make is that I've paid my dues and have been placed in some very uncomfortable situations, but I've never been so upset as I was tonight. The club was poorly managed and unorganized. The spotlight was one of those portable work lamps that you would use when you're working under the hood of your car, and it was clipped onto the back of a stool facing upward, giving the performers that Bela Legosi vampire look that's oh so flattering on stage. During the show they refused to turn off the jukebox and Metallica was blasting from the back of the room while we were trying to perform. There were only about eight people in the audience and they were sitting about 50' from the stage and talking throughout the act.

The last straw was when two guys, who were so drunk that they couldn't even stand up or talk, staggered in and started yelling "Hey, fuck face! Buy me a drink!" I could see a confrontation brewing and the employees did nothing to deter these idiots so, in the middle of the act I said 'Fuck this!' and walked off the stage early for the first and only time in ten years of performing stand-up comedy.

DAY 224 - OCTOBER 18TH, 1996

This morning I got a call from the agent who booked last night's show. He told me that the club owner, who wasn't present during the farce they called a comedy show, didn't want to pay him because I walked offstage prematurely. I told the agent that the show was a disgrace and offered to speak to the owner and explain the situation.

I spoke to the owner, who was a nice man and very interested in my input. I told him that the club was mismanaged and disorganized, no one knew what the hell they were doing, and the person in charge last night was incompetent and should be fired.

The owner said, "That was my daughter."

"Oh oh... um... but the place has a lot of potential."

Shit! Déjà vu all over again.

I had to call my accountant today to figure out what I'll have to pay in taxes this year. The answer: Very little. It appears that my tax write-offs for business-related expenses will exceed my total income for the year.

That wasn't a tough obstacle to overcome. We figured out that an eraser I bought in February pushed me over the top.

DAY 225 - OCTOBER 19TH, 1996

I dropped by my parent's home before I left for my show tonight and sat down with my dad while we watched a college football game on the tube.

"So how's it going out in LA, son?"

"I'll tell you the truth Dad, there are a lot of days that I feel like crying... Any progress I make seems to come at a snail's pace while my savings are on 'E'... Often times I wonder if it's worth all the sacrifice. I'll get depressed, and think about giving up and coming home... but then I'll do a show, and people will come up to me and tell me that I did a great job. They'll tell me to be patient, because I'm bound to be a success. It's those little things that keep me going. Their words of encouragement give me a faint glimmer of hope when I think that I'm wasting my time and it's just enough to inspire me to hang in there."

"How do you know these people aren't bullshitting you? You can't believe what anyone says in Hollywood! They're all full of shit! Half of 'em don't know what the hell they're talking about! I wouldn't listen to those idiots!"

Gee, thanks for the pep-talk, dad. You took my faint glimmer of hope and snuffed it out like a cigarette butt.

It's my dad's 50th high school reunion this weekend, so his ex-football teammate, Joe Morelli, was in town and stopped by my parent's home while I was there.

Nebraska was playing. They're having a good season, but quite a few of their players have had run-ins with the law over the last couple of years. As we watched the football game, Joe told us that he figured out that the big red "N" on the Nebraska football helmet stood for "Knowledge."

That's funny. I wrote it down.

At the house, I happened to check out the front page of the local newspaper, *The Wakefield Item*, and saw a strange headline for this relatively quiet town.

"BIZARRE WAKEFIELD H.S. INCIDENT SPARKS PROBE"

It seems that two high school students, fourteen and sixteen year old girls, were caught while they were involved in a bizarre ceremony where one of them drew blood from the other's arm with a tourniquet and hypodermic syringe, then drank the blood in what appeared to be some kind of occult ritual.

Gee, all of a sudden, catching your teenage kid with a six-pack of Pabst Blue Ribbon doesn't seem all that bad.

"Keith, is that you?"

"Ya, ma. Uh, like how come you're still up so late?"

"I've been waiting up for you... Tell me, where were you tonight, Keith?"

"Ummm... Nowhere, mom."

"Nowhere, huh? Come here young man... Look at me when I'm talking to you!... (sniff sniff) Do I smell the blood of one of your classmates on your breath? Is that your friend Timmy's hemoglobin I detect on you, son?"

"No, maaa."

"No ma, what?"

"Nooo, maaa... it's Budweiser."

"Thank God, you had me half worried to death... now go down to your coffin and get some sleep."

"OK, you bloodsucking ol' bat."

"I heard that... Thank you. I love you too."

Tonight a good friend of mine, Judge Paul Cavanaugh, presiding justice at the Malden District Court, came to see my show. He told me a funny courtroom story about a lawyer who was pleading his client out to a drunk driving complaint last week. The lawyer insisted that the defendant was pleading guilty, despite the fact that she only appeared intoxicated because there was alcohol in the salad dressing that she had for dinner that evening.

Judge Cavanaugh told me that the matter was scheduled for trial because he refused to accept the plea of guilty, rejecting it on the theory that he had never heard of someone "driving under the influence of lettuce" before.

Everyone's a comedian now.

DAY 226 - OCTOBER 20TH, 1996

I leave for Los Angeles tomorrow. I've had a great week and I got to perform almost every night. I spent the afternoon at my parents' home where we had a get together in honor of my mother and sister's birthdays, which are five days apart this week. My dad proposed that we have a drink of this twenty-one year old scotch that he's been saving for years.

You have to be shitting me! He's finally gonna open that bottle? He's had it forever. When I graduated from Boston College, I suggested that we break open the good scotch.

"Not today. I'm saving that for a special occasion."

When I got my law degree and later passed the Massachusetts bar examination I asked, "Dad, what do you say we celebrate with that expensive scotch you have?"

"You stay away from my scotch! I'm waiting for an important event."

I swear, if Frank Sinatra ever rose from the grave and rang our doorbell, when my father answered the door, the conversation would probably go something like this...

"Hi there pal, my name is Frank."

"Frank?... Frank *Sinatra?* Of course I know who you are. I'm a big fan! But I thought you were dead?"

"Well ya, I've been dead for quite some time, but I was given a short reprieve to emerge from the tomb and, as you can imagine, things can get pretty dusty down there (cough, cough), so I'm a little dry and I sure could use a drink."

"Of course Frank, come on in! My name is Jack. It's nice to meet you."

"I'm sorry, Jack, my shoes... you know, the dirt..."

"Oh, don't worry about that Frank, my wife will clean the floor. Come in. Now what can I get for you?"

"Oooh, is that a bottle of Royal Salute, Jack? It's my favorite. I used to go crazy for that booze. I'd love a belt of the stuff!"

"Oh no. I'm sorry, Frank. Not *that* bottle. I'm saving that for a *special* occasion."

My Uncle Dick and Aunt Viola are over for dinner. So is Uncle Vito. My two uncles are a contrast in lifestyles that make you question the so-called "experts" when it comes to advice on health.

Uncle Vito doesn't drink and has never smoked a cigarette in his life. At seventy-two years old, I can still hear him on the treadmill in his next-door apartment for forty-five minutes every single day. That's in addition to the sit-ups and push-ups that he faithfully performs on a strict schedule. Uncle Vito is very cautious about the food he eats and takes great care of himself.

Now, for some reason, my uncle has suddenly developed an irregular heartbeat, prostate problems and a variety of other ailments for which he has to take medication on a daily basis. No wonder the poor man is discouraged. He makes all the sacrifices that are recommended for a long and healthy life, but they could not prevent his health from deteriorating.

On the other hand, my Uncle Dick used to be a heavy drinker for years, has smoked Camels without filters since he was in high school, and covers his food with enough salt to de-ice a runway. He never wears a coat when most people are bundled up like Eskimos and the guy has never been sick a day in his life.

Go figure.

Aunt Viola is no different than most people when she asks what celebrities I've run across while living in Hollywood. Kelly's the one that rubs elbows with all the movie and television stars because she's employed as the first assistant to a movie producer. She frequently has to attend meetings and dinners at expensive restaurants and exclusive clubs that all the celebs frequent.

Every week I hear, "Paul, you'll never guess who was sitting beside me last night. Annette Benning and Warren Beatty!"

Or, "I can't believe it! There was Hugh Grant and Elizabeth Hurley, walking past me as Rob Reiner was getting off the elevator!"

Denzel Washington... David Schwimmer... Goldie Hawn... Paul Sorvino... Kevin Spacey. The list goes on.

Me? The day Mel Gibson does his wash in our laundry room or Madonna has a craving for Kentucky Fried Chicken will be the day I run into someone important.

"Say, Uncle Dick. I heard you bought a new snow blower."

He corrected me. "It's not a snow 'blower,' it's a snow 'thrower,' Paul."

My sister-in-law Cindy asked, "Paul, what's the difference between a 'blower' and a 'thrower?'"

I couldn't let the opportunity pass. "As long as you don't know the difference between a 'blower' and a 'thrower,' do you want to play catch in the bedroom?"

Sorry, I can't help it.

DAY 227 - OCTOBER 21ST, 1996

New England was pummeled with a Nor'easter over the last two days. Record breaking monsoon-like rains fell, along with gusting winds that caused many homes to lose power, and hundreds of residents had to be evacuated because of rising flood waters.

My parents drove me to the airport early this morning and the rains were torrential. My mother said, "We're lucky, this could have been snow. Thank God for that."

It's only October, ma. We could have a mid-afternoon thunder shower on a ninety degree July day and my mother will remark, "We'd be in big trouble if this was snow!"

When it snows, though, she doesn't say, "Good thing it's only snow. If this was a meteor shower, we'd be in some serious trouble!"

L.A. Misérables, Too

or "Don't complain about shoveling snow. It could be molten lava... then you'd be sorry."

The newspaper showed several photographs of flooded-out homeowners getting evacuated by the National Guard, being lead along in small aluminum boats on raging rivers that once were streets. For some of the refugees this is a little taste of success. After all, how many people can truly say they have both a boat *and* a house on the water?

I have a six hour flight in the most uncomfortable seat in the history of flight since Wilbur Wright had to lay his body across the wing of the first airplane at Kitty Hawk.

There are six seats across in this Boeing 757, three on each side of an aisle that's so narrow I got whacked on the head and shoulder by every piece of carry-on luggage that was carried past my seat, and then again with the food and beverage carts once we were in the air.

Besides that, to be politically correct, the airlines no longer have a maximum weight limit for their flight attendants, and every time they walk down their aisle, past my seat, I get hip-checked like Mario Lemieux. I don't get it.

When you bring a piece of carry-on luggage onto the plane, at the boarding gate they have a metal cage that has the same dimensions of the overhead compartment. If your carry-on bag doesn't fit inside that cage, it's too big and you are required to check your bag. The airlines should have one of those baskets that's the same width of the aisle and require the flight attendants to sit in it. If the flight attendant's ass is wider than the aisle, they should work in ticketing.

Problem solved.

There is absolutely no place to put my arms. The only three people who could sit side-by-side comfortably in these three seats are Kate Moss and a jockey, with the armless Venus d'Milo in the middle seat. As luck would have it, the guy sitting to my right has the wingspan of *Sesame Street's* Big Bird.

I don't know what it is with airline food and food service, but it's never a good experience for me. Today they served a breakfast that sucked all of the moisture out of me and made my mouth so dry, I swear they made the omelet with baking soda, cotton balls and kitty

Paul D'Angelo

litter.

By the time the flight attendant came by with the beverage cart, after what seemed like hours later, I'd been forced to suck on a Wet-Nap damp-towelette for moisture and lean across the other two passengers to lick the condensation off the inside of the airplane's window to survive.

By day, a mild mannered Assistant District Attorney...
By night, a wild and funny guy!

By JAMES M. GILMARTIN
and
EUGENE A. SYLVESTER

WAKEFIELD - In his role as an Assistant District Attorney in Essex County, Wakefield native Paul Murphy spends each and every day presenting his case to a judge and jury. At night, and outside the courthouse, Paul D'Angelo presents his case to a judge and jury of a different kind in his other role — that of a standup comedian.

These two individuals are in reality one and the same person. His real name, of course, is Paul Murphy, and it is this Paul Murphy who has lived most of his life in Wakefield.

However, it was as Paul D'Angelo that this local funny man recently headlined a comedy night at El Torito's on Route One in Saugus.

For the audience who came to listen that night, it was — as one of them put it — "an evening of non-stop laughs." And as far as El Torito's Manager Sean Rooney was concerned, "This was one of the best crowds we have ever drawn."

The overwhelming consensus of those in attendance for Murphy/D'Angelo's performance was that this was a young comic who was about to make it big. One person went so far as to say that "We're looking at the next Jay Leno here. Look out, Johnny, 'cause Paul's on his way."

What the audience found most appealing (and most amusing) about D'Angelo's material was the fact that it centers on "a day in the life" of the average person. He takes normal everyday experiences — such as going to the dentist or trying to find the fastest lane at the local supermarket — and makes them sound absolutely hilarious (and somewhat mythical).

D'Angelo uses much of his material to comment on the state of today's society. He tells his audience that "Young kids are starting to have sex too early these days. My nephew got a girl in trouble and had to get married. They had the bachelor party at Chuckie Cheese."

This up and coming comic also has a totally different side to him, and in a recent Daily Times Chronicle interview at the Peabody District Court, Paul Murphy talked about his two distinctly different jobs.

He was found in the third session of the courthouse looking very much the young competent ADA — which is completely opposite from his appearance when he steps out on stage.

However, one thing that becomes quite apparent is that there is a great similarity between being at the front of a courtroom and being on stage. One major difference, though, is that instead of young women serving margaritas in skimpy uniforms, there are now court officers in full dress (and very official) uniforms.

Murphy is also aware of the similarity, and said, "Before I performed for the first time, I had prosecuted 50 to 60 jury trials, so the last thing I worried about was getting up in front of an audience."

DAY 228 - OCTOBER 22ND, 1996

Our refrigerator is a dinosaur. And the Ice Age lives-on in the freezer. There has to be four inch thick frost built up on the walls. Kelly tried to defrost the freezer while I was away. She had chipped away the ice down to the bare wall in one area of the freezer, then somehow pressed the palm of her hand against the exposed metal surface and her hand stuck to the metal like someone sticking their tongue to a frozen flagpole on a frigid winter day.

She told me that she couldn't remove her hand for what seemed like minutes, until she finally ripped it off. Her hand's still red and tender and it occurs to me that Kelly may be the only victim of frostbite on record in the history of tropical Southern California.

DAY 229 - OCTOBER 23RD, 1996

To tell the truth, I was not looking forward to returning to Los Angeles after this last trip home. Not because I had such a good time with my friends and family, but because I felt that I've accomplished so little in the seven months I've spent in Hollywood and I didn't look forward to the continuing frustration that I've been experiencing. I think it really hits home when person after person asks me what's going on in Los Angeles and I don't really have anything extraordinary to tell them.

I have to say that maybe the reputation that I'm slowly building is finally paying off and things are taking a change for the better. Today I have a meeting with two management companies that I'm very interested in to represent me. I also had to postpone a meeting with a third manager who wants me to make a commitment to him. I told him that I could not make a commitment until all the cards were on the table and I still had other managers and agents to interview with.

I also got a phone call from the Icehouse in Pasadena, one of the toughest comedy rooms to get booked in throughout the country, and was given a week's booking in early December. This week I've been rebooked to play the Coach House in Capistrano, primarily a music theater that seats about 500 people, and 4th and B in San Diego, a 1500 seat venue. Richard from the Improvisation is still keen on giving me opportunities to play there, but there are showcases scheduled all week that prohibit him from giving me any stage time at the moment, which I can fully understand.

Tonight, Max and I went out to the Improv for a drink. We ran into some guys we knew and ended up closing the bar. I forgot that I was supposed to stop by Ralph's Supermarket on the way home to pick up a few things for the apartment. The infamous "Rock n' Roll Ralph's" on Sunset, is open twenty-four hours a day, and has a very bizarre clientele.

At the check-out, I was poking Max and giving him the head-nod to bring his attention to the two weirdos behind us in line. One guy was about 5'2" and had long blue and green fluorescent hair. His pal was wearing a black leather jacket with a matching 'Elvira: Mistress of the Night' black fright wig. He had his head pierced so many times he looked like a lucky trout that got away from several fishermen and still had the lures stuck in him to prove it. To complete his "undead" look, the Cryptkeeper had caked, white make-up on his face.

Max put a leg of lamb that he was purchasing up on the conveyor belt. which caused these guys to go, "Ewwww!! Animal flesh! How disgusting!"

Well, you fucking health nuts! Come on boys, have yourself a hamburger or a pork chop. Get some color in your face besides that infected puncture wound on your nostril.

Ya... that vegetarian diet you're on is doing wonders for you. You look like an extra from the "Thriller" video. Houseflies look healthier than you guys... and they eat shit and garbage. How are you gonna have the energy to slam dance, or get your blood pressure up high enough so you can find a good vein to mainline?

Give us a break and keep your comments to yourself, you freaks.

DAY 230 - OCTOBER 24ᵀᴴ, 1996

I had a show in San Juan/Capistrano tonight, which is about a two hour drive with the traffic. My friend Max agreed to accompany me to the club and, when he got into my car, he appeared somewhat tentative. Upon getting into the seat, Max immediately strapped himself in, then stared straight ahead with an apprehensive look on his face.

"Max, are you nervous about something?" I asked.

"No, I'm OK Paul."

"Are you sure Max?"

"Well, now that you mention it, I'm a little concerned, because I had a dream last night that I was in a car accident and I'm being extra cautious."

"Max, do you think that, because you dreamed that you were in a car crash, that it's some sort of premonition warning you about the future?"

"Well, you never know, Paul."

Hmmmm. I thought about that one for a moment.

"If that's the case, Max, then I think I had better let you know about my dream last night. Whatever you do, don't go to your high school chemistry class in your underwear. It is very embarrassing, especially if Loni Anderson's the teacher because, when she bends down to kiss you, you're staring at her cleavage and, when you finally notice that she has these big, vampire fangs, it's too late, and then you try to scream for help but nothing comes out… and… and that's all I can tell you because that's when I woke up. From that point on, you're on your own… but don't say that I didn't warn you, my friend."

Max didn't loosen his seat belt, but he did loosen up.

The club was packed. There were over five hundred people in the audience. Some were standing in the back and all of the private boxes were filled. It was nice for me because I got to stretch out and do about an hour and ten minute show, which went very well.

Max and I were almost home when I realized the strange irony of my life. I just completed a show in which I had the complete and undivided attention of more than five hundred people, while I indulged myself by talking about anything I wished, for over an hour. I made them all laugh and feel good for a while, and I got lots of praise when I was done. The management was extremely pleased and talked about booking me again in the future, while some of the people who were leaving at the same time I walked out shook my hand and asked for autographs.

The irony was that, when I got in my car, all I could dwell on were about a half dozen routines I did that I felt needed improvement. After agonizing over the work I needed to do on those jokes, I blasted several of my favorite CD's over the car stereo while we flew down the highway and, with total disregard for the performance I had just given, spent the entire ride fantasizing about what it would be like if I were a rock n' roll star and it was *me* playing that guitar and singing those songs.

At one point in our ride, Mick Jagger was singing, "You can't always get what you want..." which was appropriate for my mindset.

Hell, knowing the way my mind works, I'd probably do the same thing if I *were* a rock 'n roll star. I'd be riding in the back of a limousine after performing the last of four sold-out shows with three encores at the Hollywood Bowl or Madison Square Garden... with two beautiful groupies drinking champagne on either side of me... but my mind would be a thousand miles away, thinking, "Man... if I were only the Pope. That would be a great gig. You get to wear that big hat... Ya, the Pope, that would be cool." (sigh)

DAY 231 - OCTOBER 25TH, 1996

Either someone, or someone's dog, urinated in the elevator the other day and now, for $800.00 a month, I have to smell the scent of urine every time I leave my apartment. If I wanted to ride in something that smelled like urine every day, I could have stayed in Boston and got a subway pass for a lot less money.

DAY 232 - OCTOBER 26TH, 1996

Kelly and I drove to San Diego today because I'm scheduled to perform at 4th and B, which holds about 1500 people. I did a show here during the summer as a feature performer and they brought me back this time as a headliner.

The place was jammed and there were three other comedians and a host scheduled to go on before me. One of the comedians was pacing back and forth and pulling his hair out in the dressing room. Apparently he was paying some guy to tape his set with a television-quality camera so he would have a high-grade promotional tape for distribution to booking agents or the like. He kept looking over his set-list as he fidgeted around the room, full of anxiety. Kelly mentioned that, since he was so concerned with his presentation, it may look better if he removed his ratty looking jean jacket and tucked in his dirty T-shirt.

That's all he had to hear.

"Do you really think so? I don't know. I was going for that look, but... maybe you're right... Ohhhh, I don't know!" and he spent the next twenty minutes agonizing over the decision of whether to leave on his dungaree jacket or go with the T-shirt, because everything had to be perfect for this taping and each detail was critical to its success. He put the jacket on... then he took the jacket off... then he put it on again and looked in the mirror... then he took it off... then he tucked his shirt in... then he pulled it out again... then he put the jacket on with the shirt out... then in... then took the jacket off and tried the T-shirt tucked and untucked for the hundredth time, hoping to achieve fashion Nirvana for this critical videotaping that had to be juuuuust right.

Then, after tormenting himself with that strategic judgment about his appearance, he went out on stage and talked about having sex with his dog for five minutes. Yes, that's correct... He was fucking Fido. Giving his dog a bone. Nice job.

The material kind of makes the outfit irrelevant, don't you think? I can't be sure, but I'm willing to bet, that the gig at the big theater for the Jewish Anti-Defamation League banquet will be determined by whether or not your T-shirt is tucked in.

Oh, I get it. Screwing your pet with a jacket on is in bad taste, but bestiality with a tucked-in T-shirt is... well, sort of "whimsical and cutsey" in a way.

This reminded me of a show that I did in Boston a couple of years ago. I was hosting at Nick's Comedy Stop, where I had my own show for seven or eight years, and the place was filled with about three hundred people on that particular evening.

Before the show began, I was approached by a relatively new comic that I had never worked with before. He told me that he was one of the scheduled performers that evening and told me that tonight was very special for him. He pointed to the audience and told me that his whole family had come to see him do comedy for the first time.

I could see an entire row of well dressed, middle-aged people, patiently waiting with their hands folded on their laps. Alongside them were four older aunts, probably well into their seventies and dressed entirely in black, with black kerchiefs on their heads and wearing black nylons, looking like they just came over from "the old country."

He told me needed a huge favor. This comedian asked me... for this one night, *please, please!*... if I could just put him on somewhere in the middle of the show, because he really wanted to impress his family. "Please, Paul! Please! Pretty please! It's *soooo important to me!*"

"Of course," I told him, without hesitation. I would be glad to accommodate him and give him a nice slot. Not at the beginning, when the crowd hadn't been warmed-up to its optimal level, and not near the end, when the crowd may be getting burnt-out from sitting through too many acts.

No. Not for you, my friend. I will put you right smack in the middle of the pack, when the audience is at its peak, because I have an appreciation of wanting to make a positive impression on your own flesh and blood. What could be more important to a performer than to do your best in front of those you love most... your family, here to watch the comedic prodigy that they raised and nurtured?

And I did just that. The crowd was enthusiastic. I gave him a wonderful introduction and brought him onstage. Good luck, kid. Knock

L.A. Misérables, Too

'em dead. Make your family proud!

He then proceeded to step on the stage and tell a story about his girlfriend getting a yeast infection, or some kind of nasty female plumbing disorder, which he described in vivid detail, before informing the audience that she had to insert a vaginal suppository into her "gaping pussy." Then, when he went down on her that night, he explained how he somehow got the capsule stuck between his teeth while he was "eating her out" and... OK, OK. Please! Do I need to go on with this? You can only imagine.

I remember standing at the back of the club with my friend, Gary, and laughing my ass off while I stared at the old ladies, clutching their rosary beads, making the sign of the cross, and frantically praying for God's forgiveness on their nephew's immortal soul, lest he spend eternity painfully burning in the flaming depths of hell.

Good thing I gave you that primo spot, my friend. And *thank the good Lord above* you weren't wearing a jean jacket!

CHAPTER TWELVE
Same as it ever was...

DAY 233 - OCTOBER 27TH, 1996

I was looking through a free L.A. entertainment newspaper to see if there were any good bands playing. Here are some of the actual names I came across... Human Waste, Spastic Colon, The Humpers, Sluts for Hire, The Sweaty Nipples, Pink Torpedo, The Butthole Surfers, Woodpussy, Backside, The Muffs, Schlong, The Assholes, Cousin Lovers, Penis Flytrap, Crimson Crowbar, Fuck (honest!) and Cherry Poppin' Daddies.

When I was a teenager, we spent hours in our room playing "Louie Louie" over and over again to see if he was singing *"Tonight at ten, I'll lay her again"* or not. And very few people knew that Steely Dan was actually the name of an antique dildo. Then Led Zeppelin's Robert Plant said he wanted a girl to squeeze his lemon till the juice ran down his leg and we thought that was real cool, knowing that we didn't have to make a diligent search for innuendoes in rock n' roll songs any longer. The words to disco songs took that concept to another level ("Push, push in the bush...") and now adolescent boys can jerk off to the ads for bands because their names are so explicit.

DAY 234 - OCTOBER 28TH, 1996

I'm back on my old schedule. I didn't get any spots at either the Improv or the Laugh Factory this week. I have no other shows in the area anywhere in sight. The bills are due this week and I'm scrambling to cover them. I've heard nothing from any of the management companies or agencies that I sent my press kits and videos to since I had three or four of them returned to me. There are showcases being presented almost every night for the upcoming pilot season and for the Aspen Comedy Festival... but I still don't have representation to set up any showcases for me.

There were two significant developments of notice last week regarding my search for representation, however. About a year and a half ago I came to Los Angeles for a month and a half, staying with my friend Patty Ross. One of the reasons I came out at that time was because the owner of one of the big comedy clubs in Boston told me that he was very close with an agent/manager in LA who worked for a prominent firm. He told me he recommended that this person take a look at me. This was something that he'd never done for a comedian in his past twenty years of running comedy clubs, but he told me that he felt confident in my abilities, so he went out on a limb for me, which I really appreciated. Based on his strong personal endorsement, I planned a trip to Los Angeles so I could showcase for this agent, who would be anticipating my arrival. This, I believed, was the intelligent way to relocate. Do the showcase. Get competent representation. *Then* move out when everything was in place, so you could hit the ground running and not waste any time floundering in this city.

The first thing I did when I landed at LAX was place a call to that agent's office, announce my arrival, and give him a number where he could reach me because, at the time, he was "in a meeting."

I waited for a week. I got no return call, so I called again. He was in another meeting and, once again, I left my phone number and was told he'd call back. Another week went by... No call. I left several more messages, but was told that he was in several more "meetings," and he never returned any of my calls. After doing this for a month, I decided to go to his office in person.

Patty informed me that was just not the way things are done out here, but I told her that I was going home in a couple more weeks and I had nothing to lose. What was he gonna do… call me less? When I spoke to the firm's receptionist, I was told that this agent was in a meeting (I should have seen that excuse coming a mile away) and I told her that I would wait for as long as it would take to see him… and wait I did.

After about an hour he came out, introduced himself, and apologized for not returning my calls because he'd been so busy. We set up a night to showcase at the Laugh Factory and he said he would call the club and arrange it. The day of the showcase came and I had not heard anything from either the agent or the comedy club. I called the club and they told me that no such showcase had been scheduled, so I somehow begged them to set one up and I called the agent's office to inform him that I had procured a date on my own. That date came, he never showed up and, a couple days later, I was on my way back to Boston.

I recently learned that this agent had left that big firm and started his own agency. I also heard some very good things about him from other performers so I decided, what the hell, I'll give him a call and see if he remembers me. I did, his secretary put him on the line immediately, and he couldn't have been more cordial to me, even to the extent of putting one of his biggest clients on hold to finish our conversation. We left it off that I would send him a video and press kit and he promised to get back to me. I really had a good feeling about this guy and vowed that I would sign with him if he showed an interest.

That was over three weeks ago and I hadn't heard anything from him so, on the day I returned from Boston, I decided to call. His secretary told me that they never received the press package. I was disappointed, but at least that explained why I got no response from the agent, so I drove over that afternoon and hand delivered another package to his office. That was last week and I'm still waiting for a call.

While I impatiently waited, I got a phone message from a club manager that I did a show for this summer. He's a great guy that I've become personal friends with and he was extremely happy about the performance I gave at his club in front of four hundred people. Since then, he has gone out of his way to help me out and recommend me to various industry people. His last connection is currently in limbo, so he called to say that he knows a big-shot personal manager in Los Angeles that represents several prominent national comedy celebrities and he was going to make a call to him on my behalf.

I was in contact with this manager within the hour and, soon after, I was on my way over to his office for a meeting. I brought my press kit, videos of my NBC *Friday Night Videos* taping, a fifteen minute spot at the Ice House, and a forty-five minute taping at Boston's Comedy Connection, my *L.A. Misérables* manuscript, and the sitcom treatment I wrote based on the book about a lawyer who gives up his profession to move to Hollywood and work as a comedian.

He looked over the treatment for a few moments and told me what just about everybody has told me since I got here, "The networks are dying for a decent sitcom about the legal profession. Why don't you write a sitcom treatment from the point of view of you as an assistant district attorney moonlighting as a comedian at night?"

As obvious as it seemed, I don't know why I hadn't thought of it before. Everyone seems intrigued by the fact that I used to be an ADA and lawyer. I just think that I've always separated the two careers, at first out of necessity and, subsequently, because I was conditioned to do so, I suppose. I had great respect for this man who had been able to recognize the potential of creating a series based on my true life experiences. To me, at the time when I was living that double life, I was caught up in the harsh reality of trying to balance two, totally opposite careers. I was too personally involved to recognize the uniqueness of my experience. I took it for granted and it took someone who was looking in from outside the experience to bring it to my attention.

From the time I returned to my apartment from his office, I sat down at my laptop and began to write a treatment and the outline for a pilot episode of a situation comedy based on my experience of prosecuting criminal cases in a busy courthouse by day, and building a career as a stand-up comedian by performing most every night. It wouldn't be

Paul D'Angelo

that much of a stretch for me to come up with something. I'd just take a collage of the characters I encountered and the substance of my everyday experiences, add in a little exaggeration and imagination to make it more interesting, and put something together. It's certainly more fascinating than this non-existence I now lead: renting movies, playing video games, calling for spots without success, and waiting for phone calls that never come.

I finished the treatment, as the manager suggested, and I've completed the outline of the pilot episode of *Paul D'Angelo: Comedian at Law*. Now I'm ready to write the script for it.

And oh, by the way, it has been a week and I'm still waiting for his fucking call.

DAY 235 - OCTOBER 29TH, 1996

I am a marketing executive's dream. A stereotypical man.

After typing late into the night, I turned on the TV, just to see what was on, and I was channel surfing when I came across a movie that was just beginning on HBO. It was the movie that Cindy Crawford starred in with William Baldwin called *Fair Game*. The movie got horrible reviews and every critic absolutely panned "Cindy Supermodel's" acting debut and, for once, the critics were right on the money. It was truly terrible.

Yet I stayed up until 2:30 a.m., watching every last minute of the movie, and the only reason I stayed up was just to catch a fleeting glimpse of one of Cindy's nipples, in dark lighting, for what seemed to be the minuscule length of time it takes a hummingbird to beat its tiny wings but once.

It was well worth it. I went to bed happy and dreamt sweet dreams.

DAY 236 - OCTOBER 30TH, 1996

This is too funny. Last night, Kelly was invited to attend the world premiere of a new movie with her boss. After the movie, they met some people for drinks at the Four Seasons Hotel in Beverly Hills.

L.A. Misérables, Too

While Kelly was there, she ran into Nick DiPaulo, who she grew up with on Boston's North Shore. Nick and I became good friends when Nick started doing stand-up comedy in Boston about the same time that I did in the mid/late-'80s. He later moved to New York City and then Los Angeles a few years ago.

Personally, Nick is one of my very favorite comedians in the whole country. I think Nick and I share a similarity in what we think is funny and we both have a sarcastic approach to comedy, but Nick is much more edgy and political than I am. I admire the fact that he has a strong point of view and defends it. There are definitely some valuable underlying messages in his humor.

When Kelly saw Nick last night he joined her and her boss, the movie producer, and he and Nick hit it off. He told Nick to drop a videotape off at his office to see if he could help him out. Nick delivered a forty-five minute performance tape to Kelly this afternoon that was recorded last year at Punchlines in Atlanta, Georgia. Even though we have seen his act numerous times, live and on television, we still laugh at Nick, so Kelly brought the tape home for us to watch.

While we were eating dinner Kelly popped the tape in and we watched it for about forty minutes. It was near the end of Nick's set and he started into a routine about Bill Clinton when, suddenly, the video image changed into a XXX porno movie with two couples going at it, side-by-side on a couch for about a minute before the image returned to Nick delivering the punch line.

We looked at each other astonished. You've got to be shitting me! There are people screwing right in the middle of Nick's tape! This is hilarious!

I stopped laughing long enough to pick up the phone.

Kelly said, "What are you doing?"

"I'm calling Nick to tell him about the little 'surprise' we had."

"You can't call Nick!" she pleaded. "It's embarrassing!"

I said, "It will be a lot more embarrassing if he doesn't know that clip is on his videotape and he gives a copy to NBC or HBO for their approval."

She agreed and I called Nick to tell him about the tape. I asked

Nick if he ever watched the tape all the way through and, as I suspected, he told me that he hadn't. I highly recommended that he watch the tape before he sent it out to anyone important and began laughing again. He asked, "What? Is there porn on it?"

I told him there was, as I held the phone up to the TV and played the tape on the VCR, so Nick could hear his voice telling a joke on the audio track that, without warning, switched to two women simultaneously screaming, *"Oh my God! Deeper... Deeper... Yes, yes, yes!... Ohhhhh, yes... Harder, please harder!... Yes!... Don't stop!... Yes!... Yes!... Yes!"*

Nick couldn't believe it. The master tape was given to him like this but, fortunately, he had not distributed it to anyone else. He thanked us and intends to edit the tape the first chance he gets.

Man, these are the things you read about in books... which I guess is exactly what you are doing right now. Derrrrrrr Paul.

OCTOBER 237 - OCTOBER 31ST, 1996

Halloween night. Last year I spent Halloween in Salem, Massachusetts. Salem is known as "The Witch City" because it was the site of the famous witch trials during the 17th century. There is no city in America that personifies the spirit of Halloween more than Salem, and it's a huge event every year.

This year will be a little different. Halloween in West Hollywood is unlike Halloween anywhere else. A few years ago I spent Halloween in Los Angeles. I was staying with my friend Patty Ross when she lived in the heart of "Boys Town."

I went with Patty and one of her female friends to Santa Monica Boulevard, which was only a short walk from her apartment. They close off several blocks of Santa Monica Boulevard every Halloween and all the gays dress up as women and in other outrageous costumes. As you can imagine, many of these guys work in the movie industry and they have access to fantastic costumes, not to mention the fact that quite a few of them are makeup artists.

To be perfectly honest, I was a little uncomfortable in this situation, and I told Patty and her friend not to leave me alone for even a minute as we walked amongst the crowd.

Every once in a while, I would turn to speak to Patty and she wouldn't be there. I would search the crowd in a panic, calling Patty's name like a small child who has lost his mother in a department store. Then I would hear giggling noises coming from behind a mailbox or a phone booth, where Patty and her friend would be hiding.

"Patty, cut it out! Don't do that again!"

"What's the matter Paul? Do you think they want you? Do you think you're so irresistibly gorgeous that you're going to be forcibly gang-sodomized if we leave you alone for a moment?... Give me a fucking break."

Patty has such a cute way of putting things.

Kelly and I attended the festivities for a couple of hours tonight. Halloween in Hollywood has got to be a nightmare for cops trying to do their job.

(Radio broadcast) "This is Officer Jones. I have responded to the assault on Robertson. After speaking to the witness I have a description of the perpetrator, which reads as follows: Assailant 6'3" tall; medium build wearing pink taffeta cocktail dress with matching elbow-length pink gloves; black fishnet nylons and gold pumps; lime green hair in French Twist; heavy eye makeup; suspect has full beard and mustache."

DAY 238 - NOVEMBER 1ST, 1996

I wish one of those agents would call me.

Of course, even if an agent did call, that's just the beginning. A lot of pieces would have to fall into place after that for me to any chance of becoming a TV star.

If an agent does show an interest in me, then he'd have to set-up a showcase and actually *show-up* (for a change) for my showcase... and, even if he does, I'd need to have a killer set and, even if I do, in that agent's highly subjective opinion, he has to see my potential for personal appearances as a stand-up comic. But that doesn't necessarily mean that he'll also see my potential for television...

Paul D'Angelo

And even if I sign with the agent who recognizes my small-screen potential, I have to hope that this agent isn't so busy taking care of all of his other clients that I get lost in the shuffle and he never returns my calls or does anything whatsoever on my behalf…

And, even if that doesn't happen, I have to hope that the agent has the right connections to help my career and he hasn't developed a bad coke habit that causes his own career to go down the tubes, or maybe decides to just quit this rat race and join a religious cult in Tibet, just before he sets up a meeting with the networks to pitch my script…

And, even if that doesn't happen and he actually sets up a meeting, hopefully the representatives of the network would like me and my idea enough set up a showcase and they don't keep postponing the showcase, or canceling it, or just don't care enough to honor their commitment, which they so often do…

And if they do show-up, they'd also have to see my potential, assuming of course that the execs who come to the show have the power to make such a decision and aren't merely a couple of stiffs with no pull that were sent to the showcase to screen me for more important people whose time is too valuable to waste, and so we would then have to set up another showcase for the execs that actually have real clout, and hope that *they* show up and I, once again, have a great set and they like me, and so on…

Of course that would be dependent on their own personal opinion, which could vary considerably from person to person, depending on their sense of humor, or tastes, or the mood they're in on that particular day because, hopefully, the influential network representative didn't have a horrible afternoon because his young secretary just informed him that she's pregnant, she wants to keep the baby, and insists on telling his wife, so he goes to the club preoccupied with his own shitstorm of a life and isn't really paying attention to some stupid comic onstage who has been eating frozen dinners for eight months, desperately waiting for this very opportunity, and is having the best set of his life, only to be ignored by that selfish prick who could change his future…

And assuming that none of that happens and the reps actually like me enough to set up a meeting, I have to hope they don't keep canceling because they have bigger fish to fry, like a meeting with another dumb, 22-year-old, blonde aspiring actress with big jugs, who they might possibly lure to the casting couch without *their* wife knowing…

Then I'd have to hope that they to decide to go ahead and film a pilot episode after they get the approval of about ten other levels of network executives that have to OK shit like this, because it involves the allocation of a considerable amount of money that everyone else at the studio is fighting for…

Then we'd have to film the pilot, realizing that there are only a couple of open spots for sitcoms on their network and everybody and his cousin has made other pilots that are all trying to compete for one of those precious few open spots…

And, even if we get that far, hopefully they won't schedule my show in the time slot opposite *Seinfeld* or *Home Improvement* or *Roseanne*, which would mean instant death to any new sitcom, no matter how good it was…

And then, when they finally air the show, we'd have to hope that there isn't breaking news that preempts its premier, like a hostage stand-off, or maybe the seventh game of the World Series on another channel, on the very same night as my debut, and everybody in America is watching something else, and the executives fail to take this fact into consideration when they cancel my show because of poor ratings that aren't my fault…

And assuming that none of those things happen and the show is successful, and the ratings don't suck, and it stays on the air for a while… then I guess things would be pretty good for a change, even though there would probably be an endless amount of brand-new things for me to complain about.

So I hope they call.

Listen. I know I sound discouraged, but the truth is, the most positive observation that I can make about my seven and a half months in Los Angeles is that no one of any importance has seen me. It's not like I've been showcasing week after week and being passed over time and time again. I haven't had the opportunity for any agents or managers to see me yet, so I'm still an unknown, as far as this town is concerned.

My priority is to find a way for them to see me. Bruce Hills, who runs the Just for Laughs International Comedy Festival in Montreal, didn't get a chance to see me audition before this summer's festival, and he told me that he wants to see me in October or November, when he begins auditioning performers for next season. That's great but, without a manager or agent to set up a showcase specifically for that reason, or to get me into a showcase for the talent coordinators representing the festival, I won't ever get a chance for him to see me. I will have to take the initiative.

I decided to speak to Richard, the person who now books the Improvisation and who has been very fair to me since he took over that responsibility. I called Richard and asked if I could get his advice on some matters. Richard was extremely accommodating and told me to come down to the club to meet with him.

I went to the Improv in the early afternoon, but Richard was at lunch, so I did some errands and returned mid-afternoon. Richard was in his office and was tied up with a never-ending barrage of phone calls. I waited for about forty-five minutes and suggested that maybe it was better if I returned that evening, when he had more free time. Richard told me to hang on and, soon after, we were sitting at a table in the Improv showroom and discussing my dilemma.

A half hour later, I was leaving the club with an industry showcase scheduled at the Improv for Thursday night, November 7th at 9:30 p.m., and a commitment that I would be one of the acts on the audition for Bruce Hills and Willie Mercer of the Just for Laughs festival on either November 12th or 14th at the Improv.

I spent all night creating a template for a 4X6" postcard on my computer. I brought it down to Kinko's and they ran off fifty copies for me while I typed mailing labels for fifty agencies, managers, networks, production companies, and anyone else who might be interested in either representing me or developing a show around me. I need to send them out by tomorrow morning because the Thursday night date doesn't give me too much lead time to work with.

DAY 239 - NOVEMBER 2ND, 1996

I got up at seven o'clock this morning to attend eight hours of class at traffic school, so I don't get my citation for going straight in a RIGHT TURN ONLY lane put on my permanent driving record and incur a surcharge from my insurance company. Each "student" had to stand up and introduce themselves, tell what they did for a living, and explain why they were in the class.

The instructor pointed at me. I stood and turned to face the class.

"Hi. My name is Paul... and I'm an alcoholic."

The class started to laugh.

"Oh, I'm sorry... wrong meeting."

When the instructor asked what I did wrong, I said, "The only thing I did wrong was to drive through Beverly Hills with a Massachusetts license plate in front of a cop that was a dickhead," and sat down, annoyed that I should have to go through such a ridiculous ordeal and waste a Saturday afternoon.

All I learned from taking the class was that I should avoid driving through Beverly Hills, look more closely for cops, and carry my DA's badge whenever I drive in this town.

Hey, get this. I got a call that I am going to have an eight to ten minute audition for Mitzi Shore, the owner of the Comedy Store, on Sunday night at 9:18. Great. I have done three auditions for her in three years and got the exact same response each time: "He's too polished... He doesn't need to work out his act here, he needs to get himself an agent," which, I suppose, is flattering, but it's not the response I'm looking for. I would love to have another stage in this city that I can regularly work-out on.

Kelly and I went to a movie so I could get my mind off of things for a while. They had a preview for a modernized version of *Hamlet* directed by Kenneth Branaugh. There's no culture in this town. Half of these people think that *Hamlet* is the sequel to the movie *Babe*.

I bet if I arbitrarily stopped someone in the streets of Hollywood and asked them, "What do you know about Mozart?" there's a good chance that their answer would be, "What do I know about Mozart?

Nothing at all. Heck, I didn't even know Moe could paint! *Nyuk...nyuk...nyuk!"*

Oh, a wiseguy, ay?

The Comedy Store on Sunset Boulevard

DAY 240 - NOVEMBER 3RD, 1996

I'm getting desperate to find a comedy club that will give me the opportunity to work out on a regular basis so I can stay sharp and develop my new material.

I had another audition for club owner Mitzy Shore at The Comedy Store tonight and I only had one big problem with my performance... it went excellent.

My friend Patty Ross was sitting next to Mitzy in The Original Room as I did my set. Mitzy's reaction was... well, it was consistent.

(In a nasally drawl akin to the manic-depressive hyena, Hardy-Ha-Ha in the old *Lippy the Lion* cartoon... and I quote her comments verbatim)

"Patty, why do keep bringing this guy in? He's too polished. Look... he's killing them... Look at them all laughing. He can't work this room. Tell him to come back when he's famous."

Patty asked Mitzy why she couldn't use me in the Main Showroom.

"Sure... right after he gets his own TV show. He's too professional... He's just too funny for this room."

L.A. Misérables, Too

Shit.

The good news is, if I stay in Los Angeles without getting any steady stage time, I'm going to eventually get worse and worse and, as time goes by, my shows will regularly go downhill in quality... so who knows? With a little luck, my act could someday suck badly enough to be eligible to play the world famous Comedy Store on Sunset Strip.

My confused friend Max remarked, "Paul, wouldn't it be logical to try and put the funniest comics onstage so that the paying customers will walk out satisfied that they saw a good show?"

"Max, my amigo, you seem to forget... this is Hollywood. You can remove the word 'logic' from your vocabulary."

If it's any consolation, I've read that Mitzy didn't like Jerry Seinfeld either, so I have that going for me, and I do acknowledge that this would actually be a very funny story... if it was happening to a comic other than myself.

When all is said and done, I'm not that disappointed. It would have been nice to have another club to work out in on a weekly basis. I was hoping that Mitzy would want to have me perform the Main Room, but I guess you have to achieve celebrity status first, at which point you would most likely not give a shit about whether or not you ever play the Main Room. The club is not what it used to be.

The first time I came to Los Angeles was in 1989 and stand-up comedy was still near its peak of popularity. The Comedy Store had three rooms open, the Main Room, the Original Room and the upstairs Belly Room, and was packed every night of the week. This was before the medium of stand-up was exploited like a natural resource that's stripped-mined with no concern for its future. When stand-up became popular there suddenly appeared twenty-four hour comedy channels, appearances by stand-ups on every other TV show, full-time comedy clubs that sprung-up everywhere, and comedy on various nights throughout the week at Mexican and Chinese restaurants, nightclubs, bars and function halls.

Consequently, the talent was stretched thin, like it is whenever a professional sports league adds expansion teams. There are only so many quality acts to go around so, what were once strong shows with a competent opening act, a solid middle act and a knockout headliner, became shows with open-miker hosts, middle acts that should be openers and, more often than not, headliners that should be features. The quality of the shows suffered and people realized that they could just stay home and watch all the stand-ups they wanted if they channel surfed from their couch.

In addition, the comedians' material was being burnt out at an extraordinary rate. Quality stand-up material sometimes takes years to hone to perfection. A good stand-up will constantly be adding a word, an emphasis, a pause, a voice inflection, editing out verbose language, punctuating a line with an accompanying physical action, and so forth, to perfect each routine and get the maximum impact.

A great joke, however, does not have the equivalent longevity of, say, a great song. Once people hear a great joke, it's not like listening to, for example, "Stairway to Heaven," which you could hear over and over again for thirty or forty years, and never get sick of it. A crowd that hears jokes repeated by a comedian experiences a diminishing impact because the unexpected twist that invokes their spontaneous response is no longer a surprise. They will have an appreciation for the joke, but will react to a lessening degree. Because of the long process needed to develop a joke to its full potential, people who went back over and over again to see their favorite comedians came to realize that they would not see an entirely new act every couple of months, and thereafter attended shows with less frequency. (It is amazing how many people actually believe that comedians do a totally different show every single night.)

All of these factors contributed to the end of the comedy boom. In actuality, it was probably a necessary process, similar to the theory of natural selection and the thinning of the herd, where the weaker, sickly or inadequately adapted fringe of the animals are killed by predators or are unable to survive, which leaves a smaller, but stronger, nucleus behind. The strong survive and the weak fall by the wayside, making the final product stronger.

The Comedy Store has become a victim of the paring down of comedy. Once the premier showcase for comedy in the country, it is

L.A. Misérables, Too

now a dark, brooding venue that has few, if any, industry people in their dwindling audiences. They say that the building, which used to house Ciro's. the biggest nightclub on Sunset Strip, where Martin and Lewis and all the top entertainers used to perform many years ago, is haunted by the victims of the mobsters who ran the place. Legend has it that these gangsters snuffed people out in the lead-lined Green Room upstairs, where the gunshots could not be heard in the busy nightclub, before they buried the bodies under the floor in the hallway where the service bar is located. There are also rumored to be two victims buried under the main stage, according to my friend Cha Cha. The place has an evil atmosphere now and I wouldn't be surprised to find out that some poltergeist is sitting in the audience during the comedy shows. God knows, there are enough empty seats.

"That crowd was dead. They were lifeless."

"What are you talking about? I killed!"

This worn-out comedic shop-talk may be more prophetic when uttered in the Comedy Store than in any other comedy club around.

DAY 241 - NOVEMBER 4TH, 1996

I believe I made a similar bonehead comment that was chronicled in the first book, but this goes to show you that I don't always learn from my mistakes. I was speaking to a friend of mine from home who informed me that his father was in the hospital because he had a heart attack.

My response: "Was it a *bad* heart attack?"

The appropriate answer: "No Paul. It was a *good* heart attack… you know, like 'good cholesterol.' My dad's on a respirator in intensive care with IV's stuck in his arms and tubes up his nose but, to tell you the truth, besides that, he's never looked better, believe me. He needed the rest and the attention."

I meant well.

Today I wrote, printed, and mailed fifty follow-up notices of my showcase along with a detailed biography which, I'm hoping, will help raise some interest among the industry.

DAY 242 - NOVEMBER 5ᵀᴴ, 1996

The other night, around 1:00 a.m. there was a lot of noise and yelling in the hallway outside our apartment door. The next morning there was a huge, dark stain near our entranceway and some unidentifiable black substance on the wall. I notified the manager's office and asked them to clean it up as soon as possible. When I left the apartment today there were two little Mexican maintenance men with a steam cleaner who were preparing to clean the mess off the carpet and the wall. I thanked them for coming up and said, "They really made a mess. I wonder what it is."

One of the guys shook his head, while the other one stuck his finger in the soiled carpet and then tasted it. He smacked his lips.

He said, "I think it's oil."

Great system you have there, fellas.

"Hey Amigo! Watch your step!"

"Yuck! Disgusting! What is that?"

"Ummm... It looks like shit. (sniff, sniff) It smells like shit... Ooooh, it feels like shit (lick, lick) and it tastes just like shit... I'm sure glad we didn't step in it!"

I drove to the post office to mail a follow-up notice of my showcase to all of the agencies, managers and what-not that I mailed the original invitation to. After that, I had to pick-up something in the city of Torrence for Kelly and, while I was driving down Hawthorne Boulevard, I saw a sign on a building that said, "LINGERIE RENTALS."

Pardon me for butting in, but there's a reason that they call lingerie "intimate apparel." Underwear isn't intimate anymore if you loan it out like a library book. If I was a woman who was renting some crotchless panties, I would certainly want to know who else's crotch wasn't in them before me.

Further on down the road was a storefront with a sign that said, "DO IT YOURSELF LAW." Don't you think the courts are backed up enough without letting amateurs try their hand at the legal system?

"Call the next case, Mr. Clerk."

"Certainly, your honor. Roberto versus Robinson."

"Yes, your honor... I'd like to make one of them movements there... you know what I'm sayin'?"

"Movements?"

"You know... a movement... like they do on that OJ case there."

"Oh, do you mean a 'motion?'"

"Ya... ya. movement, motion...whatever."

"Denied. Do you wish to call any witnesses?"

"Well ya.... You see, I already called a couple o' them, but they insisted on tellin' the truth, so forget about it."

"Then how are you going to plead?"

"Like this your honor... *Please!... Please don't send me to jail! I'll pay all the fines you want!... I'll hot-top your driveway for free... How's your driveway look? Does it need hot-top? I can do a nice job, no problem... or do you want cash? Just between you and me, if you know what I mean... Let me make one quick phone call, OK?"*

Damn it. No spots at the Laugh Factory again. It's been almost three months since I got a regular spot there. (About two months ago they used me to warm up the crowd for someone else's showcase.) Maybe they think I'm too funny for the room as well.

DAY 243 - NOVEMBER 6TH, 1996

I ate at the Improv last night and tried an ostrich burger for the first time. Can you believe it? Ostrich. I thought it was pretty good but, when I got home, for some reason, I had this overwhelming urge to bury my head between my girlfriend's thighs.

CHAPTER THIRTEEN
I wanna be sedated...

DAY 244 - NOVEMBER 7TH, 1996

This is my big night, the industry showcase at the Improv. I wonder if anyone of importance will actually show up in response to my mailings, but I would not be surprised if no one did. I'm just being realistically skeptical based on experience. In a profession that liberally serves up disappointment after disappointment, it helps the psyche to prepare for the worst. If nothing comes of it, then it's just as you suspected, so it's not a big letdown. If it leads to something good, then it's like a bonus.

(later in the evening)

It is now later tonight and I'm back from the show.

When I tell you that my show couldn't have gone better, I'm not lying. The response built and built until I got a huge ovation at the end of my set. People came up to me all night, congratulating me for a great performance.

When I tell you that *not one* person that I contacted from the industry showed up, I'm not lying either. What a big waste of my time.

Back to square one. Do not pass go. Do not collect any rent money.

I had to drop something off near Redondo Beach, which is about

L.A. Misérables, Too

forty-five minutes away, but it took me almost three hours round-trip because of the Los Angeles traffic. I often wondered why there were so many people in LA who find it necessary to own Ferraris and Porshes and Corvettes that go 0-60 in five seconds. It's because five seconds is all the time you've got until you get to the next red light.

Everything is relative. People will spend $100,000 on a Lamborghini just so they can experience the exhilaration of taking exit ramp at 75mph... when we po' people can have just as thrilling an experience driving a '81 Pinto with 200,000 miles on it, bad shocks, bald tires, and no brakes, and driving 30mph on the same off-ramp, for less than $500... which leaves plenty of money left over to buy yourself a pair of clean underwear.

DAY 245 - NOVEMBER 8TH, 1996

No wonder people hate lawyers. I can't say that I blame them sometimes. I'm reading (and this is not the first time that I've seen this happen) about some guy who broke into someone's home, hurt himself, and then sued the homeowner for personal injuries. Thanks to the lawyers who bring lawsuits such as this, there will come a time where all homeowners will be required to build a ramp up to the front door of the house to give access to handicapped burglars who have been discriminated against in the past.

Earlier this year, an Alabama jury awarded $150 million to driver who was paralyzed after falling asleep at the wheel of his Chevy Blazer. Starting in 1997, all new automobiles manufactured in the United States will have their headlights permanently on for safety reasons. Once again, thanks to the lawyers, all cars will also be required to have the radio blasting at all times so that idiots won't fall asleep and sue the car companies.

And, it goes without saying, the new car cigarette lighters will not get any hotter than a cup of McDonald's coffee.

Imagine, some asshole breaks into *your* home... he's in there without your permission, then sues *you* for damages. You just know that some Jehovah Witness will end-up suing some homeowner when he steps on their kid's roller-skate going up the front steps to ring their doorbell at 8:00 a.m. on a Saturday morning. It's inevitable. They already have the word "witness" in their name. Thereafter, they will be known as "Jehovah's Plaintiffs."

DAY 246 - NOVEMBER 9TH, 1996

I just finished reading Jay Leno's book, *Leading with my Chin*. Jay has some fabulous stories about the hell gigs that he did on his way to the top. When Jay started out there weren't a plethora of comedy clubs around that he could work in, so he had to take whatever opportunities came up, and there were some beauties. I was looking through some of my notes today, in the process of working on some material, and came across a notation that reminded me of an unusual request several years ago.

I was scheduled to open up for The Four Tops at the North Shore Music Theater in Beverly, Massachusetts. The event was a charity for a large Jewish association, maybe the Anti-defamation League, I can't recall, and the organizers had specifically requested to have me perform because they'd seen my act.

I arrived at the Music Theater early to do a sound check and was waiting for the crowd to file in. There were about 1500 to 2000 people who were attending the show at the circular theater with a stage in the middle. Just before the house lights dimmed to announce me as the opening act, the organizers approached me backstage and told me that they had a special request with regard to my presentation.

"Sure, no problem. What is it?"

"Well, you see, Paul... we're a little concerned with one of the jokes that you do."

"Which one?" I asked, quickly running through the act in my mind and wondering which joke they could be referring to. "Don't worry, I've promised to keep the show clean so I don't offend anyone."

"Oh, it's not that, Paul. When we saw you perform in the comedy club you did a joke about a lobster and..."

"That routine's not dirty."

L.A. Misérables, Too

"We know, we know, Paul... that's not the problem. I know there are quite a few people here, and most of them wouldn't have a problem with the subject matter, but... but there are a handful of very strict, kosher, Orthodox Jews at the show and they might be offended if you mention shellfish."

I was incredulous. "You mean I can't *talk* about shellfish?"

"It may cause a problem."

"Really? Then I guess I can't do the bit where I say that I went into a nightclub and picked up a girl who was a *pig*... she was achin' for the *bacon* so I *porked* her last night? I can't say that... I'm sorry, I'm such a ham. Shit, I can't say that either.

"By the way, did you tell the Four Tops they couldn't sing 'Sugar-Pie, Honeybunch' because there may be diabetics in the audience?"

They nervously laughed and I vowed to leave out any references to shellfish, pork, and the Holocaust.

DAY 247 - NOVEMBER 10TH, 1996

My girlfriend Kelly has been asked to play on an all-woman softball team that consists of young actresses and models that play ballgames against celebrity teams for charity. I bought her a baseball glove today, because I am acutely aware of the popular modern aphorism, "No glove, no love".

The glove I bought her was black leather. When I was a kid, I had to have a black leather baseball glove because Brian McKnight had a black leather baseball glove. Brian and I went to grammar school together at the Lincoln School and we had an uneasy friendship. Even though we were buddies, he would occasionally beat me up or steal my baseball cards. At some point, around second or third grade, my mother told me that she didn't want me hanging around with Brian any longer, but I wasn't gonna give up my good pal without a fight, even if he did push me around now and then.

"Maaaaaa! Why can't I do stuff with Brian? He's my friend!"

"I don't like him. He's trouble."

"But Maaaaaa! He's only seven years old! How do you know he's trouble? He's just a kid. You don't know nuthin'. Brian's my friend and I'm still gonna hang around with him."

"I know because I'm your mother, and I forbid you to associate with him, understand me young man?"

I wanted a second opinion.

"Daaaaaad! Ma won't let me hang around with Brian. She says he's bad. What does she know?"

My father whispered, "Paul, your mother is a witch. It's scary what she knows. I suggest you stay away from him and that's that."

So I reluctantly stopped hanging out with Brian McKnight, the small child that my mother was convinced was the demon seed.

One of my last memories of Brian in grammar school was witnessing him punching out the only male teacher in the building. Penuse Constance was a bespectacled young man who transferred to teach at the Lincoln School when we were in the fifth or sixth grade. He didn't last long. I remember getting the impression that he was not the most macho guy around. In fact, Miss Censullo, a woman who co-taught the fifth and sixth grades with him, had to coach the boy's football and basketball teams by default.

My classmates and I really didn't like him much, but our disdain was limited to making fun of Mr. Constance behind his back and wising off to him now and then. Not Brian. I don't know what it was that ticked him off on that particular day, but I have a vivid recollection of standing in line, as we waited to file back into the building after recess, and watching little Brian running up the stairs of the school so that he could reach Mr. Constance's nose and whacking him right on the schnoz with a closed fist. The teacher was holding his bloody nose in disbelief, reminding me of the cowardly lion in *The Wizard of Oz* after Dorothy gave him a "what for?" as all the little grade-school munchkins sang *"Ding dong the witch is dead..."* on the kickball field.

Even though we went to high school together, Brian and I lost touch from his suspension on.

Then, I'd say about 1988, which was over twenty years later, I was an assistant district attorney supervising the DA's office in the Lynn District Court, when I walked into the Lynn police detective's office

L.A. Misérables, Too

one afternoon. There had been a murder in Lynn that morning and I needed to get some information in order to conduct the bail hearing on the suspect that had been arrested. As you can imagine, even though Lynn is a large city with a high crime rate and has its share of murders each year, the detective's office is full of activity immediately after they respond to a double homicide, so I was left waiting at one of the investigator's desks for a half hour or so before he could find time for me.

I eventually got bored killing time and started looking at some of the papers on the officer's desktop. One document caught my eye. It was an all-points bulletin with mug shots of one of the scariest looking hombres you could ever imagine. This guy made Charles Manson look like Pee Wee Herman. According to the information on the wire, this fugitive had just attempted to hold up a pharmacy, but the cashier had thwarted the robbery by pummeling this loser's drug-crazed head with a tire iron that he kept near the cash register. The bulletin went on to describe the desperado as heavily tattooed, with a serious heroin problem and a long history of violent felonies on his record. His last known address was in Florida, but he was last seen heading up the East Coast where he had ties. He was considered to be armed and extremely dangerous.

I didn't recognize his name, but there was something vaguely familiar about him that made me stare at the pictures longer than I really cared to. That's when my eyes drifted to the lengthy lists of aliases that he had been known to go under. I did a double take. It couldn't be... it was far too coincidental, but there it was.

"... AKA BRIAN McKNIGHT"

My facial expression must have looked like I saw a ghost. I shouted to the detectives, "Guys, can I use your phone for a minute?"

"Sure Paul, go ahead."

I dialed the phone. "Hello ma, it's me, Paul. I just wanted to tell you that you were right. Never mind 'about what,' I'll explain later. Goodbye."

Never underestimate the supernatural powers of a mother.

Tomorrow's headlines could easily have read, "KELLY SAVES

STRAY DOG FROM CRACK HOUSE AND GIVES FINGER TO DRIVER WITH GUN; ASPIRING COMIC KILLED".

On the way back from throwing the softball around, Kelly was driving down Highland Avenue, past the Hollywood Bowl, when she suddenly cut the wheel and screeched to a halt in the driveway of a dilapidated drug slum, populated with a yard full of Brain McKnights, whose heads turned in a smack induced stupor towards the strange vehicle invading their hood.

"What the hell are you doing, Kelly?"

"Look. There's a cute little Lhasa Apso that looks like he's lost! No one is watching him. He could run out into the street and be killed! I have to save him!"

"Are you losing your mind, Kelly? You're going to risk our lives to save some mangy mutt? You pulled in here like we've got a search warrant and a S.W.A.T. team backing us up! Fuck the dog. I'm not going to get caught in the cross-fire of some rival gang protecting their turf for that flea-bitten stray! Now let's get out of here."

"It looks like he went into the home. He'll be OK."

"Personally, Kelly, I think he was better off in the street. It's like every summer when you read about some infant falling out of the fifth story window of a tenement. It happens consistently enough to make me think that the toddlers may be committing suicide. The kid looks at their drunken mother, who neglects her eight illegitimate children all day because she's watching soap operas with a bottle of booze in her hand. Then the baby looks at his unemployed father, who just spent the entire welfare check on crack, before he comes home and abuses the wife and beats the kids. So the baby looks out the window and reasons, 'Fuck it. I'll take my chances on hitting the awning. Geronimo!'

"That dog probably wants to throw himself in front of a car because he's depressed that he didn't end up in a quiet suburb, with a nice family, that has cute kids who throw him a red rubber ball in their big yard, and feeds him the steak bone leftover from dinner, and lets him stick his head out the window of the new BMW on the way to the beach, and has a thick rug that he can lie on while they watch TV at night.

L.A. Misérables, Too

"Instead he's got to scavenge through the trash for food because the junkies that own him spend all their money on drugs and, when they're high, they aren't lucid enough to play with him, and when they're not high, they're miserable and disgusted with themselves so they take it out on the little dog. Let the poor little mutt run out in front of Dr. Kevorkian's van and end the pain."

As we pulled out of the yard, some guy in a maroon car tried to cut Kelly off. We traveled down Franklin Street and this nut kept trying to pass us, first on the right, then on the left. Kelly was getting very aggravated at his erratic driving, so she slammed on the brakes and gave him the finger as she pulled into the left hand lane to make a turn. As the idiot drove by on our right, he pointed something at us and laughed.

Kelly said, "Did he just point a gun at us? I think he had a gun in his hand!"

"Gun? I don't care if he had *gum* in his hand. When he pointed, I ducked," although, the way things have been going out here, I contemplated following the slum dog's example and yelling, "Go ahead, shoot! Just end the suffering! You'll do me a favor! You haven't got the balls, you wimp!"

DAY 248 - NOVEMBER 11TH, 1996

Today is Veteran's Day. If you think that times haven't changed much consider this: In our United States we have one generation of citizens whose definition of true heroism is to fight and die for your country in a foreign land, far from home, while another generation's exemplar for ultimate courage happens to be Extreme Skateboarding. Not much of a stretch, huh?

I found out that I am doing a six to eight minute audition for the Montreal "Just for Laughs" comedy festival on Tuesday night at the Improv. I'm not crazy about auditioning with such a short set. For one, it doesn't distinguish between those comedians who have a significant amount of quality material that could carry a show and those comics who have only six to eight minutes of decent jokes. Second, I think a short set favors a comedian who has a barrage of one-liners as opposed to a storyteller who weaves together a string of related concepts into lengthy routines, which I tend toward being. I have to be much more selective in my choice of material because each bit will take up a disproportionate amount of the allotted time. I feel that I'm much better off if I have fifteen minutes or more to present my character and point of view, but I have to make the best of the opportunity given me.

Tonight I went to an HBO movie premier at the Director's Guild with Kelly. I saw stars George Clooney, James Earl Jones, and Forest Whitaker, a very popular actor who seems to be in just about every other movie that I watch these days.

What the hell, it's the 90's... I wouldn't be surprised to see someone like Forrest, or Eddie Murphy, or Damon Wayans, or Denzel Washington, or maybe Samuel L. Jackson, file a lawsuit alleging racial discrimination and stereotyping by the motion picture industry because he's always cast as "the black guy."

DAY 249 - NOVEMBER 12TH, 1996

I just got booked to play at the Galaxy Theater in Santa Ana this Saturday, which is supposed to be a phenomenal place. Because it's my first time appearing at that location, like I have done at many of the other Los Angeles area theaters since I relocated, I will be used as a feature, or middle act, this time and I will have to prove myself worthy of headline status. I am told that the headlining comedian is someone called "Spanky," who I believe is famous for being the eighth dwarf at Snow White's pad.

Tonight I had my audition for the Montreal "Just for Laughs" comedy festival at the Improvisation. My set was OK, but the response was not as great as I would have liked. The crowd was kinda tough, but I'm hoping that Bruce Hills from the festival will take that into consideration. As a comedian, you get accustomed to getting a response at certain points in your act which consistently invoke laughter or applause under most circumstances. When that doesn't happen, it can throw your sense of timing off because you lose your rhythm. People who watched my performance told me that they couldn't notice it, but I was personally aware of a subtle change in my tempo that made the audition flow a slight bit uneven and it bothered me all night.

I spoke to Bruce for a short time afterwards. I was originally referred to Bruce by Bill "Spaceman" Lee, ex-Red Sox and then Montreal Expos pitcher, who saw my show and told Bruce about me. We had met previously at the Laugh Factory this summer. Later in the evening, I spent about an hour speaking to Lucien Hold, the owner of The Comic Strip, one of the two top comedy clubs in New York City, along with Caroline's.

DAY 250 - NOVEMBER 13TH, 1996

> I would love to get that dent in my car fixed, but I can't afford it.
> What good is having insurance, anyway?
> I can see it now... I walk into the insurance agency...
> "Hi, you don't know me, but I'm sure you recognize the checks I send you every month... I've got a perfect driving record... I haven't got into an accident for many years... No traffic tickets or anything... I've never made a claim, even though I've paid you thousands and thousands and thousands of dollars... but now my insurance is finally going to pay-off because I got into a little accident, nothing significant, just a little dent... maybe $300 damage, that's it, very minor... and I wondered if I could get it fixed?"
> "Ha-ha-ha... What was that you said? Three-hundred dollars damage? Ha-ha-ha... Didn't you read your policy, Mr. Murphy? You have a $500 deductible and you only have $300 damage."
> "What does that mean?"
> "That basically means that we don't have to do a thing for you as long as the damage is less than $500 ha-ha-ha... Sorry, tough luck. Ha-ha-ha, ha-ha-ha."
> "Really?... OK, I'll be right back."
> I then picture myself, crazed with anger, in the parking lot of the insurance agency, putting my car into reverse and then into drive, over

and over again... slamming into the side of the agent's brand-new Cadillac Sedan DeVille yelling...

SMASH!!! "IS THAT $500 YET?"

SMASH!!! "LET ME KNOW WHEN I REACH FIVE HUNDRED, YOU ASSHOLE!!

SMASH!!! "AM I CLOSE YET, DICKHEAD?" ***SMASH!!!***

And people wonder why, when your car is broken into or stolen, and the insurance company asks, "Did you have any valuables in the trunk?"

"Valuables? In the trunk?... Hmmm. Uh, ya... oh, ya... as a matter of fact, I had some... some... uh, some golf clubs... ya, and a coa... no, a leath... no, a *long* leather coat... as well as another, much smaller, car.

"That's it... No, wait! My God, I almost forgot! *The Monet!* Dammit, they've taken the priceless Monet from my 1991 Ford Taurus!"

DAY 251 - NOVEMBER 14TH, 1996

Listen to this. Kelly's boss, the movie producer, invited Kelly and another girl in the office who works in the development department, to attend a private reading with only thirty or forty other people. The two actors who'll be reading for the parts are Madonna and Gabriel Byrne. After the reading is concluded, Kelly's boss will have to give Madonna a ride home, in his Rolls Royce of course, and he called Kelly from his car phone and told her to have a dozen roses delivered to him, so that he could present the flowers to Madonna.

Kelly called a number of florists, who all told her that they couldn't possibly deliver the roses on such short notice. Kelly didn't know what to do, so she called the florist at the Ritz Carlton and they gave her the same response. Desperate, she explained that the roses were for Madonna, and it made all the difference in the world. They went right to work and had the roses delivered in plenty of time for the event. Hey, maybe that's the secret to getting good service in this town. I think I'll try it next time.

"Hello, Dominoes, can I help you?"

"Yes, I'd like to order one large pepperoni and mushroom pizza… and please hurry because we're really hungry."

"We'll do our best, but to be honest with ya, we're pretty backed up right now…"

"But it's for Madonna…"

"Madonna! Holy jumpin' shit! Why didn't ya say so? See ya in ten minutes wit da pie… and we'll trow some extra cheese on that for da Material Girl, no additional charge… she don't know me, but you tell her that Stan from da pizza joint says hi… OK?"

Sure Stan… I'm sure that news will make her panties moist.

DAY 252 - NOVEMBER 15TH, 1996

Six-hundred and nineteen people have been murdered in Los Angeles during the first ten months of 1996. A guy wearing camouflage fatigues and carrying an AK-47 assault rifle shot his way through a Ford plant yesterday, killing several people. On Wednesday, a 29-year-old worker making a delivery to a high-rise building in LA was killed instantly when a ten foot metal beam broke loose from scaffolding fourteen stories up and struck him in the head. He didn't know what hit him. Another nut wearing camouflage pants used a rifle with a scope to randomly shoot at passerby's from a Santa Ana rooftop yesterday. He was shot and killed by police.

Suddenly, sitting alone in this little room all day doesn't seem so bad.

"Hello, this is Dominoes, can I help you?"

"Yes, I'd like to order a large pepperoni and mushroom pizza to be delivered because, frankly, I'm afraid to leave my apartment… Now please listen carefully, I will not repeat these instructions. You will be pat frisked in the lobby and the pizza box will be searched at that time, then slowly walk to apartment #210 on the second floor, avoiding any sudden movements… pass through the metal detector at the top of the stairs, put the pizza box on the hallway floor outside the apartment door and assume a spread eagle position against the far wall directly opposite the peep hole, with your hands above your head where I can see them, and await further instructions... Do not, I repeat... do *not*... attempt to remove your hands from the wall at any time or turn to look at me when the door is opened. And don't try any funny stuff... if you see my face, I will have to terminate you... Now make it snappy, Madonna's starving!"

DAY 253 - NOVEMBER 16TH, 1996

Kelly's first practice for her all-chick softball team was held this morning. I was told I might be needed to help during the practice, so I wore sweats and brought my baseball glove, which ended up being about as functional as Michael Jackson's glove, because the softballs never left the coach's duffel bag all morning. Instead, for three and a half hours, I ended up listening to a dozen twenty-year-old Valley Girls get Cosmo makeovers from a coach with huge fake tits.

I resisted the urge to go up to her, stare at her chest and say, "Hi! Are you going to introduce me to your two friends?"

Here's a sample of the crisis management that went on:

"Oh my God, Tristin! Girl, what is wrong with you! How do you expect us to play as a team for the big game tomorrow? Your lipstick has pink undertones when all of your teammates are wearing warm colors that don't clash with our uniforms!

"Listen up girls! You can get away with wearing Windy Rose, Suddenly Salmon, or Porcelain Pink Chablis with our away jerseys, but I recommend you stick with a Twilight Plum, Applesauce Gloss, or Ripe Raisin when we're in our home jerseys! Do any of you girls have some lipstick for Tristin? Devin? Bambi? Tiffany? Giselle? Thank you. See... Cinnamon Suede is your team color. You look really look good in warm lips..."

I know something else that would look good in warm lips... oops, daydreaming again... uh, where was I? Oh ya... anyway, this antithesis of a Mensa meeting went on for hours.

"Oh Darcy, I was watching the videotape of the interviews last week and you were whipping your hair way too much as you spoke," admonished the coach as she whipped her own hair like a vapid Barbie

L.A. Misérables, Too

Doll with enhanced plastic breasts.

No one was listening to a word she said. These girls had the attention span of a hummingbird on diet pills and were engrossed in looking into the mirrors that they all brought in their pocketbooks and continually applying makeup. You might think I was in heaven with all these nubile vixens around, but I wasn't very impressed. I like women that are naturally pretty and didn't attend "The Tammy Faye Baker School of Makeup Application and Basic Camouflage" and slap more greasepaint on their face than a Navy SEAL getting ready for night maneuvers. I'm not impressed with any woman that goes to a beauty salon and has to check in for an overnight stay because they can't possibly perform her glamour transplant as an outpatient procedure.

I could tell that Kelly was getting impatient because this was not what she expected. She thought they were actually going to play softball, but that was the last thing on the clueless minds of her teammates.

Tonight I performed at the Galaxy Theater in Santa Ana, a six-hundred seat venue that's one of the nicest places I've ever performed in. That all became irrelevant when my friend Max and I discovered that they had a big bucket filled with Coronas and Becks on ice in the dressing room. It's not often that comedians get this type of treatment. On the other hand, rock and roll stars get deli platters in their dressing room that's stocked with booze and other goodies. I know, because I've opened for more than forty recording artists in theater venues such as this. Ray Charles, Patti LaBelle, The Temptations, The Four Tops, Jerry Lee Lewis, Chicago, The Beach Boys, Bad Company, Huey Lewis and the News, Southside Johnny, Hall and Oates, Lyle Lovett, Rick Derringer and Edgar Winter, Joan Jett and the Blackhearts, The Oakridge Boys, Tanya Tucker, Meatloaf, REO Speedwagon, Eddie Money, Tony Bennett etc., etc., etc.

The way I got started opening for bands was this;

I have a friend I grew-up with named Bill Kenney. Bill moved to my town when we were freshmen in high school and we've remained friends for twenty five years.

For many years, Bill worked as a road manager and production co-ordinator for various the rock and roll bands. Around 1987 or '88 he was working with the John Entwhistle Band. John is the bass player for The Who, one of my favorite bands of all time, and he had gone off on a solo endeavor after one of the Who's many break-ups and/or retirements.

So one day I got a call from Bill, who was at the Canadian border with the band. He was in a panic because the customs inspectors had found a small amount of cocaine on one of the roadies and the authorities were now in the process of tearing apart the two tour buses, as well as the eighteen-wheeler carrying the band's equipment, looking for more drugs. The band was on a tight schedule and the delay was jeopardizing their commitment for that evening at a club in New York. Bill told me that, if I could give them some legal advice to help them out of this jam, John would be greatly indebted to me.

John Entwhistle of The Who needs my help? You better, you better, you bet! (That's a Who song for all of you rap fans or John Tesh fanatics)

So I stayed on the phone for a couple hours and talked them through this crisis at the border until everything was resolved and the Magic Bus convoy was on its way to the next gig. The next day I got a call from Billy, who told me that John was very appreciative of my assistance and asked if I'd like to open up for the band during their New England appearances. You better, you better, you bet!

The first show was at a venue called JR's Fastlane in Providence, Rhode Island. This was a hell gig for a comedian because it was a dance club with no seating. All the people stood in front of the stage and yelled shit out, but I didn't care, I was opening for John Entwhistle, to whom I had been introduced the previous day.

In John's hotel room, Bill said, "John, this is my friend Paul who helped us out of that jam at the border."

John shook my hand and thanked me.

My response?

"Wow, this is a great thrill. I loved you in Zeppelin!"

He laughed. "Bill, this is your bloody friend?"

The next show was at the Channel in Boston, a rowdy club whose atmosphere is closer to a cock-fight than a concert. There had been records set that day in Boston because it had been over hundred degrees with about 90% humidity that afternoon. The inside of the club had to be at least double those numbers by show time because there was no air conditioning, the place was packed to the rafters, and the stage was baking under about a hundred or so intense, thousand-watt light bulbs glaring down from overhead.

I had to do about an hour set, but the show went really well because, in those early days of my comedy career, I used to close my show with about ten or fifteen minutes of song parodies on my guitar.

I could sing like everybody who didn't know how to sing. I wore one of those harmonica holders around my neck while I played guitar and sang like Bob Dylan, transforming *Like a Rolling Stone* into *Like a Flintstone*. Sonny Bono crooned to his former partner, and current superstar, Cher, in *I Got Screwed Babe*. Zsa Zsa Gabor did a reggae number called *I Slapped the Sheriff* ("cuz I needed the publicity...") Bruce Springsteen sang about his first experience with Mexican food. *"Oh, oh, oh, my butt's on fire..."* Johnny Rivers' hit single, *Secret Agent Man*, had become a tribute to Chinese waiters everywhere, who had to endure the abuse of drunken diners near closing time, and was now sung as *Little Asian Man*. And my big closer, about a thief breaking into my apartment and taking all my things, then getting arrested by the cops and given a jail sentence by a judge. I express my sincere concern for this asshole's well-being, while he does time in prison, by singing a variation of Richie Valen's classic hit *La Bamba...* *"He's gonna take it up the bum-ba..."*

By the time I left the stage, my clothes were soaked through with so much perspiration it looked like I dove into a swimming pool. I went to my dressing room (It was the first time I ever got my own dressing room) and was immediately asked by the stage manager if I wanted anything. I asked if I could please have a beer for myself and a screwdriver for my friend.

"What kind of beer do you want?"

"Bud... naw... what the hell... make it a Heineken." And ten minutes later the guy came back with a whole case of cold Heinies, a whole bottle of vodka, a quart of orange juice, and a big bag of ice.

Whoa! Rock n' roll! Not one to miss an opportunity to drink for free, I told the stage manager to have someone bring another case of beer to my dressing room when they got a chance.

I was so psyched to have my own dressing room I invited my brothers and all my friends into this tiny, converted closet with no ventilation that was hotter than a steam bath, where we stood drinking and sweating our balls off for the rest of the night... and I couldn't have been happier if it was a deluxe suite in Caesar's Palace. At the end of the night I had my brother carry my guitar out to the car for me and I loaded the guitar case with ice and all the beers we didn't finish. Shit... I was having so much fun I left the club that night without getting paid and had to turn the car around and run back in to get my money.

My success was short lived, however, because the next musical act I opened up for was Pia Zadora and her thousand piece orchestra that her shriveled-up, elderly, multi-millionaire husband had bankrolled for his young bride to keep her happy.

L.A. Misérables, Too

The show at the Club Casino in Hampton Beach, New Hampshire, was not selling at all, so they gave away hundreds and hundreds of tickets to nursing homes and filled the room with white-haired old ladies with walkers and liver spots that they had bussed in just to fill the room. I wasn't prepared for this audience when I walked out on stage and, at that point early in my comedy career, I didn't have enough material to shift gears and do a nice, clean set for a mature crowd such as that. So I went on stage and talked about driving drunk, and smoking pot, and getting laid, and not getting laid, then ended it all with a nice song about a convicted housebreaker taking it up the ass.

"Thank you ladies, and good night!"

The booker screamed, *"You're fired! You'll never play on this stage again!"*

But I did, a couple years later... many, many times, in fact.

DAY 254 - NOVEMBER 17TH, 1996

Kelly had her softball game against the MTV *Singled Out* show staff this morning. Once again, the sport of softball was the furthest thing from the minds of these girls. The balls and bats had yet to be taken out of the duffel bag when the big bosomed coach whipped her hair and announced that the team had a strength and fitness coach as well as a physical therapist to assist during the game. Kelly ended up pulling a muscle in her leg, had enough of the fiasco, and we left early. It's just as well because the whole thing was very unorganized and the only bad news is that I spent fifty dollars to buy Kelly what now amounts to a leather oven-mitt.

I was looking through some old notebooks and I came across a notation about an interesting court case that I had in the Salem District Court, in Salem, Massachusetts, before Judge David Doyle, a great man, a great judge, and a huge Notre Dame football fan.

The defense attorney was Peter DiGangi who has since become one of the top divorce and domestic relations lawyers on the North Shore of Boston. Peter's client was accused of indecent exposure and the principle prosecution witness was an older, matronly woman, perhaps in her late-60's, but very feisty and enthusiastic.

It seems that the defendant had gone to her home, where she lived alone, rang the doorbell and, when the woman came to the door to answer it, the perpetrator was standing on her porch with his pants down and his dick in his hand, jerking off. She reported it to the police and then the same thing happened a couple weeks later. At that time she identified the defendant, either through a description or in a photo array, I can't remember which, and he was arrested for exposing himself.

Near the end of my presentation of the state's evidence, I asked my witness if she could identify the person that she saw touching himself on her porch on those two occasions. Without hesitation she pointed to the defendant, sitting next to Attorney DiGangi, as the culprit.

It was now Attorney DiGangi's opportunity to cross examine his client's accuser. It soon became apparent that, despite this woman's unflinching testimony and positive identification of the defendant, Peter intended to make an issue of her identification and attack the credibility of her observations.

"Ma'am... are you trying to tell the court that you can say, without any doubt, that the man you have identified here is the same man that was stroking his privates on your porch that evening?"

"Yes, I am."

"And you want the court to believe you can say, for certain, that this is the *same* man that you saw touching himself on your porch two weeks prior to this incident?"

"Yes."

"You mean to tell us that.... through the screen door, in the dim light of a sixty watt overhead bulb, while your eyes were diverted down toward that man's privates, you were still able to make a positive identification of his face?"

"Yes, because that *is* the same man that was on my porch before. I'm very sure of it."

Peter raised his eyebrows. "And how can you be so sure, Ma'am?"

"Because I identified his penis also, and it was identical on both occasions."

L.A. Misérables, Too

Peter became incredulous. "You identified his *penis*? Ma'am, tell us, how in the world did you identify his *penis*?"

"In my line of work I have viewed thousands of penises and I was able to identify his penis, because it was unique."

Now even Judge Doyle was raising his eyebrows, curiously anticipating the course of this line of questioning.

Peter went on, shaking his head. "Ma'am... would you please tell the court what it is that makes you believe that you are an expert on identifying men's penises."

"Young man, I am experienced in identifying penises, because I have been employed as a *head nurse* for over thirty years."

Peter just doubled over in laughter. I, in turn, couldn't help myself and burst out laughing when I saw his reaction. Even Judge Doyle had to hide his face, while the woman looked around with a puzzled look on her face and asked the court officer, "What did I say? Did I say something wrong?"

A *head* nurse... Ha ha. I'll never forget that.

Tonight, I had a private show for some business associates near Ventura, which is over an hour drive from Hollywood. I called the guy who was running the whole sha-bang and he gave me directions to the restaurant where they had rented a function room for the occasion, and he told me to be there about 8:15 PM, when they should be through with dinner.

I left about seven o'clock, which gave me an hour and a quarter to get to Ventura, which should have been plenty of time. Note the critical words here, junior detectives, which were *"should have been."*

My directions told me to take the 101 freeway north to Ventura and take the Palm Street exit. I was making good time when I saw a sign that said "VENTURA 25 MILES," so I reset my trip odometer to zero so I'd know when I was getting close. I got to the signs that indicated I was entering Ventura and I drove on, looking for Palm Street, but there was no such sign and eventually my odometer read thirty five miles as I passed another sign which said "LEAVING VENTURA."

Now, why is it that every time I miss my exit or have to turn around on a highway, it seems that the next available exit is always *at*

185

least five zip-codes, four districts, three area-codes, two time-zones and one national border away? As soon as I realized that I had gone too far, the highway became desolate, there were no lights, no buildings, no turnoffs, no signs, and no indication that the area had been developed, or perhaps even discovered. It's discouraging to finally see a sign ahead, only to get close enough to find that it says "NEXT EXIT- ∞."

You know you're lost when you start seeing dead animals on the road that aren't indigenous to the area. As you drive further and further away from your intended destination, your mind starts playing tricks on you as you ponder, "Was that road-kill an aardvark? Do they have aardvarks in California? Fuck! Where the hell am I?... Shit, what was that? I know this sounds crazy, but I swear that looked like either a Koala Bear or a Three-Toed Sloth. Fuck!"

By the time I was able to turn around, I had gone twenty-five miles out of my way, my gas gauge was below "E" and I was almost half an hour late. I got back to Ventura, drove through the town again, and *still* didn't see the exit I was supposed to take, so I decided that I better pull over and call the restaurant. The guy at the desk answered and said, "What, are you lost? They have finished dinner and they're waiting for you! I'm going to put someone from the function on the phone with you."

I spoke to the same gentleman from whom I got the directions from this afternoon and I told him that there is no Palm Street exit off of the 101.

"That's because you were supposed to take Route 126 off the 101! I told you that today."

"No sir, I was writing it down and I'm certain you never told me that... Oh, never mind. Just give me the directions."

Rumor has it that Jimmy Hoffa was last seen receiving directions to a union meeting from this very same man.

CHAPTER FOURTEEN
Livin' on a prayer...

DAY 255 - NOVEMBER 18TH, 1996

The *LA Times* is running a series of articles about the gang problem in Los Angeles. It happens quite often that some innocent people inadvertently drive through a gang neighborhood and are gunned down because the gangbangers mistook their automobile for that of a rival gang's. That's scary because I don't really know my way around LA yet and it's conceivable that it could happen to me.

To avoid any such confusion I have decided to paint my car pink, like a Mary Kay salesperson, paste a "Let me tell you about my grandchildren" bumper-sticker on the back, and stick a Garfield, suction-cup stuffed animal on my window to make it obvious that I am not a threat. Drastic times call for drastic measures.

DAY 256 - NOVEMBER 19TH, 1996

I was speaking to a lawyer friend in Boston today, mentioned Attorney Sumner Smith, and was told that he had recently passed away, which saddened me. I did my first trial ever against Sumner, who was a wily veteran. I'll never forget that day. I had just begun my job as an ADA and had watched a couple trials, but I had absolutely no experience in trying a case.

My supervisor, Dennis Jackson, was supposed to second seat me when I did my first trial so he could advise me on where to stand, when to approach the bench, when to object, how to present evidence, and all the other trial mechanics that you never learn in law school. On this Friday afternoon on a beautiful summer's day, however, Dennis announced that he would be leaving early, handed me a manila folder, told me that I had to try a driving under the influence case with Sumner Smith (which *he* was supposed to do) and walked out the door of the DA's office with his golf clubs.

It sucks to be the low man on the totem pole.

So I began a trial with Sumner Smith, without experience and without supervision, and Sumner proceeded to pummel me with technical jargon, obscure legal nuances, and shrewd trail tactics that had my head spinning. In response to Sumner's cunning strategy and sly maneuvers, the trial judge would confront me with questions that I had no answers for and I really felt like an asshole as I got my head handed to me over and over again during the course of the trial.

When the trial ended, in a "Not Guilty," of course, I felt beaten up as if I had been through a heavyweight fight. Sumner smiled, patted me on the back and said, "You'll learn, son... You'll learn." And, believe me, I never forgot the lessons that I learned that day, because the painful experiences were branded into my memory forever. I found out, whether in law, comedy or any other endeavor, when things go right, you never learn as much as when things go wrong. No pain, no gain. I went on to hold my own with Sumner Smith in many a trial after that first loss, but I always retained the lesson he taught me that day.

Recalling the story about the head nurse brought back some other courtroom memories. Another one of my favorite judges was Judge Dominic Russo. I appeared before Judge Russo off-and-on in many different courtrooms throughout my tenure as an assistant district attorney. I remember the days when I was assigned to the Salem District Court six-person jury session and the judges were all Italian... Judge Russo, Judge Joseph Furnari and Judge Neil Collichio, three of the greatest guys you'd ever meet. Every Friday afternoon, when the docket wasn't crowded, they would make homemade spaghetti sauce and cook pasta for me and the court officers. One of Judge Russo's favorite stories, which I heard him recall many times to other judges and lawyers, was about the time that I was doing a comedy show at a local bar association banquet which he was attending. I acknowledged Judge Russo in the crowd and said, "Lawyers from out of town will often come into our court and inquire about the judges that they will be appearing before for the first time. Lawyers will often ask me, 'I have a trial in front of Judge Russo today. Tell me about Judge Russo. What's he like?'"

I'd tell them, "Judge Russo is fair... He's a fair judge."

"Well how about Judge Furnari?"

"Oh, Judge Furnari?... He's a *good* judge."

One memory of Judge Russo occurred early in my career, just after my trial with Sumner Smith as a matter of fact. It seems that a lot of nuts come into the courthouse late on Friday afternoon, just when you're wrapping up a tough week and you can't wait to get out of there. I remember one time when a guy came into the DA's office, just as I was about to leave for the weekend, and informed me that he wished to confess to a murder that happened four years ago. I asked him why he hadn't reported it earlier and he told me that he didn't have the chance because he was being held against his will in the state mental hospital.

I told him that the office was closing for the weekend and he should come back on Monday and ask for me personally... and then told him that my name was assistant district attorney Dennis Jackson.

Another late Friday afternoon, just as I was walking out of the office, I heard the court officer on the P.A. loudspeaker asking for a DA in the second session. Judge Russo was on the bench and looked annoyed, as we all were. It seems that the sheriff's department had just transported a prisoner in custody for jumping bail and failing to appear for a court date.

Judge Russo asked him why he didn't show up and this disheveled guy with the crazy eyes looked around the courtroom to make sure no one else was listening, then whispered to the judge that he was unavailable because he was working undercover for the C.I.A. in Russia, receiving secret messages from a spy satellite on orders from the president himself.

Judge Russo rolled his eyes and asked me if I was requesting additional bail on the fugitive, giving me the subtle head nod that indicated to just let him go on the promise he'd show up so we could all get the hell out of there. I understood and said, "Your Honor... In the interest of national security, I believe that it would be unpatriotic to keep this man incarcerated. I suggest we allow him to return to court on his own recognizance so that he may return to Russia and continue his espionage on behalf of the United States of America."

The guy clicked his heels and saluted me. "Thank you, sir!"

Attorney Paul Murphy is a new kind of court jest

Paul Murphy uses an alias. But not for the reason that some people do. Murphy isn't a shady character who wants to hide his true identity from the law. In fact, Murphy is the law, an assistant district attorney who also happens to be a stand-up comic.

"I go by the name Paul D'Angelo when I perform," said Murphy, who appeared this past weekend at the 1620 restaurant in Plymouth. "Because I didn't think that the court would think it was cool."

Murphy, who lives in Wakefield and works in the Salem District Court, said in a phone interview that he started his second career a year and a half ago, "and within six months I was headlining."

In fact, Murphy has gone national. He not only plays such Boston clubs as Catch a Rising Star and Nick's Comedy Stop in Boston, he has also delivered his one-liners at the Comedy Store and The Improv in Los Angeles.

Murphy, whose first jobs were

Scene and heard

Constance Gorfinkle
Patriot Ledger staff

hosting roasts, said, "I've never had trouble getting up in front of people. After all, I had a hundred jury trials under my belt before I ever got up on a stage."

Murphy says that in his act, "I touch on everything from drunk driving to blind dates to the family to song parodies." One of his routines involves speaking in acronyms: "Like, I went to a TGIF party. It was BYOB, RSVP. I had enough VO and JB to send me to AA with the DTs."

In the process of creating his act, Murphy gets inspiration from many sources. But one of them, he says, is

not the Salem District Court.

"I'm in a different frame of mind when I'm in court. People can hardly believe it's me. They say, 'It's not the same guy; he's got a tie on.'"

Murphy is happy his second career is going so well. "It's good, but I don't get a don't get a chance to sleep. My schedule is crazy. I'm booked every night in August," he adds, with dates that include Carly Simon's club on Martha's Vineyard and Boston Harbor cruises.

The way things are going it looks as though Murphy soon will be busier in the clubs than in the courts. If that happens, will he become a full-time comic?

"I just might give it a shot," he said.

Years later I was supervising the District Attorney's office in the Lynn District Court. I have mentioned the city of Lynn several times but, to give you an idea, it is a relatively large city with a rather high rate of crime. Consequently, the district court is one of the busiest in the state of Massachusetts. As more and more arrests were made, introducing a growing number of new criminal cases into the system, the limited number of courtrooms were either tied-up in a hearing or severely overcrowded, the court docket was jammed to the point of being unmanageable, and cases were getting backed up further and further, with trial dates being assigned months in advance.

In response, the judiciary committee chose to send my old friend, Judge Russo, who had recently achieved success as a troubleshooter in another problem court, to Lynn in an attempt to reorganize the system and dispose of some of the backlog in an efficient manner.

Let me tell you now, this story is true. I swear to God, I'm not making this up.

The first day Judge Russo took the bench he was determined to rule the court with an iron fist and made his intentions clear to all those who came before him.

The judge addressed the crowded courtroom, announcing, "When the clerk calls your name off the court list, I want you to stand-up and yell loudly 'Here.' Understand?... OK, Mr. Clerk, call the list."

The clerk called, "Rufus Jones."

"Here!"

The judge bellowed, "Where are you, Mr. Jones? Were you listening to me when I addressed the court? I told you to stand up! Was there something you didn't understand about my instructions?... I'll tell everyone again, say 'Here' and stand when the clerk calls your name. Is that clear, Mr. Jones?"

"Yes, your honor."

He screamed at one defendant, "Are you chewing gum, sir?"

"Uh... ya... "

He admonished, "There will be no gum chewing in my courtroom! Understood? If I catch anyone chewing gum I'll have the court officer take you into custody. Next case, Mr. Clerk."

"Edward Spencer."

He yelled, "Mr. Spencer, take your hands out of your pockets when you address the court! And tuck your shirt in, you look like a slob! Do you want to sit in a cell in lockup until you feel that you are able to present yourself in a reasonable manner, Mr. Spencer?"

"No, you honor."

To another he shouted, "SIR! THERE WILL BE NO TALKING IN MY COURTROOM WHEN I'M ON THE BENCH!" then threatened, "I'm going to start filling the cells with people until you learn to behave yourselves in my courtroom!"

It wasn't long before everyone in that court was sitting in silence, with their hands folded in their laps, totally intimidated by Judge Russo. He had the clerk call another name on the docket.

"James Cumming."

"Here, your honor!"

"Where are you?"

"Here, your honor!"

"I can't see you! Wasn't I clear? I thought I told you to stand, now STAND UP!"

"But I am, your honor!"

That's when I turned around in my chair at the prosecutor's desk and saw a four foot tall dwarf who had climbed up onto the spectator's bench and was frantically jumping up and down as he waved his little hand over his head in an effort to be seen.

The whole room erupted in laughter as Judge Russo buried his head in his hands.

"Brief recess."

One of the idiosyncrasies that Judge Russo had was his tendency to regularly share a couple of little anecdotes in court that were supposed to teach the defendants a lesson, for the benefit of all those who were present.

Not only would he repeat these parables every single day, it was as if he was reciting them word-for-word from a script because, each time he reiterated them, it was exactly the same language. It got so I would sit back at the desk and mouth the words as he spoke them, knowing precisely what the judge would say and how he would say it.

His stories were charming the first couple hundred times that we heard them but, after a while, the clerks, court officers, lawyers, prosecutors, and probation officers who had to sit through the stories time and time again would get annoyed because the judge would drag them out and make a busy day last even longer.

One such lesson would be repeated whenever someone was arrested for drinking in public or being in possession of an open container of alcohol. Judge Russo would ask the defendants, "How much did that beer (or wine or booze) cost you?"

Usually, the people in this position were toothless alcoholics that lived on the streets and were picked up by the cops. They would invariably look at each other or, in the case of a single defendant, pause and think, and answer something like, "I don't know... I think the bottle o' Thunderbird was... what? Like five bucks or somethin'."

Judge Russo would then ask, "Would you like to dispose of this matter today?" The defendants would usually want to get rid of it and not have to come back to court, so they'd answer, "Yes," and the clerk would ask, "How do you plead?"

"Guilty."

The judge would then fine them $50 or $100. But before he let them go, he would inquire, once again, "Now, I'm going to ask you again, how much did that wine cost you?"

With a confused look they'd respond, "We told you... I think it was somethin' like five bucks or somethin'."

The judge would then smile and say, "But I just fined you each $50, so I'll ask you again, how much did that bottle of wine cost you two?"

After a moment of thought, their faces would light up... "Oh... It cost us $105.00, your honor." And everyone in the courtroom awaiting their case to be called would chuckle at the judge's cute little example.

"That's right. $105 is a lot to spend on a bottle of wine. Maybe now you'll think twice before you drink in public. Let this be a lesson to all of you. Good day gentlemen, next case."

Judge Russo used to *love* that little crowd reaction when he told his stories.

So now it was a year or so later, and it was my last day supervising the Lynn District Court because I was being transferred to take over

Paul D'Angelo

the supervisory position in the Peabody Jury Session. The first session was crowded, as usual, and all the personnel were anxious to blow through the long list in a hurry, because they were planning on taking me out for a little going away celebration as soon as we wrapped-up the day's business. Collectively, we all expressed our disappointment when the clerk arraigned two vagrants for drinking in public. I looked at my watch. "Oh no, here we go again."

"Gentlemen, what were you drinking?"

"We split a fifth o' whiskey, your honor."

"And how much did that whiskey cost you?"

"I think it was $4.50."

"And how do you plead?"

Both said, "Guilty, your honor."

"I'm fining you both fifty dollars apiece. You can have six months to pay those fines. See the probation officer on your way out. But... before you leave us, (I began to mimic the judge and form the words with my mouth as the clerk, court officers and probation officers rolled their eyes and laughed at me) please tell the court how much that bottle of whiskey cost you two."

A perplexed look, then, "Four-fifty."

"Think about it gentlemen. I just fined you fifty dollars each. Can you tell the people in this courtroom how much that bottle of whiskey cost you?"

Smiles. "Oh... it cost us $104.50 your honor."

On cue, the gallery smiles at the judge and the judge smiles back, content that he made his point.

"That's right. $105 is a lot to spend on a bottle of wine. Maybe now you'll think twice before you drink alcohol in a public place. Let this be a lesson to all of you. Good day gentlemen, next case."

The clerk then calls, "Martin Lewis, charged with violation of the john law and soliciting a prostitute on August 5th by the Lynn police. How do you plead sir?"

"Guilty."

The judge said, "Fine him two hundred and fifty dollars Mr. Clerk."

"Judge Russo accepts your plea of guilty and the Court fines you $250, plus a 25% surcharge, as well as a victim witness fee of thirty dollars. See the probation officer on your way out."

I couldn't resist, it was my last day, and I rose from my chair at the prosecutor's table facing the clerk, who sat in front of the judge, with the probation officer to the judge's immediate right, and a court officer standing next to the bench on his left.

"Pardon me, Judge Russo, but aren't you gonna ask him how much that blow job cost him?"

The judge laughed so hard he quickly left the bench and ran into his chambers.

Peabody District Court jury session

Paul D'Angelo

DAY 257 - NOVEMBER 20TH, 1996

I have been working with my friend Patty Ross for three days now, trying to get her set-list and presentation together for her audition for the Aspen Comedy Festival at the Laugh Factory tonight.

How did I meet Patty? Patty was having a drink one night and ran into Fred Cronin, who was another assistant DA in the Peabody office with me. Freddie thought that Patty was very funny and she told him that she always wanted to be a stand-up comedian. Fred told Patty that I worked in his office and I would be happy to help her out. She called me the next day, we met for lunch, and I took her under my wing, helping to write some of her material, introducing her to all the club owners and bookers in the Boston area, and putting her on stage whenever I could.

We became best of friends and I always told Patty that when she could learn to be herself on stage, she would be a success, because she has a very unique personality. I've tried to assist her ever since, attending her shows, preparing her for big showcases, and basically lending my organizational qualities to her because her character is rather undisciplined, which is actually a big part of her charm. We put together a tight set that established her unique point of view, and I wrote her some additional lines to strengthen a couple routines, then I made her practice in front of me over and over again until she got it down perfect.

It paid off. Tonight Patty kicked ass and impressed all the people from HBO, as well as a number of other heavy hitters from the entertainment industry. They were all fighting over Patty, begging her to sign with them and making promises of sitcoms and development deals. I think Patty's career is going to take off now, so remember that name. By the time this book gets published, if it does, I have a feeling that Patty will be a well-known personality and I'm extremely happy for her.

When I got home I was furious. As I turned the corner of the hallway to my apartment, some dog had peed on the wall and there's a little dog turd on the carpet. Both pieces of evidence are right next to the apartment where that Chinese guy lives with his two, little white poodles. Sometimes this idiot just lets the dogs wander the halls and Kelly has caught them peeing in the building twice.

That inconsiderate bastard... I'll get him.

DAY 258 - NOVEMBER 21ST, 1996

I was supposed to play golf today and I was really looking forward to it. Today is also the first day it's rained heavily since I moved here over eight months ago.

When it rains, it pours.

I took Patty to Universal Citywalk to celebrate her successful showcase and we spent the afternoon there. On the way home, she asked me to stop at the Thrifty's. When we were in the parking lot, there was a woman on crutches who was futilely trying to open the hood of her car in the pouring rain. Patty suggested that we give her a hand and we went over to try and help.

The woman told us that her driver's side windshield wiper had fallen off and she couldn't drive in the rain. She thought the broken wiper might have fallen into the engine compartment, but it was nowhere to be found. Patty had the idea to take the good windshield wiper off of the passenger side wiper arm and put it on the driver's side so the woman could see well enough to get home safely.

I went over to the passenger side and tried to take off the one good wiper blade, but it wouldn't come off. I tugged at it. I pulled on it. And, like the master mechanic that I am, I tried to force it off. Nothing. Then I saw a little plastic tab that looked like it might release the wiper from the arm. I pulled it. I pushed it. I bent it. I forced it. And it broke off in my hand. Shit! I pretended to keep working and, when no one was looking, I slipped the broken piece into my jacket pocket. The wiper slipped off easily now... Too easily.

"Oh goody! You got it!"

"Ya... ya, I got it all right."

I slid the one good wiper on the driver's side arm, but there was nothing to hold it on anymore.

I said to the woman, "If I were you I'd go straight home, because it looks like this wiper is screwed up also. There should be a little plastic tab that keeps it from falling off, but it looks like it broke off. It's a good thing I noticed. You're going to have to replace them both."

"Thank you sooo much. Thank you. Thank you. I can't thank you enough. You're so kind."

"No problem. Remember, don't let that other wiper go."

Patty and I went into the Thrifty's.

"That was very nice of you, Paul."

"Not really," I explained, as I pulled the broken piece of the windshield wiper out of my pocket. "I broke this part off of the good wiper when I was taking it off. It holds the wiper on."

Patty laughed and said, "Oh great. Way to go, Paul. Her car is probably wrapped around a tree as we speak. Heh heh heh."

I felt very guilty as we walked into the parking lot.

Patty didn't help by yelling, "Is that a windshield wiper on the ground, Paul? Do I hear sirens? Do you hear them Paul? The sirens? Heh heh heh. Don't feel bad, Paul, she was already crippled, how much more could she hurt herself. Heh heh heh."

Just call me "Mr. Badwrench."

DAY 259 - NOVEMBER 22ND, 1996

The phone rang at 3:30 a.m. last night. I got up out of a sound sleep and answered it. From the buzzing noise in the background I could tell that it was someone on the security phone in the lobby trying to get buzzed into the apartments.

"Ya."

"Hey man, is Doug there?"

I said, "There's no Doug here. You've got the wrong apartment." (click)

I went back to bed. A minute later the phone rang again.

"Ya."

"Yo, is Doug there?"

"I told you he doesn't live here!"

"Man, I really got to see him. Do you know which apartment he lives in?"

You have got to be shitting me? Can this guy be that stupid? There are over three hundred units in this building and he thinks I know where "Doug" lives? Not only is he an ignorant asshole… he is a *persistent* ignorant asshole. I was ready to scream at him… but no, wait. I waited for my sleepy brain to clear, because somehow I knew I could use this asshole to my advantage.

Got it!

"Ya man… I know Doug. Doug lives in 207 with some Chinese guy and his dogs. Give him a call. The Chinese guy can be a jerk when he just wakes up, so be tenacious and bug the shit out of him."

Perfect.

I won't be having Thanksgiving with my family back in Boston this year. Our Thanksgivings are heavy with tradition. Not this year. They'll be no Bloody Marys at my brother Jay's apartment. No traditional Wakefield-Melrose football game. No cocktails after the game at Oliver's. No martinis with my dad before the meal. No incredible feast prepared by my mother, who will yell at us all for having a buzz on when we sit down to dinner, my father included.

I got a Thanksgiving card from my sister today. She wrote, "Thanksgiving won't be the same without you. For one thing, they'll be one less drunk at the dinner table."

Cute kid, my sister.

DAY 260 - NOVEMBER 23RD, 1996

I took Kelly to see The Fabulous Thunderbirds at the Galaxy Theater in Santa Ana tonight. The Galaxy is the theater that I did a comedy show at last week, so I figured I'd have no problem finding it, and I didn't. I also found my way home, despite Kelly's help. Thank God I've learned that one of the keys to avoid getting lost in California is to totally ignore any assistance with the directions that Kelly might give me.

Even without her coaching, navigating around Los Angeles is

tough enough with all these damn freeways running into each other... "Ya, take the 10 to the 101 to the 134 to the five to the 405 to the 25 or 6 to 4... blah, blah, blah..."

"Paul! What are you doing? Take that exit! The 405 is that way!!" (points right)

(Calmly... because I know better) "No Kelly, that's the 105, not the 405. Close. You're only off by three hundred. Thanks anyway."

(three minutes later)

"Paul, we're really lost now. The sign says we're on the 501."

"No, Kelly. That's not a street sign. That's a billboard with a Levi's blue-jean ad."

"Oh, you're right."

(short time later)

"Paul, how are we going to get to the 10 from here? You took a wrong turn. We're on the 67. We're lost now."

"The 67? There is no Route 67. Where the hell are you getting these numbers?... Oh, I see. You were looking at a bank clock. It's 67 degrees out... and just wait a second... oh, look, we're not on the '11:15 Freeway' now either. Listen, I really appreciate your help, Kelly, but I'm switching off the auto-pilot and I'll take it in from here, OK?"

I had to make a stop at the massive Thrifty's pharmacy to pick up some toilet paper for the house and it took me quite a while to find the correct aisle. The toilet paper was in the section with the napkins and shoe polish and batteries and dust mops and light bulbs and a million other things I don't normally associate with toilet paper.

It would make more sense to stock the shelves according to body parts. The suppositories, Preparation H, and laxatives are all together, so why don't they reorganize and make one large "Ass Aisle," with hemorrhoid cremes, Bean-O, Gas-X, Ex-Lax, Ammodium A-D, Depends adult-diapers, Glade air freshener, and eight-packs of Charmin Ultra and White Cloud? And since it would only be a small addition, why not could consolidate the "Ass Aisle" with the "Armpit Section" and throw the deodorants and antiperspirants in with the ass products?

The "Head and Face Aisle" would naturally have toothpaste, toothbrushes and dental floss, Listerine and other types of mouthwash,

L.A. Misérables, Too

Visine and contact lens stuff, hair care products, allergy medicines, Oxy-5 and zit treatments, head cold remedies, shaving creme and razors, makeup, lipstick, Chap-stick, etc.

Then there would be the "Penis and Vagina Aisle" with diaphragms, contraceptives, tampons, Maxi-pads for heavy days, mini-pads for light days, Vagisil for feminine itching, FDS feminine hygiene spray, and Masingill's douche for the women, and condoms, crab soap, *Penthouse*, *Playboy*, hand cream and tissues, for the guys.

I wasn't a management major in college for nothin'.

I bought an eight-pack of toilet paper that should last us for a while. I noticed that the pharmacy also sold single rolls of toilet paper, apparently for those people who are trying to quit the habit.

DAY 261 - NOVEMBER 24TH, 1996

My friend George was in town visiting his sister and we were invited over for dinner. There were several other guests there as well and we were all sitting around after the meal. George mentioned that he is leaving for Paris on Wednesday and talk turned to his many trips to Greece, Amsterdam, Paris, Rome and Germany.

George's sister, who was raised in Israel when their father was in the foreign services, turned to me and asked, "Have you been to Europe, Paul?"

I suddenly felt a bit self-conscious when everyone looked at me and awaited my answer. I didn't want to feel like a cultural misfit, so I lied. "Europe? Uh… Yes, of course. I've visited several countries, as a matter of fact."

"Euro-rail?"

"No," I answered, slightly embarrassed, "Epcot."

DAY 262 - NOVEMBER 25TH, 1996

Timthy cut my hair today. I specifically told him that I didn't want it too short this time, but he didn't listen. He cut my hair so short it was not so much a haircut as it was a biopsy.

Paul D'Angelo

I spoke to an old friend today, Jonathan Friedmann, who is one of my best pals from law school. Jon and I shared a special bond because we were singled out for out chauvinistic behavior by some feminine activist law school classmates that took themselves way too seriously and wrote a letter to the school newspaper.

It started like this:

Jonathan and I were in the same class and it was getting near the mid-term finals of our first year at Suffolk University School of Law. You didn't have to see the movie *The Paper Chase* to know that we were all under an awful lot of pressure. I became the release valve for my class, because I always found a way to get in trouble that first year. There were several incidents, but I got the most notoriety by sneaking through the hallways late at night and posting signs outside all the classrooms that said:

> ATTENTION GIRLS!!!!
> HAVING TROUBLE STUDYING FOR YOUR
> LAW MID-TERMS?
> WELL DON'T WORRY, FEEL FREE TO
> GO THROUGH MY BRIEFS AT ANY TIME.
> CONTACT PAUL M.

Now this is a pretty innocuous stunt under normal circumstances, but we had a few broads... oh, I'm sorry, "women," in our class that were radical feminists and were constantly interrupting class to point out anything that was remotely sexist. To tell you the truth, the rest of us were kind of getting tired of their militant antics, including most of the other women, so I probably did it intending to piss them off, and it worked.

That same week, in criminal law class, our professor was discussing a case in which a woman, who had been continually abused by her husband over a long period of time, had retaliated and killed him in his sleep. In fact, that incident and the ensuing trial was the basis for the movie, *The Burning Bed,* starring Farrah Fawcett.

While discussing crimes of passion, in which a defendant's responsibility for their conduct is mitigated by unusual circumstances or provocation, thus making it difficult to prove that this person was able to form the specific criminal intent necessary to convict, the professor raised the question of what actually constituted sufficient provocation. If it was reasonable to assume that a woman who has been beaten daily for, say, a couple of years, could be justified in killing her husband to protect herself, what about a woman who was only abused four or five times over the course of a year?

A heated discussion began and the feminists were being particularly vocal. Then the professor pointed at Jonathan and asked him where he drew the line. Jon jokingly answered, "I think the average, prudent and reasonable man beats his wife about twice a month." Well, that was all they had to hear. When class ended the "Femi-Nazis", which is what Rush Limbaugh calls them, circled Jon and wouldn't let him leave the class until they gave him an earful.

The next week, the following letter appeared in the law school newspaper:

> *To the Editor,*
>
> *The rampart immaturity of the male population at Suffolk Law has been a source of constant irritation. Such comments as "the reasonable man would beat his wife" and "don't worry, you'll have no trouble getting a job with that body" can be heard echoing throughout the corridors.*
>
> *The most obnoxious exhibition of immaturity was a recent advertisement inviting all law school women having trouble studying for midterms to go through Paul M's briefs.*
>
> *I find it most disheartening to observe such a disparity in maturity between the women and men at this school. What form of immunity have the women acquired against the "virus" that seems to only attack the Suffolk male? What is it that is causing this regression in men?*
>
> *Perhaps it is a vicious reaction of the male hormone testosterone which is rebelling in this hostile environment of academic overload!*
>
> *A Conscientious Objector*

Ha, ha, ha!!! That's something to be proud of!
How many men can say they've been called a "virus" in print?

DAY 263 - NOVEMBER 26th, 1996

My cousin Paul at ICM took me out to lunch at Barney's Greengrass in Beverly Hills, a place I could never afford to eat at since I took my vow of poverty and moved to Hollywood.

After lunch, Paul had to buy a necktie for his lawyer's birthday. The ties were $80 to $100 and I saw shirts for $360 and one for $495! I looked to my right and there was Attorney Robert Shapiro. I said, "So, this is where you get all those nice suits?" Then I told him that I had been a trial attorney in Boston, but gave it up to become a comedian in Hollywood.

He laughed and said, "Ha! Another lawyer who wants to become a comedian!"

I wanted to ask him if the Simpson jury thought DNA stood for "Disregard for Negro Athlete," but I had a brief flash of good taste and didn't.

I got a 10:40 spot at the Improv tonight. There was a showcase before me and, as usual, the room emptied out like a fire drill as soon as it was over. I am not exaggerating when I say there were six people in the audience when I went on stage. I basically listened to myself talk for ten minutes and it was pretty depressing.

After that horrible experience I had to get out of there, so Max, my friend Henry Phillips and I went for a couple drinks at the Mustache Café across the street. Henry told us that he was listening to one of those sex-talk radio shows on the way over and some girl called up and said that she was nineteen years old and still a virgin. The host commended her for her chastity but, later in the conversation, the girl admitted to having anal sex and servicing guys orally on several occasions, yet she still considered herself a virgin. Ya, technically that's true, but... really? I remarked that her virginity should have a big Roger Maris asterisk next to it. As in:

L.A. Misérables, Too

MOST HOME RUNS: SEASON

name:	home runs:
Roger Maris* (see below)	61
Babe Ruth	60
Jimmie Foxx	58

note: * 162 game season (others 154 games)

LIST OF LOCAL VIRGINS

name:	age:
Brenda Boyle	17
Gina Spinnoza	20
Joannie Jones	19*/** (see below)
Leslie Landers	18
Jane Jennings	21
Sally Smith	15

note: * took it up the ass / ** gave blow jobs

CHAPTER FIFTEEN
I'm livin' in my own private Idaho...

DAY 264 - NOVEMBER 27TH, 1996

Thanksgiving Day in the Hollywood Hills. By the time I rubbed the sleep out of my eyes on the West Coast, I would already be drunk and late for dinner if I was still on the East Coast.

When it was time for bed last night, Kelly was tossing and turning fitfully.

"What's the matter Kelly?"

"I can't sleep. I keep thinking about all the poor turkeys that have to die for us to celebrate Thanksgiving and it's making me very sad and upset."

Great. We don't enough problems to worry about: the future of my career, paying the rent and buying food, surviving in a crazy city three thousand miles from home, spending the holidays away from our families... now it's Turkey Awareness Day and I have to atone for the blood that's on my hands from the great fowl massacres of Thanksgivings past.

Mass graves are being unearthed in Bosnia, millions are starving in Asia, whole villages in Rwanda are being hacked to death, and people are being gunned down in the streets not far from where we live, but my girlfriend is a turkey "right-to-lifer" who feels guilty for all the in-

L.A. Misérables, Too

nocent feathered "victims" who are brutally slaughtered for the purely selfish reason of feeding your famished family and friends.

How utterly senseless. Maybe next year she can round up some ex-Greenspeace fanatics that used to sabotage whaling ships in their rubber Zodiacs, load up a pickup truck with environmental zealots carrying wire-cutters, and infiltrate a turkey farm, cut holes in the chicken wire, and free the doomed birds into the wilderness so they can get ripped apart by coyotes, run over by automobiles, and shot for sport instead.

No turkey is losing sleep over the fact that I gave up a secure, normal life with two steady incomes to move to Los Angeles and consider myself privileged to have the opportunity to do a show in front of six comatose people for a $12.50 check. So fuck the turkeys. I would like some white meat, a little dark meat, and a drumstick, with the skin, along with my mashed potatoes, squash, peas, cranberry sauce and yams, so that this majestic bird, lying stuffed on the serving plate in front of me, shall not have given his life in vain.

(later) No such luck. My parents sent me some money to take Kelly out to eat on Thanksgiving and we made dinner reservations in the main ballroom at the Four Seasons for a big buffet with turkey, prime rib and all the trimmings but, when we called to confirm, we were told that there was a mix-up because the only table available was for brunch on the outdoor patio. I'd rather starve than spend fifty bucks a person for an omelet, salad and sushi bar on Thanksgiving! We called a bunch of other restaurants and they're all booked up, so we are sitting in our apartment feeling bad for ourselves. The good news is that there may be one less turkey that has to sacrifice his life for our dining pleasure. I hope the bird woman of our own private Alcatraz is happy.

It was 4:30 p.m. and we had stubbornly refused to eat anything all day when I finally broke down and drove to the Boston Market on Sunset and LaBrea to get us some take-out turkey dinners. After all, what's Thanksgiving Day without turkey? When I pulled in there was a line going out the door and into the parking lot like a bread line in Russia, about which I had mixed emotions. I didn't want to wait in this long line, but it was good to know that I was not the only loser in Los Angeles without a life. After twenty-five minutes standing in line the manager called out, "Ladies and gentlemen, we're out of turkey!"

Fantastic! I wonder if Kelly would be upset if I took her to a homeless shelter for Thanksgiving dinner? There's plenty of food, it's free, and I'm certain that I would qualify financially.

"Honey, it's me. Listen… wash all the make-up off your face, put on your dirty, ripped jeans, muss up your hair, black-out one of your teeth with an eyebrow pencil, piss yourself, and I'll pick you up in twenty minutes… Don't ask."

DAY 265 - NOVEMBER 28TH, 1996

I have a friend named Randy Pryor who I met while working on Norwegian Cruise Lines. Randy is a magician/juggler who spends most of the year on the high seas, but he's in town for a month or so during the holidays. Randy is performing all week at the Magic Castle, located just down the street from my apartment, which is the Hollywood clubhouse of the Academy of Magical Arts and the world's most famous private club for magicians and magical enthusiasts. Randy has invited Kelly and me as his guests, and we are bringing Patty Ross and her mother, who is visiting. We picked them up and drove up to the valet, who informed us that our casual dress was unacceptable at the club. Women had to wear dresses, evening gowns, or pant suits, while men were required to wear suits or sport jackets and ties, so we had to leave to change and come back for the later show.

I put on one of my suits for the first time in months and realized that I had gained some weight as the result of my depression. Hell, the closest I've come to breaking into show business so far has been to park in the spot marked "Reserved for Tom Hanks" at the Blockbuster Video store. I could hardly button my pants, the jacket feels tight, and the sleeves are short on me. I look like Pee Wee Herman in his two-sizes-too-small suit with flood-length pants. I'm even more depressed to know that the only thing on my body that's getting thinner these days is my hair.

L.A. Misérables, Too

The magic show was cool. I have a friend that does magic in Boston, but he's not at this level of professionalism yet. I've seen him perform at children's birthday parties where seven year old kids are pointing at him and yelling out, "It's in his hand! Look! There! It's not magic! It didn't really disappear, it's right there in his hand!"

His act went over like wax toilet paper.

DAY 266 - NOVEMBER 29TH, 1996

When you get to be forty, you start to worry about things you never worried about before in your life, like heart attacks. I read an article today which warned that 1) sexual activity 2) angry outbursts 3) strenuous physical activity 4) and stress caused by fear or panic are among the primary triggers responsible for a high percentage of all heart attacks.

With those factors in mind, here's an example of a high-risk scenario that I should make an effort to avoid in the future:

"Damn you and your new positions! How ridiculous is it to have sex on an exercise bicycle?"

"Don't snap at me, buster!... Shit! Peddle faster, I think I hear my husband's car in the driveway!"

Ironically, I'm old enough to worry about heart attacks, but I still get an occasional blemish, like I'm a teenager. Right now I have a Chernobyl-nuclear-radiation-leak-mutant-sized monster zit on my ass... affectionately named *Godzilla*... that's so big it looks like a third cheek.

DAY 267 - NOVEMBER 30TH, 1996

A courtroom recollection:

One day I was filling in for another Assistant DA in Lawrence District Court, which is a large city north of Boston that has a population predominantly comprised of minorities. There is a large Spanish speaking community in Lawrence, consisting of mostly Puerto Ricans and Dominicans, which causes some significant communications problems in their extremely busy courthouse.

An arrest was made late in the afternoon and the police brought the defendant in to be arraigned for breaking and entering a house. I watched the presiding judge arraign the Spanish-speaking defendant, who was being held in custody and standing, handcuffed, in the prisoner's dock.

The colloquy went something like this:

"Sir, you have been arrested and charged with breaking and entering a dwelling during the nighttime, which is a felony in the Commonwealth of Massachusetts. Do you understand, Mr. Lopez?"

"No, I no understand. I no speak Eengleesh."

"Sir, I want to remind you of your right to remain silent. Anything you say in this court may be used against you in a later proceeding. Understand, sir?"

"I no speak Eengleesh."

"You have the right to a trail by jury..."

"I say, I no understand... No speak Eengleesh."

"You have the right to an attorney. If you cannot afford an attorney, one will be provided to you. Are you going to get your own attorney?"

"Me no understand... I no speak no Eengleesh."

Frustrated, the judge turned to the clerk sitting in front of the bench. "Mr. Clerk, this man claims that he doesn't understand me. Do we have an interpreter to assist him in this arraignment proceeding?"

"No, your honor", said the clerk. "All of the interpreters are tied up in hearings and trials today. I suggest that we hold Mr. Lopez in custody at the Lawrence House of Correction overnight and arraign him first thing tomorrow morning, when we have an interpreter available."

Suddenly from the dock came a high pitched plea,

"I SPEAK A LEETLE EENGLEESH!... ME SPEAK A LEETLE EENGLEESH!"

L.A. Misérables, Too

DAY 268 - DECEMBER 1ST, 1996

I got a call from one of my best pals from home, Paul Lang, who lived with me for a couple of years after his divorce. Paul asked if I had any shows coming up and I told him that I was playing this Wednesday through Saturday at the Ice House in Pasadena. I inquired as to whether Paul had ever heard of the Ice House before.

"Have I heard of the Ice House? Are you kidding? I *lived* in it for over five years!"

What kind of a response do you expect from a guy who says he locates his ex-wife's house by following the flying monkeys?

I was scheduled to appear at the Laugh Factory at 10:30 tonight but, the show was running long and Howie Mandell dropped by to do a guest spot, so I didn't get on stage until after 11:30 on the Sunday night after Thanksgiving, when there were only twelve people left in the audience. Maybe the Los Angeles Clippers are used to playing in front of crowds this size, but I'm not.

The Ice House in Pasadena

DAY 269 - DECEMBER 2ND, 1996

I went to bed, and was half asleep, before I suddenly bolted upright when I realized that it was December 2nd and I totally forgot to

Paul D'Angelo

pay my bills. I got up and started writing out checks and my stomach got increasingly upset as my checking account balance got closer and closer to zero with each debit.

Maybe the check writing process would be less aggravating if they left more room in the bottom-left-hand-corner of the checks for notes and comments. You could blow off a little steam if you could make out the rent check and write: "Notice: From now on I am deducting one dollar off the rent due for every roach I find in my fetid apartment; for every irresponsible tenant that lets his dog use the hallway like a litter box; for every day that I have to take the stairs because the goddamn elevator doesn't work; for every inch of water the bathtub backs-up whenever we take a shower; for every burn-hole in our carpet; and for every square foot of scum floating on the surface of our swimming pool. Here is your rent check for $8.00. You're lucky I gave you that much. See you next month."

On your life insurance premium check: "If I die young, that would really suck for me and my family, but you'd lose a lot of money because I didn't contribute all that much. If I die an old man, I get to live a long life, but I get screwed because I'll end up paying you guys a lot of money every year that I could have spent on something else. Either way I'm fucked. I hope you're happy."

On the check to a charitable organization: "I am only contributing this money because you sent me so much tear-jerking junk mail pleading for help over the last year, that you made me feel guilty. Please take me off your mailing list in the future. You have obviously made the mistake of confusing me with someone who gives a shit."

On your car insurance premium check: "I get a speeding ticket for going 45 in a 35 zone and you surcharged me for the last three years. Don't you drive in this town? There are a lot of nuts on the road. You should pay *me* a bonus every time I make it home without getting into a major accident. Not that I would be able to squeeze a fucking nickel out of you greedy maggots if I did get a dent in my fender. How do you sleep at night?"

On the check for your monthly car payment: "I can't believe this piece of shit, sorry excuse for a motor vehicle you sold me. After only

L.A. Misérables, Too

25,000 miles I just had to spend $250 out of my pocket for four new shock absorbers because the suspension was shot. What a friggin' lemon. I hope this check bounces as much as my car did."

On the check for your student loan payment: "You know, if I went to class and studied instead of watching *The Three Stooges*, going to keg parties every night, and trying to get laid, maybe I'd have a decent job today and would be able to pay this stupid loan off before I'm eighty-five years old, in a rest home, with drool on my chin and sitting in my own shit, but hey, what can I say... it was worth it."

On the check to pay your parking ticket: "Bite my ass!"

DAY 270 - DECEMBER 3RD, 1996

I drove by the Laugh Factory on Sunset Boulevard before noon and saw a bunch of aspiring comics sitting outside the club, waiting to sign-up for this evening's open-mike auditions. The Laugh Factory has open-mike night every Tuesday that's open to anyone, as long as they are among the first twenty people in line at 6:00 p.m.. If you are lucky enough to make the cut, the reward is three minutes of stage time and, at the end of the amateur segment, you get to stand in line again so you can get your set personally critiqued by the club's owner, Jamie Masada.

When this practice first began, the competition for spots was not nearly as fierce. Eventually though, people began to arrive earlier and earlier to insure that they would be among the first twenty in line come six o'clock. Five o'clock soon became four-thirty, and then three o'clock, and eventually noon, and so on and so on until people were actually sitting outside the club from about 9:00 a.m. on when I first arrived in Hollywood this spring.

Last week I expected to see one of my friends from Boston in line, but he wasn't there. When I called him, he told me that he had arrived at the club with his sleeping bag, notebook of material, books and magazines, around 7:15 a.m., and he was already too late to make the cut.

People were now getting in line at 4:00 a.m. and waiting for *fourteen* hours for the privilege of one-hundred and eighty seconds of spotlight. That works out to over four hours and forty minutes of waiting for each minute of performing. God forbid you have to sneeze on stage… you will have wasted an hour of your day.

Patty Ross called me from her the dressing room on the set of *Roseanne*. She got a speaking part on the television show this week. What a show-off.

I've seen it all now. This evening I was driving down Sunset Boulevard and saw a hooker working the streets in a motorized wheelchair. She had a pair of 68-DDDD tits, spilling out of her low-cut leotard, and she was buzzing around the street corners looking for action. That's determination. The sitting position does save wear and tear on the knees. Either that, or she thinks she found a legal loophole around the city's street-walking criminal ordinance.

"Your honor, how can my client be charged with street-walking when she can't walk? I ask that this matter be dismissed."

Only in Hollywood could someone be the victim of the world's first drive-by blow job.

DAY 271 - DECEMBER 4TH, 199

I had to set the alarm clock for 5:00 a.m. because I was scheduled to be a guest on Groove Radio 103.1, broadcasting from Santa Monica, from six o'clock to 9:00 to promote the shows at the Ice House that begin tonight.

When I arrived I found out that the format this morning is called "Poorman and The Love Doctor" in which listeners call in for advice from the celebrity guests on love problems and sexual issues. Poorman, the DJ, is assisted by an actual MD (which, as an attorney, I believed stood for "Malpractice Defendant") named Danielle, who gave serious medical advice to the callers' queries. My input was not nearly as helpful, but I played along. Some examples of my counsel:

Caller: "I'm gay and, now that Hawaii has become the first state in the nation to legalize marriage between same-sex couples, I plan to get

L.A. Misérables, Too

married to my boyfriend. Do you think we could adopt a child?"

Me: "Sure, that arrangement shouldn't cause any problems. I can see it now: 'Dad, can I borrow the car?' 'I don't know, ask your father.'"

Caller: "I'm a lesbian and my girlfriend wants to move in with me. Is this a good idea?"

Me: "Can I ask you a question? Will you two leave open cans of tuna fish around the apartment for potpourri?"

DJ: "Would you like a free ticket to the singles night dance Friday night?"

Lesbian caller: "No, I don't think I'd fit in."

Me: "Go ahead... You never know, you might have a penis flashback."

Female caller: "I think my boyfriend Gilbert is cheating on me. Am I wrong to be so upset?"

Me: "It's terrible to be in that situation. I know how you feel. It's like that movie. You're home alone at night, wondering 'Who's eating Gilbert's Grape?'"

Female caller: "I'm horny all day, every day. All I think about is sex twenty-four hours a day, seven days a week. Do I have a problem?"

Me: "Honey, you'd need a traffic helicopter to control your rush-hour sex drive.... and, by the way, my address is..."

Caller: "I'm gay and I want to know if I can get HIV if my partner goes down on me."

Doctor: "So far, it has been established that you cannot contact HIV from fellatio, but if there is a cut and any bleeding occurs, it can be transmitted through the bloodstream."

Caller: "So, what should I do to be safe?"

Me: "Make sure your boyfriend doesn't have a chipped tooth."

Gay caller: "My boyfriend is upset at me. How can I get him to like me again?"

Me: "Bend over backwards to please him, open up to your boyfriend, suck-up to him as often as possible, and swallow your pride."

Caller: "Is it OK to kiss my girlfriend right after oral sex?"
Me: "I think that would be a matter of taste."

At one point we had a party line going with Robin Leach of *Lifestyles of the Rich and Famous*, who was on the air from New York. He was promoting the premier of his new show on the USA network and he agreed to dispense advice to the listeners with us.

A male caller stated that his wife was experiencing vaginal dryness and Robin got in on the act and he suggested, "Try WD-40!"

Everyone cracked up because he was such a good sport.

Near the end of the show, one caller identified himself as "Rex" from Hollywood, and his voice sounded suspiciously familiar to me. My only friends who knew I would be on the radio were Patty and my friend Max. Max from Hollywood. "Rex" from Hollywood. Hmmm, I wonder. He said he has a problem with "penile curvature" and his penis is considerably bent at an awkward angle. I had a hunch about this call, so I gave this guy a hard time.

"I don't mean to be insensitive, but do me a favor and tell me what bar you'll be drinking this weekend, because I want to make sure I'm not standing at the urinal to your left in the men's room...

"Hey, 'Captain Hook,' weren't you in that movie *Twister?*... The good news is, you can screw around corners... Would you mind if I call you, 'Boomerang Boy?'... In my other career as an Assistant DA I dealt with thousands of lawyers and criminals, so believe me, I know something about crooks, but not like the one you have in your unit... I'm sorry, I hope you weren't expecting any straight answers."

When I got home, the first thing I did was dial Max's phone number.

"Hello."
"Hello, is Rex there?"
Max laughed…

L.A. Misérables, Too

Bagged!

I feel bad that I'm not working regularly, but it has recently occurred to me that I have met very few people in the entertainment field that are actually working. It seems like everyone I meet in Hollywood is either waiting to hear from someone or another; has something in development; is involved in negotiations; is between projects; is trying to work out a deal; has something pending; is in the process of attempting to get something or another financed; or is considering a number of different proposals.

Who the hell is working?

I dropped off a sitcom treatment to a management company in Beverly Hills this afternoon around 4:30. I found a space with a parking meter on the street, put money in the meter, then ran into the office building, leaving my friend Max waiting in my car. I ran back out in less than five minutes. My car had been moved to another parking space about forty feet down the street and Max was sitting in the driver's seat looking nervous.

"What's going on Max?"

"An asshole wrote you a $40.00 parking ticket."

"You're kidding, right?"

"I wish I was. I'm sorry. I didn't see him."

"But I had time on the meter."

"Ya, but there's a small sign behind the tree that says (in small print) 'No parking from 4:00 to 6:00 PM for white cars whose total sum of the digits of the license plate are not a factor of five on an even numbered first Wednesdays of an odd numbered month during a waning moon occurring within 30 days of the winter equinox,' so you're fucked."

"And where were you, Max?"

"I didn't see him."

"Didn't see the... the... the human... the human-sized human?"... for a total lack of a vocabulary under the stress caused by the sudden possibility of a financial crisis.

"I was in the car, but the guy snuck up from behind in my blindspot."

"If I may... I must say, that is one Helen Keller-Stevie Wonder-Ray Charles-José Feliciano-sized blind-spot you have there, my friend."

For want of a quarter... the meter was lost. For want of a valid meter... a ticket was written. For issuance of a ticket... a fine must be paid. For payment of a fine... a check must be written. For a check to be cashed... there must be money deposited. For money to be deposited... there must be an income. For income to be... uh... incoming... there must be a job. For a job to be offered... there must be a showcase. For a showcase to be set-up... there must be an agent. For an agent to be interested... there must be a showcase. For a showcase to be set-up... there must be an agent. For an agent to be interested... there must be a showcase. For a showcase to be set-up... there must be an agent. For an agent to be interested... there must be a showcase... Wait a second, I think the record's skipping... let me check...

Nope, it isn't.

That's encouraging.

I'm a whiz in the kitchen. I pulled the paper back to open a cylindrical container of those Pillsbury "Poppin' Fresh" dinner rolls and I jumped about a foot in the air when the thing popped open. I'm so skittish. From my reaction, you'd think I was working on a friggin' bomb squad in Beirut.

I have to move off this busy street and get some peace and quiet. It's constantly noisy on Hollywood Boulevard. I don't want it to sound like I'm complaining, but today I was talking on the phone in my living room while outside my apartment horns beeped, sirens wailed, tires screeched, buses belched, car alarms blared, people yelled profanities in foreign tongues, and trucks ground their gears, and my friend on the other end actually asked me if I was calling from a phone booth off the freeway.

I YELLED, "NOOO, I'M NOT... I'M STANDING IN THE MIDDLE MY LIVING ROOM, THANK YOU VERY MUCH."

I have a show at the Ice House tonight, but I have an upset stomach that has kept me running to the bathroom. I can't get sick during the show, so I drank some Pepto Bismal or, as I like to call it, "Liquid Cork." I gulped it straight from the bottle, which means that I should be going to the bathroom again in, say... the early spring.

Tonight was Groove Radio Night at the club and my new friend, Poorman, the radio host from this morning, is the guest host for the comedy show. He introduced the first act, a woman comic, by telling the crowd that, if they yelled loud enough, she may show them her tits. Before he brought me to the stage, he promised any woman in the audience a Groove 103 T-shirt if they were willing to remove the shirt they were now wearing and put the Groove T-shirt on in front of the crowd. One girl actually went on stage and stripped down to her bra to get the free T-shirt. Needless to say, by the time I got to perform, the crowd was in such a frenzy, the room had the atmosphere of a cockfight in Saigon.

DAY 272 - DECEMBER 5TH, 1996

I have been living on the West Coast for almost nine months and I've shown absolutely no sign of losing my thick Boston accent. I still can't pronounce an "R" to save my life. I still sound like, "Paaahk the caaahh in Haaahved Yaaahd."

Today I went into the Virgin Records Megastore and asked the woman behind the counter if she could tell me if a particular movie had been released on video yet.

"Sure, which movie is that?"

I said, "*Swimming with Sharks* with actor Kevin Spacey."

She wrinkled her nose, expressing obvious confusion.

"Swimming with Shaq?"

"Ya, it's a movie about treading water with a 7'2" basketball player... No, no, no... *Swimming with Sharks*."

"Swimming with Shocks?"

"That's right, in the film, someone throws a hairdryer in the swimming pool... No, no, no... Sharks! ... Sharks!... Sharks! You know, sharks!"

I performed the *Jaws* theme while I attempted to form a fin on my back with a magazine that was on the counter.

"Bum-bum, bum-bum, bum-bum, bum-bum, bum-bum..."

(smiling) "Ohhhhh! Sharks! Right, *Swimming with Sharks!!*... No, sorry, we don't have it."

That was a waste of time.

My life; a phone conversation:

"Hello, this is Ab-Roller abdominal fitness hot-line, how can I help you?"

"Ya, I bought this Ab-Roller a couple months ago, and the ad said you were guaranteed to lose weight and inches off your waist in a month, but I've been doing it every day and I've seen no progress, so I want my money back."

"Sir, if you read the guarantee closely, it only applies if you have followed our two-step abdominal-reduction program faithfully throughout that entire month. Do you have the instruction booklet that came with the apparatus?"

"I'm looking for it... Ya, here it is."

"Go to the part that describes our two-step abdominal-reduction program."

"OK...I'm reading it."

TWO-STEP AB-REDUCTION PROGRAM
Step #1: Use Ab-Roller, as instructed, on a consistent basis.
Step #2: Eat a lot less.

"Eat a lot less? What do you mean, 'Eat a lot less?' I'm not gonna give up eating... I don't need a Marky Mark washboard stomach like the guy in your ads, but I don't want this waistline of mine to get any worse, while I occasionally indulge myself in some... let's call them... 'happy foods.' This is ridiculous!"

"Well see, there's your problem, sir. You have to make a commitment to the program or it's just not going to work for you."

"But on your television infomercial you guaranteed results... You guaranteed you'd lose inches of fat."

"You will... if you follow the recommended program."

"This is bullshit. You'd lose weight and inches if all you did was stop eating without using the Ab-Roller, right?... Am I correct?"

"Well, of course, but..."

"Then you *admit* it!... See?! I'm so much *smarter* than you people... I'm not one of the naïve fools who buys into your bullshit... You can't fool me, I'm smarter than you."

"Yes, you are, sir... much smarter. Now enjoy the useless new Ab-Roller that you foolishly bought with little money you don't have. Good bye."

People's stupidity continues to amaze me. I'm watching the six o'clock news. A couple weeks ago, a news anchor read a story about a young woman from Irvine who was arrested for plotting to kill her identical twin sister, who looked exactly like her.

As he read the story, a photo of the suspect was displayed in the background over his shoulder.

At the end of the piece, the anchor stated that the victim asked that her face not be shown.

Think about that one for just a second

Tonight he was reporting a tragic accident on a Los Angeles highway in which a crane operator involved in bridge construction lost control of a massive steel beam that weighed several tons, and it dropped on the van of a passing motorist, who was killed instantly. They showed a picture of the vehicle involved and the entire front-half of the van was crushed as flat as a pancake. The anchor felt it was necessary to add that the police reported that the driver was not wearing his seat belt.

Now, would it really have made a difference if he had his seat belt on? If this poor bastard was wearing a flak vest under a suit of armor, a football helmet, welder's safety glasses, goalie equipment, and the car had an airbag in the roof, he still would have been as flat as a flounder after this mishap. I suppose the fact that he ate bacon with his breakfast this morning and was a heavy smoker contributed to his untimely demise also.

It was raining lightly when I left for the Ice House tonight. Before I got two blocks from my apartment there was gridlock in the streets. Cars were crawling along a foot or two at a time and traffic was backed up in every direction.

Paul D'Angelo

Shit, I thought I was going to be late for the show. There obviously must've been a major accident that occurred up ahead. I made a couple of quick maneuvers and tried to find an alternative route to the 101 freeway, but the entire city was congested. It took me twenty minutes before I finally got on the ramp to the 101 and, as I merged into traffic on the freeway, I saw that the traffic was bumper to bumper for miles ahead. I started to panic because it was getting close to show time and I still had a good drive ahead of me.

Eventually the backup dissipated and traffic began to flow normally but, by then, I was already tense, aggravated and running fifteen minutes behind schedule. That's when it dawned on me that there was no accident, there was no construction, there was no natural disaster… the entire community had come to a standstill because there was a light drizzle… a thin layer of moisture on the road about the density of the sweat on the outside of a cold bottle of beer.

What is it with these Southern Californians?

They all love to surf, but they don't want to hydroplane.

Aren't they basically the same thing?

CHAPTER SIXTEEN
The fool on the hill...

DAY 273 - DECEMBER 6TH, 1996

My friend, Paul Caputo, called me from Boston to tell me that they were having their first big snowstorm of the winter. He mentioned that he hates the snow, but his dog loves it and told me about an incident that happened on Thanksgiving Day.

Paul's Aunt stayed up late the night before to bake a homemade cheesecake for the Thanksgiving dinner. There was so much food at Paul's mother's house there was no room left in the refrigerator. When the aunt arrived with the cheesecake they couldn't fit it in the fridge, so Paul placed it just outside the backdoor until dessert was served, because it was cold outside.

Well, I guess someone let the dog out during dinner and she walked around to the back of the house and proceeded to eat the entire cheesecake.

I exclaimed, "Oh my God! She must have shit!"

Paul said, "No, she was fine. She didn't even throw up."

I said, "I meant your aunt, bonehead."

Paul D'Angelo

DAY 274 - DECEMBER 7TH, 1996

What a long, strange trip it's been. I started out the week as the feature act at the Ice House, meaning that I was the middle comic in the show. By tonight, I had become the headliner, at one of the toughest clubs in the country to get into, which is no small feat.

There was one show Wednesday, one Thursday, two Friday, three tonight, and one show tomorrow night, Sunday. All of the shows went phenomenally well for me, except for the late show Friday night when a table of tough-looking, Mexican gang-bangers became loud and disruptive and everyone working at the club was afraid to confront them, including me. I didn't want the hombres to "bust a cap in my ass".

A bad show will eventually pass from my memory.

A bullet would most certainly stick in my head… or body.

DAY 275 - DECEMBER 8TH, 1996

David Rattigan was a Boston-area newspaper writer who wrote a couple of features on me back in 1994 and later became a friend of mine. I was just making a copy of an article that Dave wrote for *The Massachusetts Lawyer* and came upon an interesting example of how I sometimes used humor to prove a point during a trial:

> …*as in the case of a man who caught a neighborhood teenager breaking into his car, called the police and held the kid until the police arrived.*
>
> *When the man arrived home that evening, he'd observed the teenager on the steps of the house next door, highly intoxicated. Suspicious, he checked his window a few minutes later, and saw the kid breaking into his car, trying to steal his stereo.*
>
> *At the trial, the young, zealous defense attorney got the man to admit that, when he went into his driveway to apprehend the young thief, he'd brought his nine-iron along with him.*
>
> *"He was embarrassed about it, but admitted that he did," said Murphy, who hadn't known about the golf club until that moment.*

L.A. Misérables, Too

"(The defense attorney) tried to make him look like the bad guy. She really zeroed in, trying to take the focus off her client.

"The judge asked if I had any questions on redirect examination. At that point the jury was a little confused, and I wanted to impress upon them that this was not the issue, but more of a smoke screen," explained Murphy.

"So I got up and said, 'Just one question, sir - Why did you choose the nine-iron for that shot?'

"Before he could answer I said, 'No further questions.' The jury laughed and understood the point that I was trying to make. They came back with a guilty verdict in 10 minutes."

DAY 276 - DECEMBER 9^(TH), 1996

I called my friend Christine in Boston to wish her a happy birthday yesterday. She was drinking eggnog, with Christmas music playing in the background, decorating a ten foot Christmas tree with her husband and family, putting up the bulbs, tinsel and blinking lights, with a star at the top and nicely wrapped presents piled underneath in their festive, new holiday home. She asked how our Christmas was going. All I could say is, "We have a candle that *smells* like a tree."

You know you're poor when the only decorated Christmas tree you can afford is to use raspberry-red, lemon-yellow, and orange-orange *Trix* cereal as ornaments, and glue them to the pine tree air freshener that used to be hanging from the rear view mirror of your car.

I really miss participating in the Christmas traditions, like picking out the Christmas tree. Well, actually, it's not as if the act was all that traditional for me because I had a fake tree. I didn't get bundled-up, bring the family together, and go out in search of a perfectly shaped tree on a beautiful, snowy night, but I made the best of it.

I would have a couple rum and eggnogs with my friends. Then we'd put on our winter coats, climb up to my chilly attic, look around under the eaves, and then I'd suddenly point and proclaim excitedly, *"That one! The phony tree in the cardboard box! It's perfect! We'll take it!"*

Fa la la la la, la la la la...

DAY 277 - DECEMBER 10^(TH), 1996

It has been raining for days and I went to the Laugh Factory this evening to hang out for a while. During the show a huge sign fell off the side of the building and crashed to the sidewalk. Jamie, the club owner, and a bunch of comics ran out in the rain to check out the damage. I told Jamie, with a smile, *"And if I don't get any spots next week, the sign's gonna come down again, understand?"*

DAY 278 - DECEMBER 11TH, 1996

It's still cold, rainy and miserable and the weather fits my mood. All I need now is a total eclipse.

I called the Laugh Factory to see if I got any spots this week. I asked the kid who answers the phone if they had fixed the sign yet, he said they hadn't, and I told him what I had said to Jamie last night. He left to check out the list, then got back on the phone and said that it looks like I'm gonna have to knock the sign down again because there was nothing for me.

My big afternoon consisted of accompanying Patty to the Laundromat down on Sunset. We walked in and Patty started throwing all her clothes in the washers. At about the same time, we started to sniff the air and make faces like we both drank sour milk.

"I smell urine."

"Pew, stinky! Me too. Where's it coming from, Paul?"

We looked around and saw this homeless guy, sitting on the floor in his underwear, drying off with a wad of paper-towels he got from the dispenser on the wall after he gave himself a bath with the water from the drinking fountain, while all the clothes he owned were in the drier.

Patty, wearing a pair of old, tattered sweat pants that most people would be using to polish their car with by now said, "No one understands what we're going through back home. No one would believe how we live. They think it's so glamorous for us, living in Hollywood, because they watch the E! Network every night. They think we're going to movie premiers every evening, attending swank Hollywood parties, and rubbing elbows with celebrities… and here I am, in a laundromat, putting my clothes into the same washing machine that that disgusting bum just used for his filthy things."

"Just hope he used the hot water, Patty. Hot water kills cooties… although I'm pretty sure he has a very hearty strain of some seriously rugged cooties that have survived much worse."

"Remind me to bring you along again. Will you do that for me, Paul? You giant pain in my fat ass."

C'mon, sing some Christmas carols with me, Patty!...
"We're living like scum, hanging out with a bum,
Washin' in a winter wonderland..."
C'mon, everybody join in...
"I'm dreaming of a white-trash Christmas..."

DAY 279 - DECEMBER 12TH, 1996

There is absolutely no food left in this apartment so I decided to make out my Christmas cards so I could at least lick the glue on the envelopes for breakfast.

I'm tired of living like this, but hey, money isn't everything. And if you ever think money is everything, remember this: After he ran out of $100 bills, Thurston Howell III had to wipe his ass with palm leaves just like everybody else.

DAY 280 - DECEMBER 13TH, 1996

I wonder how my life would different if I had never tried stand-up comedy and, instead, joined some big law firm like *Harpo, Chico, Groucho, Comet, Cupid, Donder, Blitzen and Feinstein.*

I got many offers from law firms to work as a trial attorney. I remember one lawyer who tried to lure me away from the District Attorney's office. We had a case together in which two Portuguese friends were highly intoxicated, left a club to take a leak in the alley, and decided to compare the size of their manhood. When one of the drunks proclaimed himself the winner, his "best friend" took out a knife and cut his penis off. Honest, true case. The severed penis was reattached by surgeons, but I don't know if the victim ever regained function.

We had a trial date scheduled that had to be postponed because the judge explained that there was no Portuguese interpreter available for the victim. When we addressed the judge I said, "Your honor, we have everyone here for trial and I'd hate to postpone it to another date. If you want, I can interpret for the victim."

The judge moved his eyeglasses down to the end of his nose and, looking over the glasses curiously asked me, "And you can speak Portuguese, mister district attorney?"

I answered, "No, your honor, but I'm pretty sure his testimony will be…

'AHHHHHHHHHHHHHHHHHHH!'"

He banged his gavel down and said, "This is not one of your comedy clubs, Mr. Murphy!" as he tried to suppress a smile he couldn't hide.

The most amazing thing about that case was that the charges were eventually dropped, because the victim refused to testify against his best pal who had sliced his penis off. That is *truly* a close friendship. As far as I'm concerned, you can be my best pal since childhood, but if you so much as wave a sharp object anywhere within the general vicinity of my dick; a can opener, tweezers, a set of keys, even a jagged hangnail… you're gonna be on my shit-list for a very long time.

I stopped working out for the last month and a half in a funk of self-loathing and I have gained a couple pounds around the waist. Last night I hit a new low by baking a whole plate full of chocolate-chip cookies and eating most of them while I sat on the couch and watched television like a lazy lump. Determined to whip myself back into shape, I went into the apartment complex's gym this morning, hopped on the exercise bicycle, and didn't stop until I was totally exhausted.

Proud of myself, I looked at the digital display on the bike, which told me that, at the rate I was peddling, I had burned something like 12 calories over the last half hour… Twelve calories? You're shitting me. I believe that my effort was approximately equivalent to canceling out *maybe* one chocolate chip in just one of those dozen and a half cookies I ate, which means that my career as a supermodel is about as promising as my career as a comedian.

DAY 281 - DECEMBER 14TH, 1996

I was out at a club last night and saw an actor on a popular television show that comes from Peabody, Massachusetts, where I used to supervise the DA's office at the district court for five years. I approached him, introduced myself, and told him that I was friends with two of his best pals that he grew up with... and, right in the middle of the sentence, he turned his back on me and started talking to a girl with big breasts while I stood there like a fucking schmuck.

I learned that in Los Angeles, tits trump most any competing interest.

That's right. Tits trump... drugs high... movie producers wild.

DAY 282 - DECEMBER 15TH, 1996

Sign that the romance stage of the relationship is over:

I'm searching through the apartment and Kelly asks what I am looking for. I said, "I'm trying to find a magazine to read in the bathroom."

She says, "I have to go in there to put my makeup on. Make sure it's not a stinky one."

Listen closely and you can hear the apartment door slamming shut behind a whipped and demoralized winged cherub named Cupid, leaving in frustration and holding his little nose.

DAY 283 - DECEMBER 16TH, 1996

Christmas season means loads of toy advertisements on television and in the newspapers. Amazingly, with all the new toys, Malibu Barbie remains one of the most popular dolls of all time.

I can see why. I didn't appreciate how accurate the doll was until I had lived in Southern California for a while. The little doll is just like the real Malibu beach babe. She's blonde and beautiful, her head is hollow, she has plastic tits, anyone with enough cash can take her home, and there is absolutely no way possible that I could ever get inside her.

L.A. Misérables, Too

DAY 284 - DECEMBER 17TH, 1996

The *Los Angeles Times* coverage of the OJ Simpson civil trial indicates that the expert pathologist testifying for the defense admitted yesterday, upon cross-examination, that he customarily receives a fee of $2500 to $3000 a day for consulting on cases, however he was billing OJ only $1500 a day "because of the defendant's inability to pay more money." Wow, if poor OJ's legal bills keep piling up and he loses the civil judgment, I expect to see him holding a handwritten sign near a traffic light in Los Angeles that says, "WILL KILL FOR FOOD."

This town can be amazing in some respects. Several times a day I will find myself muttering out loud, "Jesus Christ!" when some beautiful Hollywood hard-body walks by.

It's a spontaneous reaction that is triggered by force of habit and I feel guilty whenever I use the Lord's name as an exclamation. However, in the true spirit of my legal background, I believe that I have found a loophole in the Ten Commandments that excludes me from guilt in these situations. Catholics are taught that, "Thou shalt not take the Lord's name in vain," "vain" taken from the Latin *vanus,* meaning empty; of no real value. Well, in the context of reacting to a beautiful woman, I mean it as a compliment, as in "the Lord has created another exquisite masterpiece on the canvas that is the human body." I'm not using the Lord's name in vain, I'm using it in celebration. And it just so happens that I live in the middle of perhaps, the world's finest gallery of female art. Therefore, St. Peter, I ask you to find me not guilty of the aforementioned violations.

What do you think?... What? OK, OK, I might have to plead out to a short stint in limbo to atone for my sins.

I went to the Laugh Factory tonight. On Tuesday evenings, after the twenty open-mike comics who have waited on the sidewalk for fourteen hours have all done their three minute sets, there are customarily two or three showcase spots in which comics perform ten minute auditions for Jamie Masada, the club owner. It's December now and, if an established comic wishes to reserve a showcase audition date now, he will get one in, maybe, mid-April, so it's important to make the best of the opportunity.

Tonight I was sitting with several comics from Boston in the upstairs balcony. One comic came all the way from some mid-western town for his showcase and he was doing so-so until he did one routine about him and his twin brother. He referred to the psychic phenomenon that twins, even though they are separated by thousands of miles, have actually been known to coincidentally experience the pain felt by their sibling.

Then the comic hit himself on the head with the microphone to demonstrate how he'd get back at his brother for one reason or another. The joke was decent, yet unspectacular but, as he continued on with his routine, the crowd slowly began to double-over in hysterics. They were going nuts and the comic started to visibly gain confidence, feeding off the crowd's reaction and feeling that he was really winning them over.

It was then that I noticed that the comic had opened a good-sized cut on his forehead when he whacked himself with the microphone. Blood was seeping from the gash, flowing down his brow and along the sides of his face, and the wounded comedian didn't have a clue, probably thinking that the bright lights were making him sweat profusely. I turned to the other comics, who were not really paying attention, and said, "Guys, look at his forehead!" Now the group in the balcony was howling along with the crowd below, while the poor guy who was hemorrhaging onstage was thinking that he was having the set of his life.

Who says comedy is a non-contact sport? You want to make it big as a comedian? Blood, sweat and tears, man. Blood, sweat and tears.

On the way home, I got behind a Yugo that had a "TURBO" sticker on the back. Why would anyone buy a turbocharged Yugo? So they can race quickly over to the K-Mart before the "blue light special" on polyester pants is over?

CHAPTER SEVENTEEN
I really don't mind if I sit this one out...

DAY 285 - DECEMBER 18TH, 1996

Santa Claus is not coming to my apartment this year. We have no money to buy presents, we can't afford decorations, and I'm not flying home to see my family until after Christmas day, so I'm just not celebrating the holiday this year. Bah, humbug!

I have poured gallons of Draino and Liquid Plumber down the drain in our bathtub, but it's still clogged. Our shower is so backed up, I'm thinking of buying some guppies at the pet store and just converting the tub into a fish tank.

As I left the apartment this afternoon, Kelly announced that she hopes I "die in a car crash on the way to my show tonight." If that's not an indication that our relationship has hit bottom, it's at least a strong suggestion that we shouldn't waste our time choosing a china pattern, picking out invitations and renting a hall.

My show was way out in the sticks, an hour and a half east of Los Angeles. I was driving through the mountains... up a mountain, then down the mountain... and, on the steep decline, they had signs posted warning drivers to be aware of RUNAWAY TRUCKS.

Apparently there are trucks that get fed up with hauling freight every day and announce," I've packed some spare tires and I'm running away to Hollywood to become a star! ... Like the "Dixie Lee" in *Dukes of Hazard*... or "Kit" on *Night Rider*... or the van on *Scoobie Doo*... or maybe like the Clampetts' jalopy... or *Christine*... or Starsky & Hutch's Torino... or Herbie... or the *Smokey & the Bandit* car... or even 007's Aston Martin..."

Meanwhile, his parents are home in their garage lamenting... "I'm so worried about him alone in Hollywood. He's got low-mileage and it's all on the interstate... that city will eat him alive."

"I can't say I'm surprised. To be frank, I never thought that kid's engine was hitting on all eight cylinders, if you know what I mean... and he could use at least six months at a 'half-weigh station' till he gets off of the high-test, if you ask me."

"But what if he ends up in one of those "snuff" films where they drive you off the side of a cliff and you tumble end-over-end-over-end-over-end until you burst into flames at the bottom of a ravine?... Ohhh, why would he do this?"

"Well dear, he always did have a lot of drive."

When it comes down to it, a runaway truck is really in no different situation than I am... heading downhill fast and praying for that one big brake.

Since I didn't die in a fiery pile-up on the highway, to Kelly's dismay, after the show I rented a video and went over my friend Max's apartment. The previews for the remake of *The Island of Dr. Moreau* showed a huge Marlon Brando sitting in the darkness, enveloped in swirling fog, just like they did with him in *Apocalypse Now*. Marlon, a superb actor, has gotten so damn fat that, in every movie he's been in for years, they prop him up behind a desk, or in a chair, in the dark or in a fog, and drape him in a small tent to conceal his monstrous bulk. It seems the last time I saw Marlon Brando standing up in a movie was just before he collapsed in the tomato patch in the original *Godfather*, filmed in 1972. He hit the ground and hasn't been able to get up on his own ever since.

I love it when people mean well, but ask obvious questions. I got up in the middle of the movie and walked to the rear of Max's tiny apartment.

L.A. Misérables, Too

"Paul, do you want me to show you where the bathroom is?"

"That's OK, Max. I should be able to find the bathroom on my own. It's the little room with all the tiles, the tub and the toilet, right? I certainly hope so, because that's the room I've been peeing in at our place."

I came home late and Kelly was sound asleep. It doesn't really matter... Since we haven't been getting along, we really don't have much of a physical relationship. If this keeps up, they could name an antiperspirant after us... like, for example, Soft n' Dry.

DAY 286 - DECEMBER 19TH, 1996

I have started to receive some Christmas cards in the mail, several of which incorporate a beautiful photograph of the people's kids. Each year, every card I have ever seen of this type shows a perfect photograph of perfect children, perfectly behaved, with perfectly adorable faces, and perfect smiles and perfect little haircuts, wearing perfect little outfits, getting along perfectly with their perfect brothers and perfect sisters, in front of a perfect Christmas tree.

Where are the families with ugly, misbehaved kids? I've never, ever received a Christmas photograph card with a picture of homely, unattractive, spoiled rotten, nasty, bad tempered children with bratty dispositions, yet I know they're out there. I've seen them.

I think that the parents with children like that take a good, long look at the kids, then look at their spouse, take another look at the kids, shake their head, and ask, "What do you think?"

(with a shrug) *"Hallmark?"*

(acknowledging nod) "Ya, I agree... Hallmark."

I had a show at the Laugh Factory tonight. Here's a funny story that would be unusual if it occurred in almost any city besides Hollywood. Dana, who was the hostess sitting patrons for the comedy show this evening, sat three attractive young women near the stage. Shortly thereafter, a party of three good looking young men, around the same age as the group of females, were looking to be seated. Trying to play matchmaker, Dana addressed one of the guys and said, "Would you like to sit next to the three cute girls in the front?"

He answered in a feminine lisp, *"Not unless the three girls have three cute brothers."*

DAY 287 - DECEMBER 20TH, 1996

When I walked outside the apartment building I almost stepped in some dog-shit left by a German Shepherd formerly known as Prince.

That's when you know you're made it huge in the entertainment field, when you are referred to by only one name and everyone knows who you are. Madonna... Elvis... Arnold... Roseannne... Oprah... Sly... Cher... Fabio... Rosie... Beavis... Butthead... Prince took it to a whole new level when he decided that he would hereafter be referred to by just a symbol.

I want to be bigger than that. I want to take this ridiculous name-game to a new extreme. I want to be so huge, so popular, so recognized worldwide, that my name is nothing. Yes, that's right... nothing at all. My name would be "   ."

That way every blank piece of paper, every empty page in a book, every clear computer screen, would be all about me. Every coat with a plain, unadorned back would become my tour jacket. Each vacant billboard would be advertising for me. Every clear, cloudless day will be the same as having sky-writers print my name across the heavens. Every woman that just lies there quietly when she's having sex will actually be screaming out my name. All the space in between the daily newspaper columns would provide me with free publicity. Every bare biceps would be adorned with my tattoo. And every time people were silent, they would be talking about *me*.... the artist known as "   ."

How clever!!! Brilliant, if I may say so myself!

Hold on. Wait a second... if that's the case, every blank check would have <u>my</u> signature on it... Shit!!!

OK. Never mind... it was a stupid idea anyway.

Kelly had a tough week. She had an infected tooth that gave her a terrible toothache last weekend, but her dentist couldn't see her until Monday. He gave her a root canal, but he didn't remove the entire infection before he sealed the tooth back up, so she was in pain for several more days until he recommended that she see a specialist. She asked her dentist what the orthodontist's name was that he was recommending.

The dentist said his name was "Eddie".

"Does the doctor have a last name?"

"Ya, but we just call him "Eddie."

He's got to be good. It's Hollywood and he only goes by one name. (see above)

DAY 289 - DECEMBER 22nd, 1996

Living with a woman for the first time in my life has given me some idea of what it's like to be married. This is what I have learned so far:

After you've had a lousy day at work... when you feel like the whole world is against you... when you're in a bad mood from dealing with assholes all afternoon... when your work-day has left you feeling rotten, grouchy and aggravated... it must be nice to know that there's someone special waiting at home for you who you can make feel just as miserable so they can share your pain.

Apparently, I'm that special someone.

DAY 290 - DECEMBER 23RD, 1996

Christmas is coming, then I'm going. I'm leaving for Boston the day after Christmas and I'm returning on January seventh. I won't be missing much. In Hollywood, it is said that, "anyone you can get on the phone at Christmastime, is not worth getting a hold of in the first place."

DAY 291 - DECEMBER 24TH, 1996

I can't believe it. I wait around for months to get stage time at the LA clubs and I got a call today to do a twenty minute set at the Improvisation on Christmas Eve. Who the hell is going to attend a comedy show on Christmas Eve? The audience, if there is an audience, would have to be drawn from those people of the Buddhist, Muslim, Mormon, Jehovah Witness and Hindu faiths (all of which are *huge* supporters of stand-up comedy, by the way); atheists (who are going to be in a foul mood because they didn't get any presents, not to mention the fact that they have nothing to yell out when they're having an orgasm); Jews (many of which leave town on vacation during the Christmas holiday); and maybe a couple of down-on-their luck, destitute losers who are wandering the streets and contemplating suicide because they have nowhere to go on Christmas Eve, then see a light on in the window of the Improv, so they happen to drift in.

There might also be a few half-in-the-bag, stragglers who visited their family on Christmas Eve, had too much to drink, got into an argument with the relatives, and need to get out of the house for a while. Even the waitresses, bartenders and staff are going to be resentful about having been scheduled to work on Christmas Eve. In other words, no one who could possibly be out tonight will be in a good mood to watch comedy.

I saw a column in the *LA Times* announcing the Laugh Factory's annual free Christmas Day dinner "for struggling and/or lonely comics, actors and others in the entertainment industry." There are four separate seatings, which shows you how many of my peers qualify under the heading of "struggling and/or lonely."

The article goes on to note that, "The menu includes turkey and all the trimmings, plus on-stage comedy." Hey, I'm surprised I didn't land that stellar gig too. If there's a comedy crowd anywhere that's better than a collection of Buddhists, Muslims, Mormons, Jehovah Witnesses, Hindus, suicidal depressives, and bitter drunks, it has to be a group of "struggling and/or lonely" people on Christmas day.

I did all my Christmas shopping in two days, except for my parents, and I have no idea whatsoever what to get them. This happens every time it is my mother's birthday, my father's birthday, Mother's Day, Father's Day, and Christmas. I never, ever know what my parents need and no clue what they could possibly want. I am totally stumped

L.A. Misérables, Too

as to what would make them happy. I have been so frustrated at times that I have actually contemplated getting my parents hooked on drugs, just so I will always know exactly what they would need, want, and appreciate on each and every such occasion.

Shopping for them would instantly be a snap.

(ding dong) "Hi, mom! Look what I got you! Hope you like it. Happy Mother's Da...."

(snatching the present away and frantically ripping open the wrapping paper while she slinks off to the bathroom, mumbling) "Ya... ya... ya, thanks, Paul.... ya, thank you... Love it...sorry, gotta go..." (bathroom door slams shut and locks)

"Bye, mom! Enjoy!"

The Hollywood Improvisation on Melrose Avenue

(later) I couldn't have been more wrong about the show at the Improv tonight. To the surprise of everybody there, the club was rather busy, with over sixty people in attendance. Since it was Christmas Eve, I wasn't in the mood to perform jokes from my regular set-list, so I tailored my entire act around the Christmas season and winter in New England. Near the end of my set I saw the red light at the back of the showroom go on, indicating that I had two minutes left, and I informed the crowd that I had to wrap up.

My show had gone over so well, people immediately voiced their protest and several patrons yelled out for me to stay on, which really made my night. When I left the stage and went to the front lounge, several of the comics and managers, some of whom I had never met prior to this evening, came up to me and congratulated me on my set. What a pleasant surprise. I had looked upon the evening with trepidation but, when I left the stage, I felt like I had shared a very special moment with these people. Moments like this make the struggle and sacrifice worth it somehow.

DAY 292 - DECEMBER 25TH, 1996

This was not a traditional Christmas in any sense. I slept late, worked out, and then packed for my flight tomorrow. I got my well-traveled luggage out of the front storeroom and looked at the beat-up, leather garment bag that had been given to me as a present at my going away party when I left the Essex County District Attorney's office. I remember showing the beautiful gift to my mother, who advised me, "Don't bring that bag on the plane with you. They'll steal that in a second!"

In my usual sarcastic tone I replied, "What am I going to do with it, put it on display in the 'Expensive Suitcase Exhibit' at the Murphy Luggage Museum?"

My poor mother is often the recipient of my fresh retorts. Some examples:

After I arrived in Miami to catch a cruise ship, I realized that I forgot to inform my parents that I would be out of town, so I called my mother from the airport.

"Hi, Mom. I just got off of a flight and I wanted to let you and Dad know that I'll be away for a couple of weeks."

"I'm glad you called. Did you arrive safely?"

"No, I'm actually calling from a mountainside in the Andes, where I'm eating the flesh of the other passengers to survive, but the dead

L.A. Misérables, Too

guy next to me had a cell phone and I thought I'd give you a call to say 'hi' before we carve up his fat ass for dinner."

"Don't be a wise-guy."

"Sorry, ma."

On a trip to Boston with my parents, my mother asks, "Let's get something to eat. Paul. Where would be a good place to get Chinese food around here?"

"My guess would be a Chinese restaurant."

"Don't be a wise-guy."

"Sorry, ma."

I'm on the phone with my mother. When she asks what I am doing, I tell her that I'm heating up some food.

"Are you hungry?"

"No, I just felt bad for the food. I thought it might be getting a bit chilly in the refrigerator."

"Don't be a wise-guy."

"Sorry, ma."

As I put my jacket on and hug my parents, getting ready to head home after a visit to their house, my mother holds up my key-chain and warns me, "Paul, don't leave without your car keys!"

"Mom, thank God you reminded me. I hate it when I drive the car half-way home and suddenly realize, 'Shit! I forgot my car keys!' and have to turn around and come back for them."

"Don't be a wise-guy."

"Sorry, ma."

As I blow on my soup, she'll ask, "Is it hot?"

"No, mom, I'm trying to arouse the soup."

"Don't be a wise-guy."

"Sorry, ma."

My other large suitcase used to have four little wheels on the bottom, so you could pull it behind you, but they lasted maybe two trips. After that, one wheel was locked in a permanent right hand turn, another was stuck pointing in the opposite direction, one broke off, and the other wheel was frozen and wouldn't turn at all, acting as a brake and leaving a black skid mark behind me as I struggled to tug the bag along like a stubborn Doberman that doesn't want to go for a walk. The bag got me so frustrated that I eventually knocked the remaining wheels off with a hammer. Such is the life of a comedy gunslinger. Have jokes, will travel.

Kelly and I spent Christmas night watching a horror movie at the Sunset 5 cinema, a far cry from last year's Christmas night when we sat in the front row of the Broadway production of the Who's *Tommy* in Boston's Colonial Theater. On the way out of the cinema, the people sitting behind us told me that I frightened them more than the movie because I would jump out of my seat whenever something scary happened.

Like a little kid, I left the light on in the kitchen when I went to bed, apparently assuming that the glowing 40 watt bulb will be an effective deterrent to any insane, homicidal-maniac, demented, meat-cleaver wielding, mass-murdering, psychopathic serial-killer who may want to butcher me under cover of darkness.

CHAPTER EIGHTEEN
Say goodbye to Hollywood...

DAY 293 - DECEMBER 26TH, 1996

I flew home today.

I'm quite sure that the women who work the gates at the airport have heard it all before, but I got one to laugh out loud this morning at LAX before I boarded the airplane bound for Boston.

There was a long line at the check-in because of storms in the Midwest and it was rather hectic at the gate when I stepped-up to the counter and addressed the stressed-out American Airlines employee.

"Hi."

"Good morning, sir... I must ask you, have you received any gifts or packages from a stranger?"

I answered, "Yes ma'am, I have."

She looked up at me, surprised by my answer and very serious.

"And just who would that person be, sir?"

I said, "Santa Claus... but what's that got to do with my seat assignment?"

My flight arrives in Boston at 4:30 p.m. and I have a show tonight at 8:30, which doesn't give me much time to spend with my family. My flight was very uncomfortable. If the woman sitting to my left spreads her legs like she spreads her arms, I predict that she'll have a lot of children. She pinned me against the wall of the plane with her girth and my entire right side was frozen solid from the cold over the six hour flight. When I walked off the plane I looked like a stroke victim.

I only got to spend a short time with my parents before I left to perform at Nick's Comedy Stop at the Kowloon restaurant in Saugus. I have six shows scheduled in the next four nights and, best of all, I get to work with my good friend Patty Ross, who is also home from LA for the holidays and booked to appear as the middle act with me on each night. This should be a lot of fun.

DAY 294 - DECEMBER 27TH, 1996

I went to the gym with my father today. On the way home he gave me one of his famous father-son pep talks to boost my confidence and lift my spirits.

"So, is anything happening out there in Los Angeles?"

"Nothing yet, Dad. It's been pretty frustrating, but I'm confident this year will be different and everything will fall into place."

"What's the use of living out there if you're not doing anything? You could be doing nothing here."

"Dad, that's where the opportunity is. Things will change when I sign with an agent."

"Don't take this the wrong way, but what agent would want to represent you? You're a nobody."

"Dad, everybody who's somebody was nobody to begin with... and please explain how I can possibly I take that statement the *right* way."

"If I were an agent I wouldn't want you. Nobody knows you in California, who the hell would go to see you?"

"Thanks for the ride, Dad. I'll call you tonight. Bye, Dad. Love ya!"

And I sometimes wonder why my ego can dance on the head of a pin, with plenty of additional room for parking.

My dad is the best guy in the entire world, a fantastic father, and my best pal who only wants the best for me and he hates to see me struggling. I just seem to be a little touchy lately. Hair-trigger is more like it.

It's not their fault. Most people think that you get an agent the way you get a lawyer. You walk into their office and say, "I want you to represent me." Easy as that. No problem.

And there's another reason I can't get mad at my dad... There are two axioms which help define the parent-child relationship and explain why, as a child, no matter what you become, no matter what you accomplish, no matter what you create... you will always be their kid and, therefore, you will always be critiqued and questioned.

The first truism that applies is, "First impressions are difficult to overcome."

The second would be, "Familiarity breeds contempt."

Do you ever wonder why your parents sometimes question your competence? Do you get the feeling that your parents display a lack confidence in you from time to time? It's because they saw you grow up. They were there right from the beginning...

Your parent can look you in the eye and say, "You don't want us to worry about you? You want us to believe in you?... Did you forget? We knew you when you used to shit your own pants *and sit in it*... for almost three years!... Tell me, how smart is that? Is that intelligent?

"Your father and I have seen you cry, kick and scream, stomp your feet, and throw a tantrum in the middle of a busy department store... Is that logical? Is it mature?... Tell us, does that sound like someone we shouldn't be concerned about?

"We remember when you used to believe in the Easter Bunny... and the Tooth Fairy... and Santa Claus. Does that sound like a person who has a grasp on reality to you? Or someone who's very gullible? Huh?... Which?

"We watched you pick your nose and eat it... And, knowing that, you can't understand why we ask you if you're eating right?"

How can you blame your parents for worrying?

I have a meeting scheduled with a manager/agent shortly after I return to Los Angeles. I was highly recommended to him from several people and he showed an interest in representing me, asking that I give him some materials to consider. Three and a half months ago I dropped off a videotape and press kit to his office and I was told that he'd get back to me. I was hoping that he'd call, because I felt like he might be the right guy for my career. Three and a half months later... and no phone call.

Then a friend of mine asked him, just before the holidays, why he hadn't shown an interest in me and called me back. He replied that he *was* interested and added that he had talked to me just a week or two previous. This guy was so busy he thought that he was in contact with me the week before, when there had actually been three and a half months of me waiting for the phone to ring while I lived on macaroni and cheese and Pop-Tarts and considered blowing the landlord's Doberman for a month's rent.

"In the midst of difficulty lies opportunity." *Albert Einstein*

My poor, poor parents. How'd you like to have a son like me? It can't be easy. Forty years old and he gives up a promising career as an attorney to move 3000 miles away, live like a bum, and do comedy in a place where he can't get on stage to save his life? My poor parents. I don't blame them for being concerned.

This happened last year. My mother is sitting in her living room with her friends, having a discussion about their children. One women says, "My son just got his master's degree from the Harvard School of Business. He graduated *summa cum laude* and has a job offer on Wall Street starting at $250,000 a year. Not that he needs the money, his wife, the former Miss Pennsylvania that he met at Princeton, comes from a very wealthy family. You remember meeting her with the Kennedys on their 150' yacht in Newport last summer, don't you Frances?"

Another of my mother's friends says, "My daughter just moved to Barcelona, Spain. She speaks four languages and they asked her to be the curator of the national museum. She has three beautiful children that have all been pre-accepted to Ivy League colleges, even though the oldest is only six years old, and her husband is the CEO of an international finance company that grossed $5,000,000,000 last year despite the global recession. They'll be living in a medieval castle on the former royal estate after they get back from their vacation in the south of France with Prince Ranier and his family. Her only regret is that she'll have to quit the Boston Symphony Orchestra to take this position."

"That's too bad."

"Yes, horrible."

The third friend informs them that, "My son, the doctor, just completed his residency at Mass General and will be taking over as the head of the brain surgery unit at the Leahy Clinic. When he's not devoting all of his free time performing his duties as the chairman of the city council and donating his services to cancer patients in the free clinic, he plays classical piano, so he just purchased a rare Steinway for his mansion in Chestnut Hill where he lives with his wife, the attorney who just got a four billion dollar settlement against the tobacco companies and is on the cover of *Time* magazine this week as their Woman of the Year."

This is precisely the moment when I burst through the door, her oldest son, and announce, *"Hey ma, look! I got rollerblades!"*

My poor parents.

It dawned on me that I had a Peter Pan complex about two years ago. I came home from a comedy show. It was late, maybe 2:30-3:00 a.m., and I had been drinking with some friends in the Faneuil Hall Marketplace in Boston. I had a good buzz on, which I decided to compliment with a little roach that I found in an ashtray. Then I cranked up my amplifier, plugged in my Fender Stratocaster, blasted an old Led Zeppelin album on the CD player, and played along with *You Shook Me*.

The phone rang, but it was ringing for quite a while before I could hear it, pick it up and answer, "What's up?"

It was the neighbor in the building next door, about 25' outside the window of my apartment. "Keep it down over there God-dammit! It's three o'clock in the fucking morning and you're making a racket with all that noise!"

"Oh ya? I always gotta listen to you coming home drunk and fighting with your wife every night... When you stop screaming at her, I'll turn down my music!"

Moments after I slammed down the phone, I stood there stunned, as it occurred to me, "Shit. I'm thirty-eight years old! At this point in my life I'm supposed to have my life together. I should be married... have a family... be raising some kids that look up to me as an example... have a steady, regular job... with a retirement fund... and a house with a mortgage... and be saving for my children's college education by now...

"Na, fuck it...

"*You know you shook me babe... you shook me all night long... wah wah wah wah...*"

DAY 295 - DECEMBER 28TH, 1996

People ask me how my first Christmas was in California. I tell them it was just like... well... it was like a Wednesday.

I have working out all the time lately. I usually work out every other day or three times a week, but I got so depressed and down on myself that I stopped for two and a half months. Then I started looking in the mirror and feeling doubly bummed-out because, not only was I a loser, now I was becoming a chubby loser.

What can I say? It's discouraging... very discouraging... I'm willing to bet that if Tony Robbins, the master of the power of positive thinking, were in my shoes, he'd be up on a ledge threatening to jump.

He's full of crap anyway, with that walking over the hot coals trick to prove mind over matter. I swear I saw a guy that looked *just* like that phony at the beach one day, walking gingerly across the sand with a towel under his arm going, "*Ooooh! Ahhhh! Owwww! Ahhhh! Ooooh!*" just like everyone else.

DAY 296 - DECEMBER 29TH, 1996

We sat around my family's table telling funny stories with my cousin Paul, my comedian friend Patty Ross, and "The Prune," who I have known since I was twelve years old when he coached my Babe Ruth League baseball team. Prune has been like family to me ever since.

Once you meet the Prune, you are guaranteed never to forget him. He's rotund, but in a solid way, making him an imposing figure. His curly, stark-white hair and beard give him the appearance of a cross between Kenny Rogers and Santa Claus. Prune's deep voice is made even more distinctive by punctuating his speech with numerous "Prune-isms" and he has a personality that is boldly unique, sometimes abrasive, always attention grabbing, and is such that he draws attention, good or bad, wherever he goes.

While I was in California, I was flooded with phone calls from friends at home proclaiming, "I just saw your buddy Prune on the TV. He's been on all week."

Here's the scoop. Months ago, Prune told me that he ran into a local television anchor who he met when I was acting as a master of ceremonies for a celebrity roast/fundraiser some years ago.

Like everyone else who has ever had contact with the Prune, she recalled meeting him through me and their talk turned to Prune's weight. He informed the anchor that he intended to start a new diet, which consisted of taking a recently introduced pill that was claimed to induce significant weight-loss. The TV anchor told Prune that her station was interested in investigating the validity of the weight-loss assertions and asked if Prune would agree to participate in a controlled study of the drug's effects. He was to be interviewed initially, then re-interviewed in a follow-up segment a couple months later, to demonstrate the before-and-after results of the popular new diet.

Prune was filmed at his current weight and the introductory interview was aired on the local news in the Boston area. When I returned home, about two and a half months later, Prune appeared to have actually *gained* weight since his appearance.

"Prune, what the fuck happened?"

He shook his head, only slightly embarrassed. Prune never really gives a shit about anything enough to let it bother him.

"What can I say. I never took the pills. I've been eating like a pig and I gained twenty pounds."

"But what's gonna happen when they interview you? They can't see you like this! You're a disgrace!"

"I know. They called. They're coming in next week to film be for the follow-up. I'm screwed."

Not exactly. The Prune always seems to fall into shit and come up smelling like roses. When the anchor showed up, she was shocked at Prune's weight-gain. In a panic, Prune claimed that he couldn't take the pills because they made him dizzy, hoping that the reporter would accept his excuse for not following through with the diet.

Her reaction was, "Fantastic! This is even better! We'll do an exposé on the harmful side-effects of the controversial new gimmick diet that could be a threat to people's health!"

Prune tried to intervene so he could explain, but it was too late. He was already caught in a downward spiral from his spontaneous revelation about the pills. They had a microphone in his face and a camera focusing on him as he sunk deeper and deeper into the quicksand of his little fib. "Ya, and when I was driving my car, I had to pull over to the side of the road before I got into an accident because I felt disoriented... etc.... etc. they made me feel nauseous... etc.... etc."

Next thing you know, they had him on the TV every night for a week.

He received calls from the doctor who developed the pill, screaming, *"What are you doing to me? You're ruining me! The calling me a quack on TV! What the hell are you doing to my business?"*

His friend was refused by his pharmacist when he tried to get a prescription for the diet pill filled. "Didn't you see the guy on television? He's been on the consumer reports all week. These things will kill you!"

We all had a good laugh at that one.

Nobody but my friend, the Prune... The one-and-only. There's no one else like him. He's in a league of his own. Yup. They broke the mold when they made him.

Thank God.

It's a frightening thought, but among my friends, I just may be the most sane one of the lot... which is roughly the equivalent of being the best behaved inmate on death row, I suppose.

(Author's note: *And, as luck would have it, Prune's blatant falsehood ended up being prophetic... the pills were actually making other people sick, they took them off the market, and the lucky bastard ended-up looking like a hero*)

L.A. Misérables, Too

Portrait of a Court Jester

by Elizabeth Hardy

What does a young attorney do when he's not in the courtroom arguing a case? Play eighteen holes at the country club? Wax the BMW? Go sailing?

Perhaps most do such things, but when attorney Paul Murphy of Water Street isn't standing in front of a jury, he is standing in front of nightclub audiences telling jokes.

An unusual combination? Murphy doesn't think so. He feels that as a comic he is using skills acquired from doing jury trials. "I have about one hundred jury trials under my belt," he says, "so public speaking comes naturally."

As supervisor in the Assistant District Attorney's decided to try his act at an "open mike" night in Stitches Comedy Club on Commonwealth Avenue in Boston. The laughter and applause lured him back "four or five times" until he found himself booked into a "Comedy Riot for Top Comedians."

Despite this success, Murphy found it difficult to get booked into Boston comedy clubs on a regular basis because, "I was the new kid in town and the agents didn't know me."

After a few short months off the circuit, Paul Murphy re-emerged in the Fall of 1985 as Paul D'Angelo, bringing with him an amplified acoustic guitar and he has been booked steadily ever since.

On a recent Saturday night, Murphy the D.A. in the dark conservative suit, became D'Angelo the comic in a Flintstones sweatshirt and jeans, captivating a packed house at Stevie D's in Middleton.

He considers the club "home turf" and credits some of his success to owner Steve Daddario. "He gave me a shot and has done well by me. While I've done well by him. He put me up (on stage) on Halloween of 1985 without even seeing my act." Now D'Angelo is a main attraction or "headliner," selling out every time he performs there.

Although he doesn't mention being an attorney in his act, a lot of D'Ange-

staff photo by Michael Galvin

Paul Murphy, a.k.a. Paul D'Angelo, plays the straight man by day as an

Paul D'Angelo

DAY 297 - DECEMBER 30TH, 1996

I drove up to Magnolia-by-the-Sea, near Gloucester, Mass., where my family has a home, to visit my cousin Paul. We took a ride near the ocean and, as we were traveling through town, a squirrel ran right in front of the car I was driving, stopped, looked at us, and tried to run back across the road like an idiot. I jammed on the brakes and almost sent my poor cousin flying through the windshield, trying to avoid the nut-gathering rat.

You know that these fanatic animal-rights activists are winning the war to fuck-up the public's sense of priorities when you hesitate, even for a fraction of a second, to consider the options of: 1) Do I run over the bushy-tailed rodent? or 2) the pregnant woman pushing the baby carriage?

I spent the afternoon with my cousin and my Uncle Vito and my uncle's friends, listening to them tell stories. My uncle has a terrific sense of humor and is a great storyteller. For years, he used to run the Meadow-Glen Twin Drive-In Theater in Medford, Massachusetts. The patrons of the drive-in were either families who were going to see a movie with their kids or couples who were going to make-out in the car.

The theater was on a large expanse of land-fill and, when my uncle was working the box-office and would see a car pull up with a girl who was well-known to "put out," he would direct the couple to park in the rear in hopes that the bouncing vehicle would help to pack down the earth. Uncle Vito claims that his motto should have been, "The Meadow-Glen Drive-In, the friendly family theater. If you don't have a family when you drive-in, you'll have one by the time you drive-out."

I worked there part-time while I was going to high school. I remember that I was being paid $1.85 an hour and one of my jobs was to fix the marquis when the students from nearby Tufts College would rearrange the letters on the sign. Overnight, *Boxcar Bertha* would be transformed into *Bertha's Big Box* for the entertainment of the morning commuters.

L.A. Misérables, Too

My parents and Uncle Vito

DAY 298 - DECEMBER 31ST, 1996

Tonight is New Year's Eve. I hate New Year's Eve.

My memories of New Year's Eve are being left alone with a baby sitter when I was a kid and thinking that my parents had abandoned me and were among the thousands of partiers in Times Square, as I watched the ball drop at midnight. I spent several New Year's Eves during my high school years puking in a snow bank after I drank too much. Then I spent several New Year's Eves during my college years puking in a snow bank after I drank too much. I spent one New Year's Eve in Florida, where I ended up puking in a sand dune because I drank too much. Then there were the dateless New Year's Eves, which were slightly better than the New Year's Eve when I caught my girlfriend with another guy and punched him in the nose in front of his twenty or thirty friends, who proceeded to throw me headfirst into a snow bank where someone had just puked after they drank too much. And it all goes downhill from there so, when I started to do comedy, I was glad for the opportunity to work so that the night wouldn't be a total waste.

It was minus twenty degrees wind-chill tonight. People in Southern California have no idea what winter can be like here. Their only taste of winter is watching reruns of an old Andy Williams Christmas special with fake snow falling in the fake background of the television studio that's a comfortable and toasty 72°.

And there's Andy, in his brightly colored V-neck sweater singing, *"Chestnuts roasting on an open fire, Jack Frost nipping at your nose..."* ... and the people are going, "Isn't that adorable? Jack Frost *nips* at your nose! Wouldn't it be wonderful to spend a winter in New England? We could have Jack Frost nipping at our noses!"

I got news for them. When it's bitter cold, the wind chill factor is -10°, gusts of frigid air are whipping down the neck of your coat, you can't feel your fingers or toes, your nose is running like a leaky faucet, your nuts are shriveled up like raisins, and that lump in your throat just happens to be your scrotum, Jack Frost doesn't *nip* at your nose... he'll bite your damn nose right off of your frigid, frozen, frostbitten face... then spit it out 'cause you got frozen snot all over your upper lip.

Take a hint... There's a reason folks are *"dressed up like Eskimos."* It's friggin' cold outside!

This would have been a good time to work on a cruise ship for a couple of weeks. I love the Caribbean. It's all incredible but I do like some islands more than others. I had a bad experience in San Juan, Puerto Rico, although it may have been partly my fault... I don't know Spanish very well.

I handed a kid my camera and said, "Take my picture."

And, apparently, he misunderstood and thought I said, "Take my camera."

DAY 299 - JANUARY 1ST, 1997

Kelly called from Los Angeles to tell me that her boss took her and some of his friends to the Santa Anita racetrack for the afternoon. Her boss and his buddies are serious gamblers that really know what they're doing. Before they place a bet, they have studied the results of the horse's last ten races, the results of the jockey's last ten races, and the

L.A. Misérables, Too

results of each of the competition's last ten races. They know if the horse runs better on a dry or muddy track, on a cool or a hot day, over a quarter mile or a half mile, when there's a full moon or a new moon. They know the last time the horse took a shit and if the jockey is getting along with his wife that week. They have a full injury report and have been informed of the horse's training regimen prior to the race, including his eating habits and blood pressure charts.

Kelly bet on the horses that had cute names, looked pretty, had jockeys wearing cool colors, or steeds that she had a "funny feeling" about.

The guys lost… Kelly picked five winners.

See. You gotta have a system.

DAY 300 - JANUARY 2ND, 1997

I visited my friend Dugie tonight. I always have a ton of laughs when I hang out with ol' Dugie Russell, who is a court officer in Gloucester, Massachusetts.

Dugie's daughter came in later in the evening. She told me that she was getting a divorce from her husband, Charlie. I remarked that it seemed like yesterday when I was at her beautiful wedding and Karen said, "Ya, it was a nice day… but, hey, what can you do."

That's when I looked over at Dugie, whose jaw went slack and his eyes stared unfocused into space as he thought, "$2000 for the band… $3000 for the hall… $1500 for the flowers… $2200 for the open bar… $4000 for the caterer… $340 for the cake… $1000 for the limos… $500 for the champagne… ya, it was a 'nice friggin' day' alright."

Dugie told me the story about seeing my brother Chris' license plate, which was 464-C. That sequence struck Dugie as significant because he said that he used to live on 464 Clarke Street, so he played 4-6-4-3 (the three representing the letter c's position in the alphabet) in the lottery for a week without success.

The day after he stopped playing the number, it hit.

"See! I knew that number was going to come up! I knew it! 464-C and 464 Clarke Street. That was no coincidence! I knew it!"

"Dugie, get a grip. Really. Probably twelve million people played the lottery last week... there's thousands and thousands of possible combinations of those numbers... Do you think that God looked down to the earth when it was time for those randomly picked numbers to be chosen and said, "Let's see, what numbers will I have come out this week in Massachusetts. Oooh, what's that? Do I see Dugie Russell looking at Paul's brother's license plate? I think that's the combo I'll go for... now that that's taken care of I'm on to those floods in Northern California, the growing hostility in Rwanda, the car bombing in Beirut, and genocide in Africa."

Dugie playing judge at my Court Jester DVD photo sessions

DAY 301 - JANUARY 3RD, 1997

I visited my friends who have a beautiful, seven month old baby girl. Parents are all the same when it comes to their children. Theirs is the cutest. Theirs is the brightest. Someone's baby drools while they squirm in their highchair, with applesauce smeared all over their face, goes "Mpghudhfjkjcnd" and the parent will claim, "Did you hear that? She just said "cactus" in Czechoslovakian! She's brilliant! Our child is a prodigy!"

L.A. Misérables, Too

"Ba ba ba ba ba."

"See, see! Now she was starting to sing that Beach Boys song! It was on the radio last week and she picked it up. *Ba-ba-ba-ba Barbara Ann, ba-ba-ba...*"

"Augggghhhhhhh... Ugghhhhhrrrrrr."

"That's right honey. Listen to her! What did I tell you, she's so advanced for her age. She's doing the death scene from *Othello*. She's going to be an actress!"

When I did my show at Giggles I asked a guy in the front what he did for a living. He was a helicopter pilot for the Navy. Fantastic. When a guy says he's an accountant, an engineer, stockbroker or computer programmer you know the conversation is generally going nowhere, comically speaking.

"Where do you patrol?"

"I patrol off the Florida coast and spend most of the day looking for drugs."

"Don't we all... What was your most exciting mission?"

"We located the last remaining MIA from Operation Desert Storm. His plane went down and we found him stuck in the mud after almost six weeks."

"Six weeks stuck in the mud? He had to be hungry and... and soggy."

"He was dead."

NOTICE: *As the entire crowd suddenly hushes in anticipatory tension, we will break for an in-depth look into the mind of a stand-up comedian as he reacts to the guy's comment and formulates a plan to bail himself out of an uncomfortable situation.*

The following are just some of the thoughts and considerations that went through my mind in approximately one quarter-of-a-second; in the midst of a potential crisis; while alone onstage in front of a crowd of complete strangers; who worked hard all day; who've all been downing a two-drink mandatory-minimum amount of alcohol; and who have forked over a significant chunk of their hard-earned money for me to amuse them.

And in that ¼ of a second, I contemplated...

Paul D'Angelo

("Oh shit!... awkward moment... Fuck! What do I say? Why did I choose this career? Maybe my parents were right... Well it doesn't matter because you can't bale out in the middle of a show, so you better think *fast*, Paul... The guy in the crowd mentioned death, so the audience is going to be vulnerable and therefore in a defensive posture, so this can be a sensitive subject if you don't handle the situation appropriately under these particular circumstances given all the variables of the crowd, the venue, your mood and the overall atmosphere of the evening, so it has to be something clever and original, but not so offensive that it alienates the crowd... and you better think of it *right* away or it's not going to appear completely spontaneous to the audience, and you might lose their respect if it doesn't happen in the blink of an eye, so quickly sift through every single idea, memory, recollection, thought, dream, notion and image that you've ever had in your head, and can still remember on something less than a moment's notice, and see if you can weigh all of the possible options, make an accurate association that people can relate to, and come up with an appropriate response that was absolutely unanticipated, yet is expected to be delivered in a totally improvisational manner that appears to have been rehearsed a thousand times, and is likable, yet effective, in getting your point across to a diverse, dissimilar, eclectic and mostly unrelated collection of people... male and female, old and young, blue collar and white collar, tired and wired, sober and wasted, single, married, widowed and divorced, attentive and preoccupied, skeptics and believers, optimists and pessimists, rich and poor, locals and visitors, black and white, intellects and morons, educated and uneducated, happy and grumpy, bashful and Sneezy ... no sweat... like right aboooout *NOW!*...)

"Oh, of course. Stupid me... I wasn't thinking. I guess being hungry was the least of his problems, wasn't it? My bad."

The grade?: Average at best, but at least it bailed me out of tricky situation. It also brought back a memory of a similar circumstance when it all came together perfectly.

I was headlining a show at Dick Doherty's Comedy Vault in the theater district of downtown Boston, a number of years ago. "The

L.A. Misérables, Too

Vault" is a downstairs room in an old building that used to be a bank. The green room for the comics, to the right of the small stage, is actually the bank's old vault, located behind a massive, and very ornate, tempered-steel door.

It's not a big room and it was packed to the max that night, the sell-out crowd was pumped, and the atmosphere was electric.

There were three or four comics doing short sets before me. The audience was great and each of their sets went well, but each one of them also came off the stage shaking their head, a little spooked by the guy sitting in the front row, right before us at center stage.

This man was massive and built like a gorilla. I don't know how he even fit at the table and/or how he didn't break his chair, because he was a mountain of a man, with a full, black beard, heavily tattooed arms the size of tree-trunks, and hands as big as a Grizzly Bear's paw. To compliment his charming ensemble, he was sporting a black leather vest with a motorcycle gang's colors on the back.

Throughout their acts, he glared at the other comics with a menacing stare and never laughed once... never reacted... never even cracked the slightest smile. Each of the intimidated comics just tried to look beyond him, addressing the rest of the audience, and pretending that Goliath wasn't there, but this hulk with the bad attitude was impossible to ignore.

When I finally took the stage I was a little apprehensive, hoping they'd be no trouble. I was only about a third of the way through a great set when, for some reason that I can no longer recall, I asked the audience, "How many people here went to college? Raise your hands."

The giant sitting in front of me bellowed, in a deep, very loud and very threatening voice that shook the room like a lighthouse's foghorn..."*I WENT TO COLLEGE.*"

Nervously, I inquired, "Really? And where did you go to college?"

He slammed his gigantic fist down on the table and roared...

"*VIETNAM WAS MY COLLEGE!*"

All the air suddenly went out of the room. The audience was frozen in fear. You could hear a dust mite sigh, as they anticipated my reply, which could either save the show or possibly get me killed.

Without hesitating, I nonchalantly replied…

"No kidding… Tell me, *how did their football team do this year?*"

There was a moment's pause and suddenly the guy started laughing so hard, I thought he was gonna piss himself. As soon as the audience saw his reaction, they erupted in relief, and that monster was a joy for the rest of the night.

Trust me when I tell you, that could have gone *much* worse.

DAY 302 - JANUARY 4TH, 1997

I went to my parents' house to spend some time with my dad and watch the NFL playoffs. The 49'ers were playing on a rainy, muddy Lambeau Field in Green Bay, Every time my mother came into the room she announced, "Oh my God! Look how muddy they are!" She repeated the statement *at least* ten times.

That's my mom… the consummate mother and housewife.

The men watching the game are thinking, "If they're going to blitz the inside linebackers, you're going to have the wide receivers in man-to-man coverage. You've got a rookie at right cornerback, and the safety's been hampered by a groin injury since the Minnesota game and can be beat long. The running back can pick up the blitz before he releases in the flat for an outlet swing-pass if the flanker is covered, as long as the right guard and center double team their all-pro nose-tackle that had three sacks in their November 3rd meeting, but they have to use the sideline because they only have one time-out left, not counting the two-minute-warning, and their red-zone offense is only rated 18th in the league over the second half of the season. The field goal kicker will be kicking into a twenty-mile an hour wind, which only makes him effective from the 35 yard line on in, especially considering the footing is tenuous where they re-sodded the field during the bye-week."

And my mother, watching the same play, contemplates whether or not they'll ever get the stains out of those nice, white uniforms.

It's interesting how generations progress. My father and Uncle Dick were football stars at Holy Cross College and both had tryouts with the NFL. As they watched the game they, informed me that they

L.A. Misérables, Too

played in an era without face-masks, when a huge defensive lineman weighed 240 lbs. and star players got $50,000 a year.

If I had children I could imagine watching sports with them in the future.

"You know, when I was growing up, there were actually still a couple white guys still playing professional basketball in the NBA that *didn't* come from Europe."

"No way, Dad!"

"It's true."

"Wow!"

DAY 303 - JANUARY 5TH, 1997

My parents are throwing another house-party because the New England Patriots are playing the Pittsburgh Steelers in an AFC playoff game. God bless my mother. She has been cooking since yesterday, preparing a big Thanksgiving-like feast because I missed the holidays at home. She's worked so hard and I truly appreciate her sacrifice and dedication, but she can't let the opportunity pass without getting in a healthy share of guilt-distribution.

I gave her a little kiss and thanked my mother for cooking. She opened the oven and pointed to the turkey.

"Do you see that big turkey? This is for you. Do you know how much work I've done just for you? I did all this work because I know you love turkey. I'm throwing this party because of you. Do you realize how much work went into this afternoon? I did this all for you. We're having this party for you, because we want you to have a nice party before you go back. This is *your* party, this is *your* turkey, and I hope you appreciate it."

"Maaaaa. If it's *my* party, how come it's all *your* friends? There are none of my friends here. All the people here are *your* friends... and they're eating *my* turkey! I hope they appreciate it. Go ask 'em if they appreciate what *I'm* doing for *them*, ma!"

Between my parents and my girlfriend, my ego has been beaten into submission. You know you're on a guilt-trip from hell when you watch the evening news and they report that a bus full of travelers left the road in Bolivia, killing all those aboard, and your instinctive reaction is, "Somehow, it must be my fault. I'm to blame. I am so, so sorry."

DAY 304 - JANUARY 6TH, 1997

I love my parents more than anything else I've ever loved in the world. They are the greatest parents in the history of parenting and I owe everything I am and everything I have to their guidance, sacrifice, generosity, kindness, example, dedication and love.

That said, during the course of a car trip with my parents they still treat me like I'm a little kid and I tend to develop a strange nervous-twitch that grows in intensity with duration of the ride.

(*author's note: The notation indicating the intensity of my twitch is noted on a scale from 1-to-10, with 1 representing a subtle jerking of the head and 10 representing a full-blown seizure and/or anxiety attack.)

"Paul, I'm cold. You can make it warmer in here if you turn that knob on the dashboard toward the red."

"I know Mom, I have a heater in my car too."

"Paul, have you ever eaten at that fast-food place? They serve hamburgers."

"Ya, Mom. I've been to McDonald's before."

"Ooooh, watch out, he's slowing down!"

"Is that what it means when those red lights in the back of the car get brighter? Knowing that will make driving so much easier for me, Mother." (twitch *1)

"I like your new car, Dad. What's this button do?"

"DON'T TOUCH THAT, YOU'LL BREAK SOMETHING!"

"Dad, I'm not seven!" (twitch *2)

"Paul, have you been eating in LA?"

"No Mom, I usually wait until I come back to Boston every two or three months … What'a ya mean, have I been eating? Of course I've been eating." (twitch *3)

L.A. Misérables, Too

"That... that *thing* you have on your face..."

"The goatee?"

"Ya, that *thing*... you remind me of someone... Do you know who you look like?"

"No, who, Mom?"

"I don't know... a bum... or maybe Charles Manson, or a child molester... or *Lucifer*. Why don't you shave it?" (twitch *4)

"Mom, I didn't grow it just to piss you off, and I'm not shaving it just to make you happy."

"PAUL, WATCH OUT!"

"I see him, Dad!" (twitch *4.5)

"No you didn't, you weren't looking... you were gonna hit him."

"Dad, do you think that I just plow right into people every day when you're not in the car to direct me? Is that how stupid you think I am?... Maaaa, tell hi..."

"HEY, HEY... keep your eyes on the road!"

"I was looki..." (twitch *5)

"You weren't looking... you were turned-around, looking at your mother in the back seat."

"But just for a split secon..." (twitch*5.5)

"How can you tell me you can see the road ahead if your head is facing in totally the opposite direction, Mr. Boston College? Is that what they taught you there? Huh?... Is that what I paid for?... That's why you got into that other accident."

"Accident?... *Accident?*... What accident?... What are you talking about? I wasn't in any accident."

"You forget that you smashed into the high school and totaled my company car?"

"You mean when I was sixteen? (twitch *6) The first week I got my driver's license?... Twenty-seven years ago? Dad, I would hope I've progressed a <u>little</u> since high scho..."

"PAAAUL, did you hear that So-and-So's son just moved into a beautiful, brand-new $450,000 house in Lynnfield?"

"Yes, I did, Mom... the house that his father, the wealthy contractor, built for him... Did you ever think that that information would be an important part of the story, Ma?... This is a good time for you to change the subject."

"... and they're putting in an Olympic-sized swimming pool in the backyard... of course they have two and a half acres... and his two sons both made the All-Star team... What good-looking kids... and his daughter is a brain with the computers. She's studying in Spain this summer... The grandparents are sooo proud..." (twitch *7)

"Maaa, I..."

"JESUS CHRIST, PAUL!!! DON'T YOU SEE THIS GUY ON YOUR RIGHT?... LET HIM GO, LET HIM GO!!!"

(twitch *7) "That's it. Dad, take the steering wheel, I don't want to drive anymore... Go ahead, take it..." (twitch *7.5)

"What the hell are you doing with your arms folded? Steer the damn car!"

"No... I'm not steering. Everything I do is wrong. You take it, I don't wanna drive your new car..."

"You two stop fighting up there! Grow up and steer the car, Paul... Act your age, you're almost fifty!"

"Maaaaaa, I'm only 43, I'm not fifty yet. You always make me older than I am." (twitch *8)

"Close enough. All I know is that I saw the Such-and-Such's the other day... what a beautiful family they have... and I have never once... not *once*, ever heard anyone in that family raise their voice or argue like you two animals do."

"Maaaa, you see them twice a year, at the most... and it's at functions and weddings and dinners and banquets... Of course they're not fighting at those places! They're on their best behavior. You don't know what they do at home when they're alone behind closed doors... (twitch *8) They could be beating the shit out of each other in there... or they could be incestuous perverts... or Satan worshippers... or they could be making amateur bondage porn with the babysitter... or smoking crack... How do you kno..."

"TAKE THIS LEFT!!!"

"I think I know where you guys live, Dad! I grew up there, remember?" (twitch *9)

"You grew up?... When?... I don't seem to remember you ever growing up..."

"Agggggghhhhhhhhh!!!!"

"Put the car in park, turn the headlights off and lock the doors, Paul."

(spasms begin)

"Paul, do you want to come in and have something to eat?"

"Sure!"

Boy, I miss them.

I'm leaving tomorrow. This trip has gone by so fast I can't believe it, but I have to say I'm a little anxious to get back to LA and keep the ball rolling. Will I miss my friends and family? Of course. Do lesbians like to play softball?

My friends Johnny Pizzi, Gary Gulman, and my former secretary, Mimi, took me out for a drink before I leave for the West Coast.

Johnny's upset because his eighteen year old daughter went away to college and went on the pill coincidentally. He just kept muttering, "I wish I didn't know. I'd rather not know. What I don't know won't hurt me. I just wish I didn't know what was going on. Ignorance is bliss. Why do I have to know?"

"How do you know, Johnny?"

"I went through her pocketbook."

Oh.

It's freezing out and Johnny dreams of moving to a warmer climate for the winter months.

"How about Florida, Johnny?"

"No way. I hate alligators."

"How about Arizona?"

"No way. I hate scorpions."

"How about Mexico?"

"No way. I hate tarantulas."

"Southern California?"

"No way. I hate fake tits."

Paul D'Angelo

DAY 305 - JANUARY 7TH, 1997

My plane arrived in Los Angeles about a half hour ahead of schedule.

I guess there wasn't much sky traffic.

I opened up the mail that came when I was away, which included several Christmas cards. One of the cards was from Joe Marchese and his wife Charlotte. Joe's an old pal and a very successful attorney. His wonderful wife sent one of those yearly-update form-letters that you only get from people who've had an interesting and prosperous year.

Here's some of the highlights that made me realize how much my life really sucks:

"…not only did the year fly by, but we were very busy. The New Year's vacation in Aruba was perfect… we did the usual island stuff, read, relax and have a few cocktails… The ski vacation in Italy was just OK… the snow was light and the people were rude… But the summer was fabulous! The Nantucket home is finally complete and the dogs and I enjoyed the island from May till October… rollerblading, fishing, swimming, sunning and boating… Joe turned 50 in October. We celebrated in Hawaii for 2 ½ weeks. We had such a wonderful time playing golf each morning and sightseeing each afternoon… We plan on doing the usual for Christmas and heading to Anguilla for New Year's… "

I love these people but, after hearing how wonderful their year was, I'm ready to kill myself. Imagine if I sent out a newsletter, recapping my 1996…

Dear whoever (like I really give a shit):

What an exciting year it was! After I gave up my two successful careers, left my friends and family, took a voluntary vow of poverty, and an involuntary vow of celibacy, and moved to Hollywood, the action has never stopped.

In March I did a little vacuuming around the house… I got most of the dried vomit up from the previous tenants of our palatial estate and, let me tell you, that rug looked fabulous! April found me snaking our backed-up toilet, doing several loads of laundry, killing a lot of cock-

L.A. Misérables, Too

roaches and making other improvements around the apartment... And that's not all!

The thrills didn't stop in May, when I had severe dysentery after stuffing my face like a pig at an all-you-can-eat burrito bar... Ohhh, how we laughed! Wish you could have been here to share the evening with us. Thank God the toilet was working again!... Summer was chock-full of activity... sweating, eating, sleeping, farting, arguing, scratching my ass, yawning, breathing, clipping my toenails, existing, trying to make ends meet, taking up space... Phew!... Where did we find the time!

One sunny June afternoon I actually walked two whole blocks in our neighborhood without being asked for "spare change" and I made a rare sighting of a woman with real breasts... and a fake head. You don't see that in Boston!

I had a little scare in July, when I developed a funny looking rash on my scrotum, but thank God it turned out to be nothing... Hey, and the fun didn't end there!... October was filled with thrills as I got desperate, swallowed my pride, and told my jokes at a coffee house in front of nine people... If you listened closely, I swear you could hear the sound of my career hitting bottom... and the hits just keep on coming!

The commotion mounted in November when we spent most of our time wondering how we were going to pay the rent. Yard Sale? Prostitution? Theft? Insurance scam? Kidnapping? Trading in white slavery? Selling drugs? I'll tell you, there's never a dull moment!...

As for entertainment, I had some crusty stuff in my eye when I woke up one morning and you can imagine the excitement that caused... and, just when you think life couldn't possibly get any more fascinating, it's time to vacuum again!... It never lets up around here! Hard to believe but, one of the days, I think it was the 14th... no, maybe the 15th... well, anyway, there was one day in November when Kelly and I didn't fight with each other, and she is promising another truce sometime in the early spring, so we have that to look forward to. I had to say, "Stop it! You're spoiling me!"...

And there's so much else to tell you... December topped off our ex-

hilarating adventure with a bang when I got to experience the shame of calling my friends and family to tell them that I couldn't afford to buy them Christmas presents... It also marked the ninth consecutive month in a row that you didn't call from your perfect little world to say 'Hi!' Thanks a lot!

Next year I'm saving up all my money so we can swing another trip to the burrito buffet and sponsor a flatulence festival. Book your flight early!... Hope your year was as triumphant and wonderful as ours. And have a Happy New Year!... Not me, I'll be working to help pay our mounting bills."

Yours with Satan,
Paul D'Angelo

Tonight, Kelly took me to Drai's restaurant for dinner. It is definitely over our budget, but we need to do something out of the ordinary for this year's newsletter. While we were eating, Don Rickles and his wife sat down at the adjacent table with another couple. Even though I hate to bother people when their eating, I have always idolized Don and love his sense of humor, so I had to go over to his table and introduce myself.

"Mr. Rickles, I'm so sorry to bother you, but I'm a comedian also and I wanted to tell you that I've admired you for a long time. Also, it's because of you that my father refers to me as 'dummy.'"

He said, *"My father called me dummy too!"*

The gentleman sitting to his left looked very familiar and I wanted to say something, but decided to keep my mouth shut before I embarrassed myself like I have a tendency to do.

One night I opened up for the country-music recording artists, the Oakridge Boys, at the North Shore Music Theater. When I finished my set and walked backstage, there were three guys dressed in Country & Western attire (cowboy hats, big belt buckles, cowboy boots and long hair) who approached me and said, "Great set! We thought you were really funny. That was fabulous. We were laughing our asses off."

Being complimented always makes me feel a little uncomfortable, so I returned their praise by saying, "Thank you, but I want to tell you

L.A. Misérables, Too

that you guys are my favorites. I'm a big, big fan. I have all your albums and I've been following you for years. It's a great pleasure to open up for you and finally meet you. I'm looking forward to your performance. Thanks again for your kind words."

In reality, I don't know one song the Oakridge Boys do, I have none of their albums, and have no idea what they look like, but I didn't want to admit it and I thought it would be a nice gesture to return the courtesy after they were so complimentary to me.

Well, shortly thereafter, the concert started and the Oakridge Boys took the stage and began singing, but not one of the guys that I spoke to backstage was among them. It was then that I looked around the theater and realized that I had actually been speaking to the lighting and sound men on the road crew for the band.

When I walked away, they must have looked at each other, laughed, and said, *"Whaaaaat an asshooooole."*

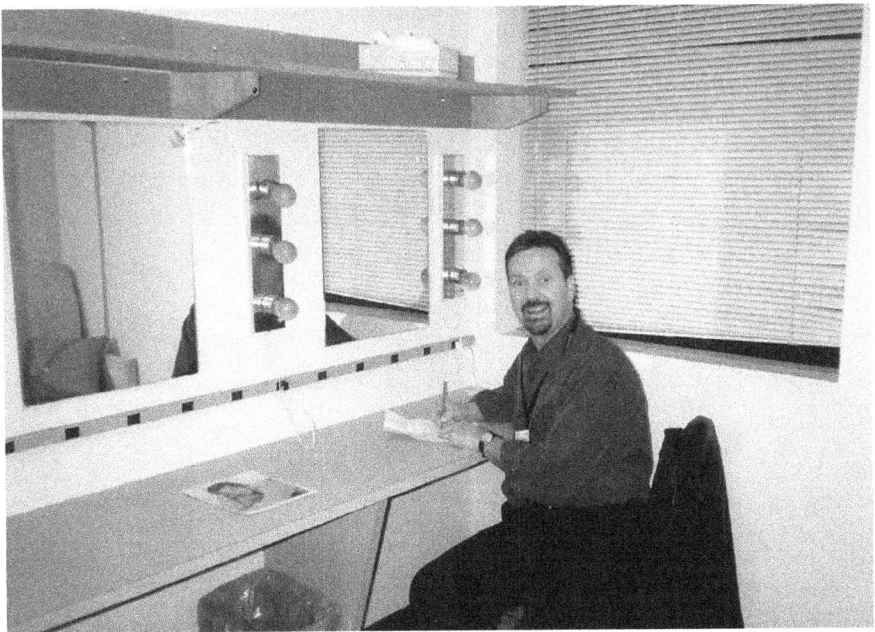

Backstage at the North Shore Music Theater opening for Engelbert

CHAPTER NINETEEN
And the beat goes on...

DAY 306 - JANUARY 8TH, 1997

Patty Ross came over with Dolly, her dog. She told me that she spoke to a friend from home this morning. He used to be a comedian, but left to establish and run a chain of diet clinics that have become very successful. Patty asked how business was lately and he told her, "Business is great, but we had a scare for a while when some asshole got on the evening news and announced that he was having harmful side-effects from the diet pill we prescribe. That fucking guy, I wanted to kill him!"

Patty was laughing. "Does he look like Santa Claus?"

"Ya! That fucking guy! He almost destroyed my business single-handedly!"

All Patty could say was, "Heh, heh, heh."

DAY 307 - JANUARY 9TH, 1997

Patty Ross invited me over for dinner last night. Her place looked great. Usually, if there's something clean in Patty's apartment, it must be new.

Patty is on the verge of signing an agreement with a production

L.A. Misérables, Too

company which would give her a development deal for a television series. I predicted, to the dinner crowd that consisted of Patty's friends... and they unanimously agreed with me... that Patty would be a First Amendment trailblazer and be the first to break the "See You Next Tuesday" word barrier on network television. And we'll be saying, with disgust, "And I remember when they could only say 'pussy' during prime time!"

Patty's friend, Carrie Snow, a writer on the Roseanne Barr Show, has a little Cocker Spaniel that she has enrolled in an "Aerobics and Socialization Program."

Only in Hollywood.

When I got back and parked on the bottom floor of the garage in my apartment building, the elevator seemed to take an eternity, and I spotted a sign on the wall that I had never noticed before.

The sign proclaimed, "NO TRESPASSING; VIOLATORS WILL BE PROSECUTED."

As a former assistant district attorney, the wording on the sign would have been much more intimidating to me if it had read, "NO TRESPASSING; PROSECUTORS WILL BE VIOLATED."

No thank you.

DAY 308 - JANUARY 10TH, 1997

I have a list of people who are important to me that I call each and every year on their birthday. Today I called my comedian friend Gary Gulman's mom to wish her a happy birthday and she told me that Gary just got a job as a substitute teacher at the local high school. He's teaching a Spanish class. Apparently, it doesn't bother the school board that Gary doesn't speak Spanish, can't read or write Spanish, and can't converse in Spanish. But why obsess on trivialities?

I know very little Spanish. Very little. For instance... I know that *bueños noches* happens to mean "good" *noches*.

I was driving through town today and wondered, "What does it tell you about a city when, at any given time, half of all the people pushing a shopping cart are not shopping?"

DAY 309 - JANUARY 11TH, 1997

I learned that a friend of mine, Mike Betts, who was a manager at Nick's Comedy Stop in Boston, where I had my own weekly show for seven or eight years, suffered a massive heart attack and died suddenly. Mike was only forty-three years old. What a shame. It's hard to believe, he was so young. He was in the prime of his life. I'm gonna miss him.

A moment of silence for my friend Mike:

Thanks.

More shocking news today. My friend George, the consummate bachelor, got engaged to be married. Now I'm the only holdout left, although I'm slowly being joined by all my married friends whose marriages have fallen apart or are in the process of getting divorced. George was only thirty-nine years old. What a shame. It's hard to believe, he was so young. He was in the prime of his life. I'm gonna miss him.

A moment of silence for my friend George:

Two tragedies in one day. I will deal with them in the only way I know how. In the words of Bluto Blutarsky, John Belushi's character in one of my favorite films of all time, *Animal House*, "My advice to you… is to start drinking heavily." What the hell, I'll get an early start preparing myself for the big New England Patriots-Jacksonville Jaguar AFC Championship game tomorrow. This one's for you, my friends!

DAY 310 - JANUARY 12TH, 1997

I watched the Green Bay Packers win the NFC championship game and then watched to Patriots clinch a trip to the Super Bowl with six Boston comics at comedian Bill Burr's apartment. These football players were getting slammed by 250lb. linebackers, running at top speed and hurtling their bulk through the air with reckless abandon, without the slightest consideration for their bodies, yet both teams made it through the playoff games without any significant, major injuries. I, on the other hand, was running into my living room to catch a big play on the television, and stubbed my toe on the couch, causing my toe to swell up and turn a horrible hue of black, blue and purple.

At game's end, the players were celebrating while I was sitting on the couch with my foot elevated and an ice pack on my injury, moaning with pain and crying out, "Drive me to the emergency room! I'm in pain! I think it's broken!"

Some athlete.

DAY 311 - JANUARY 13TH, 1997

Today is very significant because I have an 11:00 meeting with the man who could be my manager and personal appearance agent if all goes right. I'm keeping my fingers crossed. I limped noticeably out the door around 10:30 a.m.

The meeting went well. The agent suggested that he "pocket" me as a client, meaning that we will go through a courting period to feel each other out. He will try to set up various talent showcases to create an interest in me among the industry people This is called "creating a buzz," in Hollywood lingo. The agent will try to impress his potential client by showing that he has enough pull to create opportunities for me and I will have to prove to the agent that I'm a marketable commodity that can generate money for both of us. It's a start.

I was in the middle of a sound sleep during the night when Kelly shook me awake and said, "I think I heard something in the other room!"

"Hummphhh?"

"I heard something! Go check and make sure that the screen door to the balcony is locked."

"Humnnnfffgg...zzzzzzzzzz."

"Wake up! I heard a noise on the balcony! See if the screen door is locked!"

Rubbing my sleepy eyes I said, "Kelly... I'm pretty sure... that if someone is obsessed enough... *and* ambitious enough... to scale the

Paul D'Angelo

outside wall of the building to reach our third floor balcony, he's not going to be turned back by a flimsy screen door. Who do you think is out there, Jackie Chan?"

Paul D'Angelo, Essex County attorney by day, stand-up comic by night

DAY 312 - JANUARY 14TH, 1997

I eventually fell back asleep... after checking the screen door, of course, and when I woke up, I was astounded by how clear my sinuses were. I had stopped taking my sinus medication because I couldn't afford it. My health insurance has about a $100,000 deductible. I have to build a new wing on the hospital before they'll even think about sticking a thermometer up my ass.

It's so bad that I twisted an ankle playing basketball and was limping around the court in obvious pain. My friends encouraged me to go to the emergency room and get an X-ray.

"Are you kidding? I have like $100,000 deductible! I can't afford an X-ray."

After a week I was still limping and the ankle wasn't getting any better. My friends told me to get an X-ray because the ankle might be broken.

"I told you, I can't afford an X-ray with this health plan."

Two weeks later my ankle was not making any progress and I knew I needed an X-ray... so I went down to the security checkpoint at Logan International Airport, laid down on the conveyor belt, amongst all the luggage and suitcases, held out $3.00 cash and said, "Hey sky-cap... Here's a couple bucks... Can you do me a favor and check out the right ankle on the way through... Tell me if you see anything... Thanks."

Even so, after having trouble breathing for the last couple months, I decided to start taking the prescription again and figured I'd worry about the cost later.

"Kelly, I can breathe again! I can smell things! This is great!" I filled my lungs with fresh air through my open nostrils, appreciating every breath I took. "I can breathe! I can smell things! This is fantastic! Ahhh, the aromas are wonderful! Yes!"

"Paul, I'm leaving for work. You have to come down to the parking garage and move your car, you're behind me."

"No problem! I'm just so happy! I can finally breathe!"

We stepped into the only working elevator, pressed the button for 'P4,' and the door closed to take us to the basement garage. I almost gagged.

"Pewwwwww! What's that stink?" I looked behind us to find that someone had puked in the corner of the elevator.

"Augggghhhhh! Gross!"

"Kelly, just hold your nose till we get to P4!" The doors opened and we ran out into the parking garage. "I'm so glad I can breathe again! Look what I was missing!"

I hate the people in this apartment building. I can't wait until I can afford new neighbors. I already went through this "smell the puke in the hallway; live on cold Spaghetti-O's straight from the can; milk-crates for bedroom furniture; wear your socks for at least three-days or until you run out of toilet-paper; making tomato soup out of ketchup and hot water; never have any money in your pocket" stage in college. There's really no need to relive the experience for artistic purposes.

Paul D'Angelo

Late in the afternoon, Kelly called to say she'd be home late from work because they are starting production on a CBS *Movie of the Week*. Knowing that I'm a moron in the kitchen, she informed me that there's a small steak in the refrigerator that even I should be able to cook, along with some canned vegetables. No problem. How hard can it be?

I picked out a can of corn niblets and read the elaborate and detailed directions, which said, "Open can. Heat." Simple. Even I can handle that. I opened the can, emptied the contents into a sauce pan, then proceeded to stare blankly at the niblets. I fished the empty can out of the trash and read the label again.

What were those directions again? Oh ya,... 'heat'... For how long? How hot? In the oven? On the stove? On the grill? In the microwave? What level? How do you know when they're done? I reviewed my limited knowledge of cooking hints. Do they turn color? Do you stick a fork in them and, if it comes out clean, they're done? No... that's a cake. Do I throw a niblet against the wall to see if it sticks? No... that's macaroni. Does a little plastic thing pop out like a turkey? Oh hell, these directions don't tell me shit. I'll just wing it.

I started a flame and put the steak in a frying pan. How high do I put the flame? I like steak on the grill, so I put the flame up high to simulate the hibachi experience. A couple minutes later the smoke alarm was wailing its high pitched tone, which can only mean one thing, "Steak's ready!"

I put the niblets on my plate. Next time I will know enough to drain the water off first. I plopped the steak down in the corn niblet flavored puddle and cut into it. The outside of the steak was cooked like... well, it was cooked like a slow rabbit in a forest fire... charred black, but the inside was so raw it looked like sushi. What did I do wrong? Help! Considering my survival instincts, if I were one of the original cavemen, we'd still be swinging from trees.

Tonight I went to a movie with Max. I'm not advocating the use of any illegal substances, no matter how innocuous they may actually be, but I must report that smoking a joint adds an average of a ★½ to any movie. Don Knotts becomes Robert DiNiro. And, as a bonus, if you really like the movie, you can see it again and it will be just like watching it for the first time because you won't remember most of it. The only drawback is experiencing the paranoia of trying to find your seat in a dark theater when you come back from buying your third jumbo-sized box of popcorn.

DAY 313 - JANUARY 15TH, 1997

I had to move the car again early this morning. I got into the elevator very cautiously, sniffing around like a German Shepherd at a customs check-point. The coast is clear. No vomit.

Ahhh. Not so fast. When I went into the little gym room to work out, there was a used condom lying on the rug. Kind of gives new meaning to the gym terminology of "pullover." I want to work out to that guy's exercise video.

Today was very exciting for my friend Patty Ross. She has signed up with the Gallin-Morey Association, which is one of the biggest, if not *the* biggest talent management companies in the world. Patty had a one-on-one meeting with Sandy Gallin himself, the star-maker who has represented the likes of Michael Jackson, Whoopi Goldberg, Roseanne Barr, Dolly Parton and Andrew Dice Clay. Patty's biggest thrill came when Sandy Gallin received a call from Sarah Ferguson, the former Duchess of York, during their meeting, and "Fergie" was told to call back because he was busy. There's something to tell the kids that Patty never wants to have.

Patty's managers want to develop a sitcom around Patty for this year's fall season so, out of the blue, Sandy asked Patty if she was doing a show this evening. Patty told him that she had a spot at the Laugh Factory at ten o'clock and he told her that he would be there to see her. Keeping in mind that Sandy Gallin hasn't been out to personally view talent at a comedy club in years, Patty went into hysteria when she got back to her apartment around 5:00 p.m.

"Paul! Sandy Gallin is coming to see me tonight! Get your ass over here *right now* and help me put a set-list together! Help!"

Who you gonna call? Joke-Busters! I flew over to her place and led Patty through her set-list while she nervously smoked countless cigarettes. Accompanied by my first-hand coaching and her second-hand smoke, we hammered out a twenty minute routine for her big set, then Patty went out and delivered the goods. Sandy was very impressed with her and Patty is on her way to fame and fortune.

Hey, maybe that Tom Arnold wasn't so dumb after all.

comedienne / actress Patty Ross

DAY 314 - JANUARY 16TH, 1997

Just when thought it was safe to go in the water... When we woke up there was no hot water in our apartment. Kelly had to boil water in pans to give herself a sponge bath and get ready for work. I'm paying

L.A. Misérables, Too

$800 a month rent to go fuckin' camping.

Both my uncle and my mother called this afternoon when they heard that Bill Cosby's son was murdered during an apparent robbery attempt in Los Angeles, not too far from where we live.

"What are you doing in that crazy place? That city is a battle zone! You could get yourself killed walking down the street!"

I did my best to assure them that there was nothing to worry about. "Listen, LA is like any big city, it's got its problems but I'm safe, believe me. There's nothing to worry about. Besides, who's gonna rob me? I have no money anymore."

I left my apartment three minutes later to visit Patty Ross, who lives about four blocks away, but I couldn't drive down Hollywood Boulevard. There had to be a dozen police cruisers blocking the traffic, several officers were setting-up road flares, and others were cordoning off a three city-block area with the yellow police tape that typifies a crime scene investigation. I pulled alongside an officer redirecting traffic and asked what was going on.

"There are a couple suspicious packages in the area. We evacuated the neighborhood and the bomb squad is on their way."

Oh, is that all? Here I am telling my family that this place is safe yet, in reality, the image inside my head is that of the robot from *Lost in Space*, wildly waving his arms and yelling, *"Danger! Danger! Danger!"*

DAY 315 - JANUARY 17TH, 1997

OK, this is how this agent/manager thing works. The first talent manager I spoke to when I moved to Hollywood had never managed a comedian's career before. He was primarily a financial manager who was in the process of establishing a theatrical management division and, for the most part, his clients consisted of teenage beauty contestants and other young ingénues that he could surround himself with. He claimed to have a connection with a producer of comedy specials, but he was never able to get a hold of this guy in the couple months that we were in contact. After he spent the first thirty minutes of a forty-five minute meeting at a sidewalk café in Sunset Plaza gawking at women and trying to sign-up the waitress, I told him that I wasn't interested.

The second manager I met with had been at the top of the entertainment world at one time, when he managed one of the biggest names in comedy and motion pictures. It bothered me that he wanted me to make a three year contractual commitment after our brief encounter, without asking to see me perform live or learning any more about me.

I told him that I was in the process of screening managers and agents and I would stay in touch, and he continued to pressure me to sign with him each time we met or spoke on the phone. His over-the-top eagerness put me on the defensive and I later learned that he had burned a lot of bridges when he was in a position of power. None of his current clients were big names and he seemed to be "out of the loop."

One personal appearance agent initially showed an interest, then never returned my phone calls. One night he saw me perform and indicated that he wanted to get together ASAP to see if we could come to an agreement. Again, he didn't return my phone calls and generally made himself unavailable. I spoke to his assistant, who told me that they were very busy in the office and I should call at least once a week so they wouldn't forget about me. I informed him that, if I had to call once a week to remind them that I exist, they didn't want me bad enough, and I hung up. I got a call from the agent almost immediately thereafter and he made more plans that he didn't honor. Fuck him.

In the meantime, I met with several other managers, none of which were right for me, or big enough players to be part of the inner circle that encompassed those powerful industry executives who made the decisions that could jump-start an entertainment career.

Two significant players were given referrals by club owners and bookers who were familiar with my act, and I met with both. Each responded enthusiastically and told me that they'd look over my tapes and press materials and then get back to me. I was psyched because I would have jumped at the chance to sign with either one or the other. I didn't hear from either of them for over three months and pretty much wrote them off as uninterested.

At that point, one of my friends, who I had happened to do a big favor for, spoke to one of those managers about me. He told them that he was interested in representing me, but had been too busy with other clients to follow up on our meeting.

My friend hyped me and that previously uninterested manager called shortly thereafter to set up another meeting. His unexpected response made me wonder if I had given up prematurely on the other manager who seemed to blow me off, so I called him up for the hell of it. He also told me that he hadn't forgotten about me, but he'd been tied up with business and I had slipped his mind. I dropped off a tape from a show at the Ice House and he told me that he'd get back to me which, of course, he didn't.

What's with these fucking people? They express interest in me, then immediately go off the grid and enroll in the witness protection program.

In the meantime, I had the meeting with the first manager who set up a showcase to see me live at the Improvisation next Thursday night. Someone told the second managerial candidate that I was thinking about signing with about the other manager who was interested in me, so now he wants to attend the showcase on Thursday too. As soon as Patty's manager heard that the other two managers were interested, he told me to call him and *he* says he'll be there on Thursday as well. Not a nibble for ten months, then you lay down a little chum slick in the water, and the next thing you know, the sharks are in a feeding frenzy.

I just don't get this town. No agent or manager gives a shit until a rival of theirs expresses interest, then they panic because they think they're gonna miss out. These people are like lemmings… goateed lemmings with ponytails, cell phones and designer sunglasses who are inconsiderate assholes.

DAY 316 - JANUARY 18TH, 1997

Late this evening, I saw a panhandler standing on the side of the road holding an empty cup and a sign that said, "WHY LIE? I NEED

A BEER."

I've got to admire the guy's honesty… but not enough to give him any money.

I think it's so strange that I sometimes come up with humorous comebacks in my subconscious dreams. True story. The guy begging for money must have been on my mind when I went to sleep because I dreamt that, for some strange reason, I was carrying my bag of golf clubs down a Los Angeles street. A bum approached me with his hand out, asking for change, and I told him to get lost.

The bum berates me, saying, "You're so selfish and elitist. How can you go golfing when there's so much inequality and suffering in the world?"

I kept walking past him and, without missing a beat, I replied, "Hey, maybe that's why I slice."

Monday is Martin Luther King Day and maybe that's not just a coincidence because we *both* had a dream.

DAY 317 - JANUARY 19TH, 1997

I ate dinner with my friends Patty and Timthy tonight. It's always an interesting experience to be out in public with Timthy. He shows me a different side of life because he is 180° different than my usual friends.

I've often said that the basic difference between myself and Timthy is that, if a beautiful woman walked by, I would want to "do her" while Timthy, on the other hand, would want to "do her hair."

CHAPTER TWENTY
I'm all shook up...

DAY 318 - JANUARY 20TH, 1997

This is a big week. I have that management showcase on Thursday night at the Improv and I have to put together a representative set-list that will be a knockout. First of all, I have to find out how much time I'm getting. Unlike a comedian that has traditional set-up & punch-line jokes, my act is made up of routines that run with a premise, so the more time the better. I also have to convince some people to fill the room in the event that it's a light crowd. The problem is, I don't know enough people around here and I'm not in a position at the club to request a guest-list with comp'ed tickets so they wouldn't have to pay.

While I was at my desk, it occurred to me that I'd redeemed some of my frequent flier miles and requested a free domestic flight certificate from American Airlines quite a long time ago, but I never got my certificate in the mail. I decided to call customer service and the nice woman who answered told me that the certificate department had received my request on November 5th, 1996, and issued the certificate November 7th, so if I haven't got it by now it should be on its way.

"M'am, it is now January 20th. It's two and a half months after they mailed it."

"Well, that correspondence was mailed 3rd class rather than 1st

class, so it takes a little longer."

"I'm sorry, I must have missed something… Did you say '3rd class' or 'pony express?'"

That helped the nice lady to see the light and they issued me a new certificate.

I need to complain about this mail service. I went to the post office for a minute and came back in an hour. Next time I'm gonna pack a lunch.

One woman in line must have been a stripper because she paid for a money order with about six hundred one dollar bills, which had to be counted twice by the postal employee. A couple of other customers went through and, just when you think you're making progress, the worker at the window is like a short-reliever on a baseball team… they only pitch to three batters, then they hit the showers… because they'd service a couple people, then they'd take a break and leave the window unattended. I could have walked the letter to its destination by the time they got to me. I was lucky. I swear, there were rotting skeletons of people clutching letters in their bony hands that never made it to the front of the line.

DAY 319 - JANUARY 21ST, 1997

My God, it's January 21st, where does the time go? You know what this means… it's almost time to throw out that Christmas eggnog in the refrigerator.

I was looking for something in my desk draw, but I couldn't find it because the draw was full of junk. Amongst the other crap, there have to be about twenty-five books of matches from various restaurants and bars in the Los Angeles area. At my place in Boston, I have two huge, glass jars filled with matches from places that I've been to over the years. I don't know how I got started collecting matchbooks but, even before I did comedy, I used to be out on the town every single night for years, so you can imagine the assortment I amassed. It has since become a habit to grab matches if I walk into a new watering hole.

Looking at the matches reminds of a funny, true story that I later converted into a routine for my act. My law school was located on old

Beacon Hill in Boston. Each time we would finish a grueling final exam at Suffolk University School of Law, my friends and I would leave the classroom and walk straight down to the Faneuil Hall Marketplace on the Boston waterfront, where we would pound down cocktails at Lily's bar until we were hammered and ready to buckle down for the next test. The practice became a tradition used to relieve the stress during finals because it gave us something to look forward to when we started to get burnt out. Plus, it was a convenient excuse to get slammed.

One such time, I was sitting on a stool alongside the outdoor bar at Lily's and spotted a pack of matches from Buddies which, in the late '70s-early '80s, was the most well-known and notorious gay bar in Boston. Even though I had a policy to include in my collection only matches that came from places that I had actually visited, I would occasionally make exception if the matchbook itself was unusual, or if it represented a particularly unique establishment. I thought these matches would make an interesting addition to my collection, so I slipped them into my pocket without a second thought and began drinking with my pals.

By the time we left, hours later, we were all laughing, stumbling and staggering across the marketplace, heading back to the Hill. As we approached the busy street that crosses to Boston City Hall and its plaza, I was joking around, wasn't paying attention, and wandered into traffic without looking. In an instant, my roommate Richard grabbed my arm and yanked me back onto the sidewalk, just as a huge dump truck blew its horn and whizzed by me, missing me by inches.

Richard laughed, "Whew! Be careful! You almost got squashed by that truck!"

We all continued to laugh when, suddenly, my face became pale and I froze with a stunned look on my face. I began rummaging through my pockets and came up with the matches from Buddies.

My friends looked concerned. "What's the matter, Paul?"

I told my friends that I found the matchbook on the bar at Lily's and I was going to put them in the jar with my other matches. But what would have happened if I got killed by that truck? It's bad enough that I would be dead, but the cops would have knocked on my parent's door...

"Mr. And Mrs. Murphy. We're sorry to inform you that your oldest son was hit by a truck and killed instantly this afternoon. Here are the contents of his pockets. We thought you might want them."... and my parents would have been standing there sobbing, until they eventually sifted through the items and looked up at each other with their mouths hanging open in disbelief.

"Buddies? Frances, these matches are from Buddies in Boston, the homosexual leather bar. I never suspected Paul was gay. He hid that from us all these years. Paul shouldn't have been ashamed. He could have told us... we would have understood."

"Jack, I had no idea... There were no indications. He always went out with girls... always with different girls... living a lie. The *Playboy* magazines... the Farrah Fawcett poster... playing football... pretending to have no interest in Broadway shows... all just a lie, a façade to hide his real self. I'm stunned."

And I'd throw my harp down and be on my knees, pounding my fists on a cloud, looking down from Heaven, with veins popping in my forehead and screaming at the top of my lungs to the people I left behind on Earth who can no longer hear me...

"*NOOOOOOO!* THIS CAN'T BE HAPPENING! MOM AND DAD, LOOK UP HERE! CAN YOU HEAR ME? I'M NOT GAY! THERE'S A OUIJA BOARD IN THE CLOSET IN MY OLD BEDROOM! I CAN EXPLAIN EVERYTHING! TAKE OUT THE FUCKING OUIJA BOARD! THAT'S ALL I ASK!! CONTACT ME, I CAN EXPLAIN! *PLEEEEEEEASE,* GET THE GODDAMN OUIJA BOARD <u>*NOW*</u>*!!"*

DAY 320 - JANUARY 22ND, 1997

I have spent all day trying to prepare a set-list for tomorrow night. I rewrote it over twenty times and have gone over the set hundreds of times in my head. There will be four major managers and agents at my show and I need top-notch representation before I can accomplish anything in this town. This is it, baby!

DAY 321 - JANUARY 23RD, 1997

Tonight is the most important night since I moved to Los Angeles. It has taken over ten months to finally get these people out to see me. I called and got confirmations that they all would attend the showcase. I went over and over my set-list all day, making more changes and improvements, and basically working my ass off and dedicating myself to my performance to make sure that I kick ass tonight, because this is the opportunity that I've been waiting for and I'm not going to blow it.

Later that night...

Well, show's over. The good news: My set couldn't have gone better. I rocked the place. The crowd was absolutely dead for the preceding comedians, but I got at least five big applause breaks during my ten minute set. A dozen people from the audience came up to congratulate me and tell me that my set was the highlight of their night and they wished I could have gone on longer.

The bad news: Not <u>one</u> of the agents and managers that told me they would attend actually showed up, including the agent who set this whole showcase up and supposedly "pocketed" me as a client.

Which pocket did he put me in, in a pair of hip-hugger, button-fly, tie-dyed, flood-length frayed-hem bell-bottoms in the back of his closet, or the breast pocket of a paisley Nehru jacket hanging in the attic? I know shit like this happens all the time in this town, but that fact doesn't make it any easier to swallow when you're the one who's been disappointed. To those guys it's just another promise they couldn't keep. To me, it means another couple months of frozen Kraft microwaveable Macaroni & Cheese dinners. I was devastated. What the fuck do I have to do just to get someone to come out and see me?

DAY 322 - JANUARY 24TH, 1997

My thoughts for today:
As far as I'm concerned, everyone can just go kiss my fat ass.

DAY 323 - JANUARY 25TH, 1997

I worked out my muscles very hard and long in the gym today in an attempt to work out all the anger and resentment building inside me at the same time, and, I am proud to say, as a result of my efforts, I have a different outlook on the whole situation.

The way I see it now, as far as I'm concerned, everyone can just go kiss my *tight, firm* ass.

CHAPTER TWENTY-ONE
Hit me with your best shot...

DAY 324 - JANUARY 26TH, 1997

Super Bowl Sunday. My hometown Patriots against the Green Bay Packers. The Patriots lost, but they were in the game until the fourth quarter.

At this time next year, I hope I'm *not* doing this joke in my act:

"Boy, those strings of cheap Christmas tree lights I bought are just like the New England Patriots. They were only good for one season."

DAY 325 - JANUARY 27TH, 1997

Almost everything is drive-through now.

Of course there are drive through fast food restaurants, but now they have drive-through banking... drive-through dry cleaners... drive-through pharmacies... even drive-through liquor stores.

Leave it to California, where all these crazy new trends seem to start. I just read that they actually have drive-through wakes here now. Apparently, you drive-up to a window where you can view the body of the deceased and you never even have to get out of your car.

For the record, I do *not* want to have a drive-through wake.

It's not asking a lot, but I would like to go out with just a little bit

I can imagine a mother pulling up to a funeral home window in her SUV, making the sign of the cross and closing her eyes in prayer... "In the name of the Father, and of the Son, and of the Holy..."... only to be interrupted with, "MA! JOEY'S HITTING ME!

Turning to face the backseat, the housewife yells, "Stop fighting with your brother! Can't you see I'm doing something? You boys are going to have to behave yourselves for just two minutes! Can you do that? Two minutes is all I ask."

She turns back around and crosses herself again... "In the name of the Father, and of the Son, and..."

"JASON CUT IT OUT!"

The mother turns completely around in the seat and screams, "I thought I told you boys to stop it!"

"JOEY STARTED IT!"

She points at the body in the funeral home window...

"Do you boys know why that man is in the box? He didn't listen to his mother. Would you like to join him? I can arrange it, just keep it up!"

A guy lays on the horn in the car behind them... *HONNNNNNNNNNNNK*

The mother sticks her head out the window and hollers at the top of her lungs, *"HOLD YOUR HORSES, BUDDY! CAN'T YOU SEE I'M PAYING MY FUCKIN' RESPECTS HERE? HAVE SOME CLASS, DIP-SHIT!"*

That is *not* the way I want to go out.

DAY 326 - JANUARY 28TH, 1997

I haven't heard from the agent who set up that showcase last Thursday night, when he was a "no show." I thought he might call Friday, apologize and explain why he couldn't make it, but I must have been dreaming. So I called him both yesterday and today.

Both times, his receptionist told me that he was on the phone, but he would call me back in ten minutes. Both times, I waited around all day and he never returned my call. Just because this behavior is common practice in Hollywood, it doesn't make it acceptable to me when I'm in the process of choosing an agent. If this is our "courtship" period, as he called it, I think I wanna see other people.

DAY 327 - JANUARY 29TH, 1997

I'm so broke I haven't been able to afford the luxury of getting my car washed for months, but it's a mess so I splurged and went to the self-serve bays on Santa Monica Boulevard this afternoon. I soaped the car down, went over the body and wheels with the foaming brush, then gave it a good rinse.

When I drove the car out of the bay there was no place to dry it off because the car wash was very busy, so I parked it in the street to use a chamois to get all the water off. I worked on the back of the car and got the finish all shined up. I was happy because it was about time I gave the car a good washing. I made my way down the sides, wiped all the water spots off the windows, cleaned all the details in and around the aluminum wheels, and then went to wipe off the hood.

It looked like someone had dropped a dozen overripe avocados from an airplane onto the hood of my car. What the hell? I looked up and realized that I had parked directly underneath a telephone wire filled with about a hundred pigeons taking aim on my clean car.

Go ahead, everyone else has been shitting on me lately, why should you fuckin' birds be any different? Bombs away... I imagine that it must be physically impossible to accomplish this when you have a beak for a face, but I swear I saw one of the little bastards smiling.

DAY 328 - JANUARY 30TH, 1997

You know, sometimes it feels like the whole world is against me. My dad sent me a copy of *The Boston Globe Magazine* from last Sunday's newspaper. There is an article about the current state of the stand-up scene in post-comedy-boom Boston that he thought would be of interest to me. I took the magazine into the bathroom with me and read the following:

> "One of the problems for aspiring comics in the Boston area is that many of the (established headliners)... have been headliners for years and dominate the local scene, leaving others little room for advancement beyond the middler stage. The best solution for those not satisfied being worker bees on the comedy scene is to leave town.
>
> For instance, one of Boston's top rising comedy stars of recent years, Paul D'Angelo, finally decided to move to Los Angeles a year ago, sacrificing his day job as a criminal defense lawyer in the process. From 1982 to 1993, D'Angelo was an Essex County assistant district attorney who..."

Whoaaaaaaa!! Stop right there!! I can't believe I'm reading this. I headlined the Boston clubs for almost ten years, I leave for a few months and now I'm characterized as a frustrated "worker bee" stuck in the "middler" stage, so I had to leave town like a convicted child molester. It's enough of a struggle to deal with a miserable present and an uncertain future, but now they're trying to take away my past. What the hell is this, a scene from *Total Recall?* Damn, you can't expect me to fight the war on two distant fronts... That was the downfall of the Third Reich.

I have already been labeled as a "virus" and a "bee," are there any other insects, animals, bacteria, or germs that they're forgetting to associate with me?

Rodney Dangerfield's got nothing on me.

"Ooooh, I'm tellin' ya...I get no respect either... no respect!"

I was so pissed-off I needed a release to help me chill, so I went to Blockbuster video and rented a movie that I watched with Kelly.

The movie was sooooo fucking boring, I thought the VCR was on pause for an hour-and-a-half. The story dragged like a dog pulling his itchy ass across a rough carpet.

DAY 329 - JANUARY 31ST, 1997

I have a meeting with a management company on Monday. When I came to Los Angeles, I made a list of the top ten or twelve management companies and limited my consideration to that group but, from my own personal experience and the experiences of comics I know personally who have signed with one of those agencies, I have learned that it's in my best interests not to limit myself to the major management companies.

There seems to be a tradeoff between having a high-powered, big name manager or agent, with a prestigious clientele and an impressive reputation, and a manager or agent who has a qualified background and is sufficiently connected enough to be effective, but whose operation is intimate enough to make you a priority of their attention and energy.

It is also critical that the representative has faith in you, they believe in your abilities, and they have a passion to see you succeed, because you are their ticket to success. Every time I've dealt with one of the prominent managers or agents, it seems like they always have someone more important to talk to on the phone, they always have someplace more important to be, or they always have something more important to do.

Face it, if, for example, you represent, say... Jim Carey, and you stand to earn 15% of the $20 million he gets for doing a film, would you devote more effort to promote him as a client, or would you spend your time trying to convince the networks to put Paul D'Angelo in a sitcom? That manager might have enough pull to get a conference with a network executive with one phone call.

Another aspiring manager, whose focus is to make Paul D'Angelo a star, would have more incentive get Paul D'Angelo a development deal because 15% of nothing is nothing. He'd have to be more tenacious and, even though he might not get a conference with that executive with one phone call, he might succeed with ten calls, if that's what it takes. The means are different, but the ends are the same.

The three gentlemen that I'm meeting with on Monday have recently established a management company. They have impressive credentials and come highly recommended. One partner was the senior vice-president and co-head of the West Coast office for a major national talent agency. Another was senior vice-president of the music division of Paramount Pictures and he worked as the music supervisor on over 100 films, including *Footloose, Beverly Hills Cop I & II, Top Gun, Ghost, Star Trek III, IV & V, Naked Gun*, etc. He now produces television movies for CBS and is also producing a feature film. The third partner founded a production company that produced nine feature films and over 300 television shows.

These guys are among the nicest people that I've met and they seem to really believe in me. They have never put me on hold, forgot to call me back, or postponed meetings. They've showed up when I scheduled a showcase and they seem genuinely enthusiastic and hungry. I think I may have found the right management for me.

DAY 330 - FEBRUARY 1ST, 1997

I'm living a fucking nightmare. Last night I got tired of listening to our cheesy, little, pseudo-toy stereo that only plays through one cheap, tiny, plastic speaker and vowed to trouble-shoot the system to find out why there's no stereo. I had the receiver in pieces, there were wires everywhere, and I had a genuine concern that I would never get the thing back together again but, after a half hour or so, I finally got sound out of our left speaker for the first time since we moved in. "Ta da!"

I don't think ten notes of a song had been played through the two speakers before security was banging on our door.

"You're going to have to turn that stereo down. The neighbors complained that the bass is up too high."

You've got to be shitting me! Our neighbor's apartment is quaking from the deep resonance of the bass tones emanating from our audiophile-quality sound system? It's impossible. The amplifier in our stereo has about as many watts of power as a Sony Walkman. The speaker in the ear-piece of our telephone is better than the speakers that go with this poor-excuse for a stereo system. Not to mention that the volume is only turned up to "4" and it's only 9:30 on a Friday night. Get a life! Did you get a new battery for your Miracle-Ear? What the fuck is your problem? Some people just love to complain. Personally, I hate people

L.A. Misérables, Too

who complain all the time.

"Waiter, I'd like to send this piece of fish back... It tastes *fishy*."

Guess what, Einstein... that's because *IT'S A FUCKING FISH!* If you want your food to taste like a chocolate cupcake, order a chocolate cupcake, not a haddock!

Meanwhile, deafening police helicopters are hovering outside the window; ambulances are screaming past the complex like a traveling, 1000 decibel, TV test-pattern; buses are grinding their gears into metal dust under our window; and there must be a street sign in the neighborhood that says, "CAR HORN INSPECTION AREA"... but they have to gripe about my shitty little stereo.

So why don't these people complain about that asshole's shit-box with the car alarm that goes off every half hour, on the hour, at all times of the day and night? You can't possibly miss it, because it's annoying me so much I'm at my breaking point.

After we turned the stereo off and went to bed, as usual, I was awoken by the familiar sound of that goddamn car alarm about 1:30 a.m. That's when I decided, "That's it, no more Mr. Nice Guy!"

I got out of bed and opened the refrigerator. There were three raw eggs in the door that have probably been there since last summer, so I would be reluctant to eat them anyway. We're too poor to waste food.

I took the eggs and walked out onto our balcony, where I could see the headlights of a car across the street flashing on-and-off, on-and-off, on-and-off, while an obnoxiously loud siren blared a medley of its obnoxious-noise greatest hits.

"That's right! Exclusively from K-Tel Records, not available in stores, a collection of the most irritating sounds you could ever imagine, all in one car alarm!

"There's the siren, 'Aaaaiiiieeeeeeooooooooo Aaaaiiiieeeeee-ooooooooo'

"The busy signal, 'Bzzzzzzzttttttt Bzzzzzzzttttttt Bzzzzzzzttttttt Bzzzzzzzttttttt'

"The European police siren, 'Whoooooooop Whoooooooop Whoooooooop Whoooooooop'

"But wait, there's more! Order now and you'll also receive the rabid donkey, 'Heeeeeee Hawwwww Heeeeeee Hawwwww Heeeee Hawwwww'

"... and the air-raid alert 'Whaaaaaaaaaaaaaaaaaaaaaa.'

"How much would you expect to pay for a infuriating collection such as this? $9.95? $19.95? $29.95? $39.95? You should be so lucky! No, you get to have your peace disturbed on a continual basis for a paltry sum of eight-hundred dollars each and every thirty days you live here! Correct-o-mundo, all for only the price of a monthly rent check! What a deal!"

From my balcony, I squinted to see across the street in the darkness. Yup, it was that same car again. This is gonna be a tough shot past the palm tree, over the sidewalk, and six car-width lanes diagonally across Hollywood Boulevard. I wound up and flung the first egg. It landed short, splattering on the street. Damn, it's farther than I thought.

I took aim and let the second egg go... Oooh, hit the tire. Not good enough.

One egg left. C'mon Paul, just like playing the outfield. The runner's trying to score from second on a single... he's testing your arm... you've got to nail him... I let it fly.

Splat!!! Bull's eye!!! Right on the windshield!

Whoooooop Whoooooop Whoooooop, Heeeeeee Hawwwww Heeeeeee Hawwwww Heeeee Hawwwww, Aaaaiiiiieeeeeeooooooooo Aaaaiiiiieeeeeeooooooooo What's that? That's right... rise and shine you inconsiderate asshole... it's breakfast time! Your eggs are ready! I hope you like them scrambled, dick-wad!

Kelly, who has since been promoted to a development position in the motion picture production company that she works for, had to go on-sight to San Diego, where they are shooting a movie-of-the-week for CBS. Left alone this afternoon, I went with Patty Ross to comedian Steve Moore's home in Laurel Canyon, where a film crew will be recreating Steve's 40th birthday party for an upcoming HBO special that focuses on Steve's comedic manner of handling life after being diagnosed HIV-positive. There were over forty people at the party and take a wild guess who the only straight guy there was. Some people might have a

L.A. Misérables, Too

problem with those odds, but not me. My outlook was, "Well then, all the beer in the refrigerator must be for me," and I proceeded to take advantage of the free Dos Equis.

More trouble. On the way home with Patty and her dog Dolly, I got pulled over by a motorcycle cop because we weren't wearing our seatbelts.

"Why do you have Mass plates?"

"I... I... I just moved here officer... uh, a... um, a week ago. I haven't had time to get a California registration yet."

He let me go, warning me, "I patrol this area all the time. I won't forget you and, if I see you again, and your Mass plates are still on the car, I'm gonna write you up. So remember, I'll be looking for you."

Great. I don't have enough problems, I already have to watch my ass in Beverly Hills, now I'm confined to the south side of the Hollywood Hills and, should I venture into the valley, I have to avoid the police like a parole-violating fugitive with an outstanding warrant. If these run-ins keep up, soon I won't be able to leave my building unless I dig a tunnel to the outside like they did on *Hogan's Heroes*.

Things are just not getting any easier, are they?

DAY 331 - FEBRUARY 2ND, 1997

Last night I went out with my friend John Dutton, who books the comedy shows at Carly Simon's nightclub on Martha's Vineyard, the Hot Tin Roof. John spends his winters in Los Angeles and we've been hanging around a lot since he came out to the West Coast. He picked me up and I got into his Saab after I moved the mountain of empty soda bottles and cans off the passenger seat. The mess he's driving is not so much a car as it is a redemption center. Dutt was still tossing empties into the backseat and not paying attention as he kept swerving over the double solid-yellow lines in the middle of the road. He jerked the wheel back and said, "Shit, that stunt would earn me a week at traffic school."

I added, "Not to mention a couple of months of intensive care and rehab. Forget the stupid five cent returnable cans and watch the friggin' road before you get in an accident and the only thing that will end up getting recycled will be my internal organs."

We saw comedian Frankie Pace around last call at the Improvisation on Melrose. I worked with Frankie at a crazy club on Cape Cod one hot summer evening. An employee sat at the door of the nightclub, with a cash register on a table, taking the cover charges for the packed room. While I was on stage, some drunk grabbed the cash register and tried to run off down the street with it. I could see the commotion near the entrance at the front of the club, but had no idea what was going on. Fortunately, Frankie and my friend, The Prune, chased the guy down and got the register back which, thank God, meant that the place was able to pay me that night.

Kelly's been away one day and I've already settled back into my usual lifestyle. Dutt and I ended up at the Fatburger at 3:00 a.m. where I had a double Fatburger Deluxe with the works and an order of fried onion rings. And the good news is that I only have to collect twelve more receipts before I get my complimentary angioplasty. I have a feeling that burger will be in my colon until next year's Thanksgiving turkey pushes it out.

CHAPTER TWENTY-TWO
Tomorrow never knows...

DAY 332 - FEBRUARY 3RD, 1997

That damn car alarm woke me up again last night.

Shopping list: Extra Large Eggs.

I've been thinking, I returned from my trip to Boston on the 7th of January. My last show there was on the fourth. It's been almost a month to the day and the only time I've been on stage in Los Angeles is the ten minute showcase I had at the Improv on January 23rd. I realized that the Improv runs a Latino comedy night every Sunday and a black showcase every Monday night. The weekend spots are reserved for comics with major film or television credits. That leaves only Tuesday, Wednesday and Thursday for me to get spots, assuming that those evenings aren't blocked off for showcases, which they often are. The situation is similar at the Laugh Factory. I might as well be selling snow-blowers on Maui.

I had my meeting with the management company today, everything went exceptionally well, and I made a commitment to sign with them for a year. They are sending a copy of the contract for me to sign in the mail. By the time I left the meeting, did a couple errands and drove home, there were already two messages on my answering machine from my managers, who immediately made efforts to get me a showcase with a personal appearance agent. Hey, maybe things are looking up already. Who knows, with any luck, *L.A. Misérables, Part III* might actually contain something vaguely resembling progress on my part.

Whoooooooop Whoooooooop Whoooooooop, Heeeeeee Hawwwww Heeeeeee Hawwwww Heeeee Hawwwww, Aaaaiiiiieeeeeeooooooooo Aaaaiiiiieeeeeeooooooooo, Bzzzzzzzzzttttttttt Bzzzzzzzzzttttttttt Bzzzzzzzzzttttttttt Bzzzzzzzttttttttt, Whaaaaaaaaaaaaaaaaaaaaaa.

That %&#*@!!#%*$&@!!%$* car alarm!!

Excuse me, I've got to go now, the coach is signaling for a right-hander to start warming up in the bullpen. Seems my favorite customer is looking for another order of the special tossed-egg omelet.

Coming right up, dick-cheese.

To be continued...

EPILOGUE
Ba-ba-ba-baby, you ain't seen nothin' yet...

OK, I know what you're thinking, "It's been almost a year since Paul moved to Hollywood and he still hasn't made all that much progress." Ya, ya, don't bust my balls, no one said this was gonna be easy. But I'm close though, I can feel it. I might as well keep writing because it's a creative outlet for me, the process makes me feel productive, and it keeps me from initiating "Plan B," which is strapping dynamite to my torso and holding the executives of a major studio hostage until someone pays me some attention. Besides, since the publisher told me that my two books, which they characterized as a "running stand-up routine," would be marketable once I established a name for myself, if you're reading this now it must mean I've accomplished something or another, so I might as well continue into a third book because some interesting shit could finally be coming up.

My friend Patty reminds me, "It's the journey, not the destination that matters." If that's true, the stoner Dead-Head driving my van on the road to Easy Street is saying, "And what a long strange trip it's been, right dude?" while I'm in the back, whining like a little kid, *"Fuck that, are we there yet? I don't feel good… I think I'm gonna throw up. I wanna go home. Are we almost there?"*

If there's anything that Hollywood produces more proficiently than major motion pictures, it's bullshit, and I believe that if I can avoid being caught in the undertow from the tidal wave of phoniness, insincerity, egotism and game playing that's so prevalent in the entertainment business, there's no reason that I can't be surfing that very wave to success with a lot of perseverance and a little luck.

I don't have an ego, but I'm not stupid, and every week that I'm here I get motivated by seeing more and more crappy sitcoms that make it onto the air, more and more lousy "comedy" writers that turn out bland, humorless scripts, and so many mediocre comedians who are getting opportunities that I can only dream about, and it makes me determined not to give up because the time will come when I get to prove myself. And whenever things appear bleak, inspiration seems to come in many other forms. My friend Jim Roach sent me a card today with an Oscar Wilde quote on the front which reads, "Life is too important to be taken seriously." Inside Jim wrote, "Don't ever give up! I need you to become rich and famous so we can open up a "gentlemen's club" together."

And, as always, tits trump.

.

About the Author

Paul Murphy spent eleven years as an assistant district attorney, supervising several of Massachusetts' busiest courthouses, before becoming a successful criminal-defense trial attorney. The unexpected twist to this story is that, under the pseudonym of Paul D'Angelo, Paul was simultaneously becoming one of the nation's top stand-up comedians.

Paul has headlined A-List comedy clubs around the country for over thirty years and he has performed at many other famed entertainment venues that range from the legendary Friar's Clubs and the Waldorf Astoria's main ballroom in New York City, to the main showroom at Harrah's Casino and Caesar's Palace.

He has been invited as a feature performer at the Montreal 'Just for Laughs' International Comedy Festival; was named "Boston's Best Comedian" by *Boston Magazine*; and has been a finalist in a number of national and international comedy competitions, including the esteemed San Francisco International Comedy Competition.

Paul has also opened for over sixty internationally known acts, including Ray Charles, Aretha Franklin, Tom Jones, Tony Bennett, The Beach Boys, Chicago, The Doobie Brothers, Hall & Oates, Bad Company, The Four Tops, The Temptations, Jerry Lee Lewis, Huey Lewis & The News, Lyle Lovett, Kenny Rogers, Jay Leno, George Carlin, Joan Rivers and Dennis Miller.

He has entertained hundreds of prominent corporate clients all over the country, such as Ford Motor Company, Sony Music Corp., Hewlett-Packard Corp., Nike-Bauer International, Fidelity Investments, Bike Athletic Corp., CVS/Caremark Inc., American Airlines, Delta Airlines, NFL Charities, General Electric, Goldman-Sachs, Edward Jones Investments, UPS, the American Bar Association and the Burger King Corp.

Paul recently co-starred in Showtime's popular stand-up comedy movie, *The Godfathers of Comedy*, and he is the author of three hilarious, multiple award-winning books, *Stories I Tell*, *More Stories to Tell* and this book's predecessor, *L.A. Misérables: The Amusing Misadventures of a Boston Comic in La La Land*.

Gold Medal Winner, 2015 eLit Awards

Finalist, 2015 International Book Awards

'Best Comedy Book of 2016' – Best of Los Angeles Awards

Honorable Mention, 2016 New York Book Festival

Clarion Reviews ★★★★

Available at pdangelo.com or Amazon.com

Gold Medal Winner, 2016 eLit Awards

Finalist, 2016 International Book Awards

Winner, 2016 Book Excellence Awards

Silver Medalist, 2016 Global eBook Awards

 Clarion Reviews

Available at pdangelo.com or Amazon.com

An excerpt from *L.A. Misérables, Three*

DAY 374 - MARCH 21ST, 1997

I went into a music store on Route 1 and saw an old friend who works there. He says he's coming to Los Angeles to visit his brother next month and wanted to know where I lived.

I gave him these directions:

"When you leave LAX, take the 405 north, past the location of the Rodney King beating that started all the violence, rioting, looting and fires.

"Continue on the 405 and you'll go by the scene of the Menendez double homicide where the two boys slaughtered their parents.

"You'll go through the Brentwood area where OJ slashed those two innocent people to death and their blood was splattered all over the place, then you'll pass the scene of the Reginald Denny clubbing, and continue over the 10 Freeway where the ramp collapsed with all the cars on it during the giant earthquake, crushing all the helpless people inside.

"Take the Mulholland exit where the Cosby kid was shot in cold blood for no apparent reason whatsoever.

"Then drive-by (sorry, bad choice of words) drive *past* the site of the horrific Manson murders when they butchered the people and wrote on the walls in their blood... but don't take a left or you'll end up in North Hollywood where they just had the big shoot-out with the heavily armed bank robbers... instead proceed over the hills where you'll pass the hotel where John Belushi died in his own vomit.

"You want to take a left at when you get to the intersection where they just whacked Biggie Smalls, then bear right where Eddie Murphy picked-up the chick-with-a-dick and drive past two other hookers working the corners and three homeless beggars asking for change.

"You're getting close now... Pretty soon you'll see a bunch of gang members hanging out... If they're Bloods you're OK... But, if they're Crips, you've gone too far, so turn around and come back... then take a left at the crack deal, right at the burning car, and there's my building... just before you get to the bad section of town."

www.ingramcontent.com/pod-product-compliance
Lightning Source LLC
Chambersburg PA
CBHW051038160426
43193CB00010B/987